THE ROYAL GRIFFIN

THE
ROYAL GRIFFIN

Frederick Prince of Wales
1707-51

JOHN WALTERS

STEIN AND DAY/*Publishers*/New York

First published in 1972
Copyright © 1972 by John Walters
Library of Congress Catalog Card No. 72-82852
All rights reserved
Printed in the United States of America
Stein and Day/*Publishers*/7 East 48 Street, New York, N.Y.
ISBN 0-8128-1496-7

Contents

Illustrations

Between pages 128 and 129

Portion of the Herrenhausen Palace, Hanover, birthplace of the Royal Griffin—*Dr. Wolf Strache. Courtesy German Embassy, London*

Eighteenth-century scene being re-enacted in the baroque garden of the Herrenhausen Palace—*Heinz Koberg. Courtesy German Embassy, London*

Frederick with his sisters. Painting by Mercier—*National Portrait Gallery*

Frederick's barge—*National Maritime Museum*

Interior of barge's saloon—*National Maritime Museum*

Frederick Prince of Wales. Painting by Mercier—*National Portrait Gallery*

Augusta Princess of Wales. Painting by Philips—*National Portrait Gallery*

George II. From studio of Jervas—*National Portrait Gallery*

Queen Caroline. From studio of Jervas—*National Portrait Gallery*

Sir Robert Walpole. Painting by Van Loo—*National Portrait Gallery*

William Duke of Cumberland. Painting by Reynolds—*National Portrait Gallery*

George Bubb Dodington. From a contemporary engraving—*Radio Times Hulton Picture Library*

Prince George, eldest son of Frederick. Anonymous engraving after Wilson—*British Museum. Photograph John R. Freeman and Co.*

Introduction

COMMENTS ON THE ROYAL GRIFFIN

Griffin, griffon, gryphon, n. Fabulous creature with eagle's head and wings and lion's body. Oxford Pocket Dictionary

I have always hated the rascal . . . false, lying, cowardly, nauseous puppy. King George II (father)

My dear first-born is the greatest ass, and the greatest liar, and the greatest canaille, and the greatest beast, in the whole world and . . . I most heartily wish he was out of it. Queen Caroline (mother)

Pray Mama, don't throw away your wishes for what cannot happen, but wish he may die, and that we may all go about with smiling faces, glad hearts, and crape and hoods for him. Princess Caroline (sister)

The prince who never forgot an injury or remembered an obligation. Lord Hervey

A poor, weak, irresolute, false, lying, dishonest, contemptible wretch, that nobody loves, trusts, or believes. Sir Robert Walpole

His was the most vicious nature and the most false heart that ever man had, nor are his vices the vices of a gentleman. M. Neibourg (tutor)

The chief passion of the prince was women, but like the rest of his race, beauty was not a necessary ingredient. Horace Walpole

The most agreeable young man it is possible to imagine, without being the least handsome. Lady Bristol

He is extremely dutiful to his parents who do not return it in love. Augustus Schutz (courtier of George II)

We have lost the delight and ornament of his age—the refuge of private distress, the balm of the affected heart, the shelter of the miserable. George Bubb Dodington (later Lord Melcombe)

An overflowing benevolence, generosity and candour of heart, joined to an enlightened zeal for liberty, an intimate persuasion that on it depends the happiness and glory of both kings and people. James Thomson, poet

This excellent prince—possessed of every amiable quality which could engage the affection of the people—a tender and obliging husband, a fond parent, kind master, liberal, generous, candid and humane. Tobias Smollett (novelist)

He walked the streets unattended to the great delight of the people. He could enter the cottages of the poor, listen with patience to their thrice-told tales and partake with relish their humble fare. . . . Never did the illustrious maimed appeal to him in vain. Dr. John Doran, writer

He had no great parts, but he had great virtues: indeed they degenerated into vices . . . and then his condescension was such that he kept very bad company. Unnamed Mayfair Chapel preacher quoted by Horace Walpole

> *Here lies Fred,*
> *Who was alive, and is dead. . . .*
>
> *But since 'tis only Fred,*
> *There's no more to be said.*

From anonymous verses

I

'Queen Anne's Dead!'

'*Die Königin Anne ist tot!*'

These words echoed in all parts of the vast palace of Herrenhausen close to the city of Hanover in Germany. For a messenger from England, in a state of exhaustion, had handed George Louis, Elector of Hanover, a message that the queen had died. Anne's life had slipped quietly away on the first day of August 1714 causing John Arbuthnot, her physician extraordinary, to comment that 'sleep was never more welcome to a weary traveller than death was to her'. To some in the palace the tidings brought pleasure and expectation, but not to George Louis, the fifty-four-year-old elector. Although George had keenly co-operated in the machinations to ensure Hanoverian succession to the British throne, he now winced at his future prospects. For he would have to leave his compact little state of 500 square miles with a population of less than a million to preside as monarch in the great alien land whose language he could not speak.

Queen Anne had died without a direct heir; not that she and her husband Prince George of Denmark had ignored their generative duties. 'I have tried him drunk and tried him sober and there's nothing in him,' said King Charles II of Prince George. Nevertheless, as a devoted and patriotic husband he fathered seventeen children for Anne. All died in their infancy except a son named William, whose life flickered out in its twelfth year. Therefore to keep the throne protestant there was little alternative but to look towards Sophia, Electress of Hanover, grand-daughter of England's James I. So under the Act of Settlement warm and English-speaking Sophia became heiress to Anne. However, only two months before Anne's death Sophia, then aged eighty-four, expired in the garden of the family palace, making way for the kingship of her sombre son George Louis. He was a man of heavy jowls, of blue eyes that bulged. An Englishman meeting George for the first time compared him to a cold draught. Another complained he was 'so cold that he turns everything to ice'.

'Queen Anne is dead!'

The news affected the many relatives, mistresses, friends and officials of the elector in a variety of ways. For the palace was a kind of Teutonic Versailles, housing a diversity of people, each group with its own individual interests and aspirations. The women closest to George Louis, and never refrigerated by his person, were his two favourite mistresses, fat Charlotte Sophia Baroness von Kielmansegge and tall thin Ermengarde Melusine von Schulenburg. Each regarded the prospect of the move to the British court as dazzling. The fat mistress was known as 'the Elephant' and the thin as 'the Maypole'. The amorous tastes of George Louis often ran to stout women, and in 1714 Charlotte Sophia von Kielmansegge definitely outranked Ermengarde Melusine von Schulenburg in his favour. Moreover, Charlotte Sophia was probably a half-sister of George Louis, for she was daughter of his father's wicked but influential mistress the Countess Platen. Later, however, Charlotte Sophia was to emerge as second best from a battle with Ermengarde Melusine for their lover's sexual and social attentions. George gave the winner the title of the Duchess of Kendal, while half-sister Charlotte Sophia had to be content with the lower title of the Countess Darlington.

The two mistresses started without delay to be measured for splendid clothes with which to impress those noble British ladies among whom they would soon be mingling. At the same time, miles away in the grim fortress of Ahlden, the woman most detested by George Louis was told that his coming accession to the British throne would make not the slightest difference to her own domicile and mode of life. This woman was Sophia Dorothea, his cousin and former wife. Twenty years previously she had been divorced by him for alleged adultery with handsome Count Philip von Königsmarck and sentenced to life imprisonment in the fortress. The two had been intercepted in an elopement attempt. Von Königsmarck had been slaughtered on the spot, with the Countess Platen looking on from her carriage. From that day George Louis had not only completely ignored Sophia Dorothea, but had forbidden their two children ever to communicate with her.

In a wing of the Herrenhausen palace, remote from the apartments of Elector George Louis, lived his son and heir George Augustus with his wife Caroline and their family of one boy and three girls. George Augustus heard of the death of Queen Anne with sorrow, not for her but for himself; for he liked neither his father nor England. Since this father was to become George I, the son's fate would be to become Prince of Wales and eventually George II. There seemed no way of evading circumstances that would bring him closer to his father and, almost as bad, residence in England. But his wife Caroline was not displeased. Imaginative, far-seeing and loyal to the family into which she had married, she gloried in the promise of its increased greatness as ruling house of rich and much-envied Great Britain.

George Louis had disliked and disapproved of his son George Augustus even from the day of his birth. The baby annoyed him by being born extraordinarily like his mother. He had Sophia Dorothea's fair complexion, light brown hair and delicate features. True that his marriage to Sophia Dorothea was young at that time, but nevertheless she had already sunk lower in his affections than his mistresses. George Augustus in his manhood was of small stature. He loved soldiering and took inordinate pride in his reputation for bravery. Like his descendant George V he had a passion for punctuality. His movements were dominated by the clock. But, unlike George V, George Augustus was a vulgar foul-mouthed man and a boastful sexual athlete. His marriage at the age of twenty-two

to Caroline of Anspach was a love match, although throughout
her life she never objected to his keen pursuit and possession
of other women. While sharing her husband's predilections
for obscene jokes and foul language, Caroline was nevertheless
a person of unusual intellect and culture. She took particular
interest in philosophy and theology. Among the many distinguished thinkers with whom she mingled was the philoso-
pher Leibniz.

Throughout his years in the Herrenhausen palace George
Augustus had to endure the unkindness and persecution of his
hostile father. When in 1705 Caroline arrived in Hanover as
bride, George Louis insisted that the wedding should be very
quiet. Queen Anne sent the Marquis of Hertford to this as
her representative, together with a gift of tea for the bride.
George Louis received him with distant and icy politeness.
Nevertheless, the Electress Sophia insisted on holding a ball
in Hertford's honour.

Of the four children of George Augustus and Caroline,
the eldest was Frederick Louis, born in 1707. Next came Anne,
Amelia and Caroline, born respectively in 1709, 1711 and 1713.

The life of Frederick Louis, the subject of this biography,
was extraordinary from birth to death. He was born in his
grandfather's palace in an atmosphere of unnecessary mystery
and folly. Early in January 1707 Caroline's physicians told her
that the arrival of the baby was imminent, but to their surprise
he was not born until January 31st. All through January,
however, only a few showed interest in Caroline's vigil,
because court and city were lost in the madness of Hanover's
annual carnival. The elector's predecessors had taken a passionate and even lustful interest in the gaiety, carnivals and masquerades of Venice. The first elector had indeed been so
impressed by Venice that he boldly tried to transfer its atmosphere to Hanover. He renovated his palace, populated it with
sculptures and in its precincts he built an opera house of
baroque splendour. Into the court was introduced a German
version of Venetian revels. In balls and masquerades the
dancers waved torches five feet high. The drunken revellers

would between the dances retire to couches for more intimate pleasures.

Elector George Louis, disapproving of such extravagant and exhibitionist antics, tried to make carnival more restrained. But he dared not deny its boisterous and uninhibited delights to the lusty burghers of Hanover and their womenfolk. As throughout the month of January the pregnant Caroline bravely paced her palace apartment in hope of speeding the birth, the vicinity echoed with the sounds of revelry, both day and night. Nearly every evening in the opera house there were lavish, brassy opera productions or saucy comedies written in the sexual and scatalogical manner of North Germany. Throughout the old city there were gargantuan feasts, washed down by so much wine that the diners would rise to prance, to bound and to bawl in scenes resembling a Breughel painting, until belching and breathing hard from exhaustion, they collapsed or wallowed on the floor. The more important citizens would gather in the town hall for what they liked to believe were authentic Venetian revels. Masked and in fantastic fancy dress, the burghers, with their distended stomachs, tried to bow in courtly fashion to roly-poly women playing coquettishly with their fans. But generally these distinguished citizens of the 'German Venice' preferred the town hall's supper rooms to the dance floor. And they would also reveal a prodigious appetite for gambling games which often ended in unseemly brawls.

Elector George Louis presided at the more respectable carnival functions in the palace and in the town. He greeted the ovations of his loyal subjects with bows and unexpressive stares from his goggle eyes. In public he chatted politely with his son and heir George Augustus. But behind the elector's exterior worked a mind the intricacies of which would baffle the most penetrating and sophisticated of today's psychiatrists. Apparently during this January of 1707 this mind was filled with hatred and jealousy for George Augustus as the latter approached the joy of fatherhood. The question why this should have provoked such fury behind the elector's icy exterior can only be answered with guesses. The marriage of George Augustus to the brilliant and attractive Caroline was a success and had brought him happiness. The marriage of George Louis had been a failure. The birth of a son to George Augustus and Caroline would increase their popularity not only in the electorate but also in England. George Louis had never concealed his disapproval of any friendship shown by the British queen towards his son. He had been much displeased at the arrival of Anne's Garter Herald Lord Halifax in May 1706 to present George Augustus with the Order of the Garter. On May 12th of this year there were combined celebrations over the arrival of this garter and news of Marlborough's victory at Ramillies. Moreover, Hanover's relations with England demanded some reciprocity for George Augustus's garter. Thus the elector reluctantly allowed a service of gold plate to be presented to Garter Herald Halifax. The award to George Augustus was followed by an announcement that Anne would confer upon him the title of the Duke of Cambridge. This apparently caused the resentment of the elector to burn all the more. And now, in January 1707, Queen Anne was waiting impatiently to congratulate and honour his son and Caroline on the birth of their first child. George Louis, it seems, could only be infuriated and jealous at the thought of having to share so much of his electoral stage with his son and daughter-in-law. And it is also likely that the elector was also evilly envious of the connubial happiness of his son and Caroline.

When the news reached George Louis on the evening of January 31st that Caroline was at last in labour he warned his son and all other relatives and court officials to keep away from her apartments. The Electress Sophia, mother of George Louis and grandmother of George Augustus, was distressed by this command. She adored Caroline and had promised to be at hand during the agonies of her first *accouchement*. Thus the boy who was to become heir apparent to the British throne was born in the presence of only one doctor and a midwife. Representatives of George Louis stood guard outside Caroline's apartment to ensure that the worried husband, the Electress Sophia and others did not try to invade this enforced privacy. Within some hours of the birth the baby's father was allowed to see him briefly. However, the grandmother remained barred, much to her distress. Sophia suggested that since one doctor and a midwife were the only eyewitnesses of what happened in Caroline's room, there could be no proof that the baby had not been stillborn and replaced by another snatched from an unmarried mother or from a foundling hospital.

Mr. Howe, the British envoy, bothered the chamberlain of Elector George Louis for news of the mother and the baby, who he presumed was still unborn. A messenger stood near the envoy prepared to dash to a waiting coach for a gallop across North Germany to the Netherlands coast where he would board a boat for England and then speed to the court of impatient Queen Anne. But Howe was told repeatedly 'There's no news' until he succeeded in wringing from one of Caroline's ladies-in-waiting information that she had indeed at last given birth to a healthy baby boy. Nearly a week had passed before the baby's irritating grandfather permitted an official announcement of the birth to be issued. Ignoring the conventions of diplomatic courtesy, he made no personal notification of the event to Howe as representative of the British queen.

A week later King Frederick William I of Prussia, who was married to Sophia Dorothea, daughter of George Louis, arrived in Hanover on a short visit. Thereupon one morning George Louis disclosed, mysteriously, that the christening would take place in the evening of that same day in the bedroom of Caroline. The sponsors at this christening, he added, would be himself, the Electress Sophia and his Prussian son-in-law. George Louis justified this almost secret christening with the excuse that he 'couldn't endure pomp'. The father of the baby was furious, yet he dared do nothing to frustrate his own father's wishes. In Hanover the powers of the elector were supreme. At this christening, where the baby was given the names of Frederick Louis, the old electress saw her great-grandson for the first time and was delighted. Later she was to remark in a letter on the baby's 'liveliness', his 'merry blue eyes and mouth wide open to suck'. And to Leibniz, a friend she shared with Caroline, she confided the hope that 'this child will have more sense than his father'.

The christening had not been long over when the unpredictable elector announced he was off to the Brunswick Fair and that he expected almost the entire court, including son George Augustus, to accompany him. They were away at these Brunswick junketings for three weeks, leaving Caroline and little Frederick with a skeleton staff of servants. At the end of February envoy Howe at last succeeded in begging and pleading his way into Caroline's apartments to inspect the baby and congratulate the mother. Later he reported to his queen that Frederick was a remarkably big baby, and he quoted evidences from ladies-in-waiting that he was strong and healthy. Meanwhile George Augustus quietly apologised to Howe for the discourtesy he had endured from the elector in having had to wait so long to see the baby.

In the following month George Augustus was again apologising to Howe for the bad manners of his father. The patent of the dukedom of Cambridge had arrived in Hanover, together with a personal letter from Anne to its recipient. According to the rules of diplomatic etiquette, the patent should have been handed from Howe to the prince in a ceremonial manner in the presence of the elector and leading officials of the court. But the elector rudely said he would not allow this. Howe was kept waiting days with the patent while father and son squabbled over how it should be received. Eventually Howe was allowed to go to the court and give the patent to the apologetic George Augustus without any pomp or ceremony.

Despite rosy reports on the size, health and progress of little Prince Frederick by the Electress Sophia, ambassador Howe and others, he was not a healthy baby. His complexion, far from being pink and white, was an unhealthy yellow. In keeping with early eighteenth-century theories of baby care, Frederick was almost smothered in layers of long clothing and had been guarded fanatically from fresh air. He had been taken from his mother's breast to suck the nipples of some peasant woman who had been deprived of her own baby. But the early escape by Frederick from his mother's arms was fortunate. For in the spring of 1707 Caroline had three days of headaches and digestive disturbances, followed by the appearance on her face of red papules. Caroline had caught the smallpox, the disease which had killed her father (the Margrave of Branden-burg-Anspach) and stepfather (Elector John George of Saxony). Then George Augustus got smallpox also. The disease followed its course through both patients without complications. Caroline, however, was left with permanent 'pits' in the skin of her face which the thickest cosmetics failed to hide.

Frederick was still an infant when George and Caroline began to call him by the nickname of *Der Greif* in German or the Griff in their poor English. They humorously saw this pale over-cosseted little creature as something fabulous, like a griffin. The nickname stuck even when in later years many people were praising the prince as graceful and handsome. Frederick's parents were in his adulthood to call him by many rude names, including 'Fly'. But he predominantly remained the Griff—the son whose uniqueness and contrariness so often horrified and infuriated them.

At the age of two the Griff, belying his nickname, had become pretty and appealing. His hair was fair, his face had lost its yellow pallor and now had a lighter appearance. Nevertheless this infant was sickly. The attention of the court physicians delayed rather than hastened any increase in his strength and vigour. In those days in Germany doctors believed that for an infant to be kept well, regular 'purging' was vital. Doses of cruel herbs and salts disrupted the normal movements of the infant's bowels, causing weakness and hysterics rather than health and calm. This was also the time of novel medical experiment, both in Germany and England. New medicines for which great wonders were claimed were enthusiastically

brought to the attention of royalty. These included invigorating 'horse-dung possets', snail tea and curative mixtures so
secret that even kings, queens and princes were kept in ignorance of their ingredients. Not all the progressive medicine
of the age had been able to save the lives of Queen Anne's
seventeen children. And now such progressive medicine wasn't
doing Frederick any good.

At the age of two Frederick, although pretty, was groggy and
muddled. He never tried to stand. When nurses tried to raise
him on his feet he toppled over. He spoke a few words, then
refused to increase his vocabulary. At birth Frederick had been
hailed as a big baby. Now, for his age, he was diminutive and
spindly. He was pigeon-chested and his legs had a crooked
look. Finally physicians decided that Frederick was suffering
from what was known in Hanover as 'the English disease',
meaning rickets. The prevalence of rickets in England had
caused doctors to associate it with the frequent absence of
sunlight in the cloudy foggy island. Frederick, shut up in the
great Hanover palace with its high windows with heavy red
velvet curtains and hangings, had certainly been denied any
place in the sun. And probably there was no Vitamin D, the
existence of which was then unknown, in the heavy stodgy
diet pushed down the throats of German infants in that age.
Frederick was, it was claimed some eighteen months later,
cured of rickets, although for years afterwards he suffered from
physical weaknesses which rickets may have started. There is
no record of the medical treatment received by the two-year-
old patient, but it is probable that associating rickets with
cloudy England, his doctors recommended that he should be
encouraged to sit and play in the palace gardens in the sunshine,
despite the perils to infants which at that time were believed
to lurk in the fresh air.

Now we move again into that August of 1714 when in
Hanover the word had passed from mouth to mouth that
'*Die Königen Anne ist tot!*' Later messages from London to
George Louis, now virtually George I of Great Britain, urged
him not to delay his move to London. For there were fears

that without his early presence dissident Tories might try to have Roman Catholic James, the Stuart pretender, proclaimed as king. Bishop Atterbury of Rochester had pressed for such a proclamation, only to be warned to his anger that it might result in his throat being cut with those of other anti-Hanoverians. Support for George was strong in England, but it was felt this might decline if he lingered too long in his electorate.

George, usually slow and deliberate, quickly evolved plans for the move. Almost hourly from his state chambers he issued orders covering every detail of his exit from Hanover and entry into England. He decided that his son George Augustus as his heir and the new Prince of Wales would have to accompany him, much as he disliked such company. Soon he made known his commands in detail to his unbeloved son. These were that George Augustus should come to London with Caroline and their three daughters. Next came the cruel and astounding order that the seven-year-old Frederick should be left behind. There must always, insisted his grandfather, be a family representative in direct line of succession in the court of the electorate—and Frederick would be that representative. George Augustus surprisingly bowed to this order without opposition. Caroline received it apparently without demur. The Griff, an affectionate boy, would suffer painfully to be suddenly deprived of his mother, father and infant sisters. But Caroline was reminded that often staying in the great palace was Duke Ernest Augustus, a younger brother of George I, and that he would keep a loving eye on Frederick, his grandnephew. Ernest Augustus, later made Duke of York, was prince-bishop of Osnabrück.

George I made another promise which brought Caroline cold comfort. He vowed to supervise his grandson's upbringing by personally selecting his tutors and programme of studies. Moreover the Hanoverian court would continue as before in the palace, with routines, functions and etiquette unchanged. However, instead of sitting on its throne in person, he would arrange for his portrait to be displayed there. The seven-year-old Frederick, supported by officials and courtiers, would represent the elector before this throned portrait.

In early September 1714 George I began his journey to England. As he drove in open carriage from the Herrenhausen palace and through Hanover crowds lined its thoroughfares, leaned from windows and from roof-tops. Many were sobbing at the permanent departure of their elector. The sight and sound of their sobs suddenly and miraculously melted the ice of his nature. He started to weep, dabbing his big watering eyes with a lace handkerchief. George's loyal subjects were so affected by this royal revelation of humanity that they cried all the more. George Augustus, now the *de facto* Prince of Wales, accompanied his father, leaving Caroline and daughters to follow later. In separate coaches at respectful distances from the king were his two mellow mistresses, 'Elephant' Charlotte Sophia, now aged forty-one, and 'Maypole' Ermengarde Melusine, aged forty-seven. The departure of the king and those closest to him had been preceded by a long line of wagons, packed with his possessions, coaches, carriages and mounted courtiers and troops; all were moving towards the Netherlands coast from which the royal yacht would sail to England. Despite polite hints that he should hurry, the king dawdled on his journey, taking the opportunity of spending nights at the homes of relatives or friends in Holland.

Early on September 18th there was tense excitement across the sea at Greenwich on the Thames, some four miles from the city of London. There had been reports that the royal yacht, carrying King George, was approaching the mouth of the river with an escort of British and Dutch warships. The Greenwich quay was a mass of decorations and illuminated by many flares. At Greenwich Hospital and in nearby mansions were the more illustrious of the British nation ready to assemble in their grandeur on the quay when the royal yacht appeared in the river and then docked there. But England is the land where so often man proposes while fog disposes. This morning there arose such a fog that soon all plans were thrown into confusion. George I, peering from his yacht with the Prince of Wales, was annoyed that the fog had rendered his realm invisible. The Thames's most expert pilots advised that any attempts to bring the vessel through the blackness to the Greenwich quayside with its precious passengers would be too risky. Thus the king and the most important members of his party were transferred to the royal barge which was propelled by oarsmen.

Soon George I stepped from the barge, nervous and solemn. The new dynasty whose descendants in our own age, so British in character and so secure and beloved, was now established. Members of the vast crowd now gathered on the quayside, from religious and political leaders of the nation to the poor illiterate slum-dwellers, seemed instinctively conscious of the momentous consequence of the occasion when the king was at last on British soil. From the trembling and tottery seventy-nine-year-old Archbishop of Canterbury, Thomas Tenison, to the tousled trollops of the dockside, all fell on their knees in an emotional gesture of respect. Among those there were the Duke of Marlborough and two who had plotted so assiduously against the Hanoverian succession—Henry St. John, Viscount Bolingbroke and Robert Harley, Earl of Oxford. The king whose language was German and the peers of his new realm whose language was English greeted one another and exchanged compliments in French, the lingua franca of the cultured of eighteenth-century Europe. However, the prayers of the Church of England, whose faith the Lutheran George was now the Defender, were recited in English.

On the following day the new monarch with his heir, German advisers, servants and mistresses moved to St. James's Palace to surprise and to excite the curiosity of Londoners of all kinds. The new royalty differed so much from good Queen Anne. Then members of London's court and society circles were startled by the imposition upon them of George's highest-ranking mistresses, the elephantine Charlotte Sophia von Kielmansegge and tall, scrawny Ermengarde Melusine von Schulenburg. As Charlotte Sophia was then the favourite of the two with the king, fatness together with thick and lurid facial cosmetics became fashionable in the capital's highest circles. In the words of Lord Stanhope, 'The standard of his majesty's taste as exemplified in his mistress makes all ladies who aspire to his favour, and who are near the suitable age, strain and swell themselves, like the frogs in the fable, to rival the bulk and dignity of the ox. Some succeed and others burst.' The presumption of the Elephant and the Maypole, from the moment of their arrival, horrified some of Queen Anne's former court ladies who regarded them with a similar repugnance as that of children for Cinderella's ugly sisters.

Those English servants of the court who had served Queen Anne so well were pained by the influx of the new king's own servants from Hanover. Everywhere in St. James's Palace was now heard guttural German, with French among the better-educated palace immigrants. It was said that in the precincts of this home of the new British monarch English had been reduced to the status of the third language and poorly spoken at that. Conservative English eyebrows were also raised at the sight of two exotic personal servants of George I named Mahomet and Mustapha. These, arrayed in Eastern costume, were German-speaking Turks. They had allegedly saved George's life in 1685 in the siege of Vienna and then entered into his service in Hanover. Belying his name, Mahomet repudiated the Moslem religion to become a Lutheran and married a German woman.

Caroline, who in Great Britain would be Princess of Wales, lingered on in Hanover until October. Most historians have, without substantiation, attributed this to her reluctance to part from her son Frederick. Then why, if Caroline and George were so fond of their seven-year-old boy, did not they challenge and argue against the command of the grandfather that he should be left behind in the electorate 'to represent the family'? A wild and ridiculous story, also without evidence, is that Frederick was the offspring of an illicit relationship between Caroline and either Mahomet or Mustapha. This story has been bolstered by statements that Frederick had 'a dark complexion and thick lips'. It is also said that in later years, during a fierce quarrel with Frederick, the angry father shouted, 'He's no son of mine!' And there is another story that George and Caroline nicknamed Frederick 'the Griff' because in Louisiana patois this was slang for a half-caste. Yet Frederick had fair hair and a white complexion. His lips were full but not thick. It is obvious that in shouting 'He's no son of mine!' the king meant that Frederick wasn't behaving as a son should behave. Also it is obvious that Frederick was called *Der Grief* as German for griffin, and not a slang term from remote Louisiana of which this Hanoverian couple would almost certainly have been unfamiliar. There is but one reasonable explanation why, bowing to the king's wishes, George and Caroline left their son behind and never saw him again for fourteen years. They did not really care for young children. The intellectual Caroline was a bluestocking first and a mother second. Her husband was far too wrapped up in himself, in his sexual adventures, in the Army and a few other narrow interests to be bothered about boys and girls, even when they were his own. Both parents appreciated their daughters when these were no longer children. They never appreciated their eldest son. Certainly he came to them in England at twenty-one, but also as a stranger.

At last Caroline kissed the Griff good-bye and started on the long drive to the Dutch coast with an escort of mounted guards. Her two elder daughters Anne and Amelia had two days previously been driven off towards Holland in charge of nurses. The youngest daughter, one-year-old Caroline, was ill, so the mother left her behind in Hanover until well enough to be taken by a nurse to London. The princess, Anne and Amelia, landed at the then bustling port of Margate, Kent, on the evening of Monday, October 10th. Prince George hurried from London to meet them. When, two days later, the four arrived in the capital they were almost mobbed by cheering crowds in a demonstration repugnant to the jealous king. He had decided that for the present his son and daughter-in-law should have no separate home, but occupy a wing of St. James's Palace.

Frederick, undersized but of charming countenance and attractive ways, had now the dignity of being the highest-ranking personage in Hanover, as deputy of his grandfather in the electorate and its palace. The child was self-possessed, easy of manner. Nobody awed him. Grave and elderly diplomats and ministers were sometimes nervous on how to approach and talk with this exalted small boy, but he would quickly put them at their ease with gracious prattle. When the Griff went to England in his manhood his parents, sisters and other enemies would brand him as foolish and stupid. Yet in the Herrenhausen palace in those early years he could, at least on ceremonial occasions, give the impression of wisdom and self-possession. But off parade the mask fell to reveal mischief and simplicity appropriate to his years. The society over which the Griff presided was elaborate, sophisticated and interesting. The host of nobles and ladies left behind by George I carried on the Hanover tradition of ceremony and pleasure. City and court had also an international flavour because of wealthy families from other countries who had settled there in the state's heyday. The court had also many unattached women who had served the elector and family in the past in capacities ranging from ladies-in-waiting to mistresses. These had been left behind by the elector-king as unsuited to the English scene. Among them were also widows of courtiers and of officials and of army officers who had been in the service of the elector or his predecessors. Battling the ravages of age, they painted their wrinkled yellowing faces and disported themselves with an artificially youthful mien, always ready for intrigue and desperately hopeful for a final romantic liaison. Alas, these ancient ones were to make unlovely contributions towards the education of the Griff.

2

Boyhood of the Griff

George I was not a generous man, particularly in expenditure on his own family. The cost of maintaining the Hanover court was already so high that he shrank from spending much money in the education of his grandson. The court in its splendour was necessary for the king-elector's prestige on the continent. How Frederick was taught and the qualifications of his teachers did not worry the king. The boy was given a 'governor' or tutor-in-chief in the person of Jean Hanet, a Frenchman of genteel background. Other tutors were recruited from the teaching profession of the city of Hanover. The programme of the Griff's studies from the age of seven onwards seem to have been slipshod and inadequate. Although second in line for the British throne he was in boyhood insufficiently instructed in the history of the United Kingdom. His knowledge of the English language was poor and would have been worse had not Caroline prevailed upon the king to allow an Englishman, a Mr. Nicholls, to give him lessons. On the other hand, within a few years of Monsieur Hanet's arrival Frederick was speaking and writing excellent French. And from early childhood he revealed a love for music, for art and for nature.

The Griff's father, as a devotee of the Army, was a disciplinarian. But, perhaps fortunately, the boy escaped his domination, since the style of his upbringing was dictated by the king. In the Germany and England of those days boys of gentle birth were customarily bullied into submission by their elders. They either learned their lessons or faced severe beatings. But

Frederick never became the victim of physical force. If he received ill-treatment it came in the form of only indifference or neglect. When away from court functions and his classrooms he was free to wander wherever he chose within the palace precincts—and further still when he was a few years older. The gardens and orangeries of Herrenhausen were renowned throughout Europe for their beauty and perfection of design. Frederick enjoyed these, but as they were too often frequented by the élite adults of the palace, he wandered away to quarters where there were personalities of more appeal to him. These were the palace stables and the servants' quarters where he could mingle happily with stable boys, grooms, page boys and young footmen. These rough working youths taught him language and attitudes unsuited to the grandson of a king. Nevertheless his fraternisation with them almost daily gave him an understanding and rapport with working folk which was to delight the lower classes of England when in early manhood he at last moved there. In the eighteenth century, the most snobbish and class-conscious age in European history, Frederick grew up indifferent to pride of birth, indifferent to social status.

There was great curiosity in the British Isles about the small boy that the king and Prince of Wales had left behind in Hanover. Just as today the subjects of the monarch take high imaginative flights about members of her family, so in the 1700s did they dream up stories concerning Frederick. The obvious story to conjure up and circulate was that mentally he was 'not quite there'; that he would be concealed in the Herrenhausen palace for the rest of his sad life. Naturally there arose a desire to investigate such gossip. Thus many with sufficiently impressive credentials and introductions made a beeline for Hanover in the hope of being received at the palace and of seeing and hearing the mystery boy. One such investigator was British diplomat Lord Polworth, who called at Hanover on his way to Copenhagen in 1716. The Griff, then aged nine, granted an audience to Lord Polworth who continued his journey to Denmark in a state of enchantment.

He had discovered the Griff to be 'the finest young prince in the world'. Another visitor was the Hon. John Hervey (later Lord Hervey). Hervey, who was to have a big effect on Frederick's life, first as a friend and then as an enemy, was then aged twenty and on the Grand Tour which young gentlemen of the day enjoyed before settling down at home. The young man and the child quickly bathed in mutual admiration. Twelve years later, on coming to England, Frederick brought Hervey into his service.

George I himself came to Hanover in 1716 when for some weeks his own body replaced his picture on the Herrenhausen electoral throne. The king was pleased with the progress of the Griff, but most of his time was spent on other interests. Although his mistress Charlotte Sophia von Kielmansegge had accompanied him from London, the object of his affection was another mistress. It was said that this lady had been unable to migrate with the king to protestant England because of her loyalty to the catholic faith. However, such religious fidelity apparently did not discourage her from joining the king in adultery.

At the time of this royal visit to Hanover, Frederick was brought under the inspection of the remarkable woman Lady Mary Wortley Montagu, who became a famous traveller and whose descriptive, candid and often uninhibited letters are now a valued part of England's literary heritage. She met Frederick when she lingered in Hanover in the course of travelling to the Porte where her husband Edward had been appointed British ambassador. In her letter-writing Lady Mary could be vulgarly candid. For example, writing to her sister, she complained that Madame de Broglie, wife of a French diplomat, 'makes a great noise, but 'tis only from the frequency of her pissing, which she does not fail to do at least ten times a day amongst a cloud of witnesses'. Then, although welcomed warmly at the British court by both king and Prince of Wales, her private comments about them were cutting. She wrote of the prince as an irritable person 'who looked on all men and women he sees as creatures he might kiss or kick for diversion'. And to Lady Mary the king was just 'an honest blockhead'.

Anyhow, when Lady Mary Wortley Montagu came to Hanover that 'honest blockhead' King George greeted her as a loyal friend and, although she had not been invited, provided her with a suite in his Herrenhausen palace. Moreover he commissioned mistress 'Elephant' Charlotte Sophia von Kielmansegge to act as her escort and guide. She took Lady Mary to the opera, to the theatre and to a private performance of French comedy in the palace. And her keen eyes noticed the many ageing ladies of Herrenhausen and their desperate attempts to appear young. 'All the women here', she wrote, 'have literally rosy cheeks, snowy foreheads and bosoms, jet eyebrows and scarlet lips, to which they generally add coal black hair. These perfections never leave them until the hour of their death and have a very fine effect by candlelight—but I would wish they were handsome with a little more variety. They resemble one another as Mrs. Salmon's court* in Great Britain, and are in as much danger of melting away by too near approaching the fire, which they for that reason carefully avoid, tho 'tis now such excessive cold weather that I believe they suffer extremely by that piece of self-denial.'

Then this female cynic was presented to the Griff. The boy was with his tutor, who, on the entry of Lady Mary, left the room. They talked, and throughout the meeting the visitor was so charmed that she found nothing about him to criticise or to be cynical about. Indeed, she wrote to Lady Bristol: 'I am extremely pleased that I can tell you without flattery or partiality that our young prince has all the accompishments that 'tis possible to have at his age, with an air of sprightliness and understanding, and something so very engaging and easy in his behaviour, that he needs not the advantage of his rank to appear charming. I had the honour of a long conversation with him last night before the king came in. His governor retired on purpose (as he told me afterwards) that I might make some judgement of his genius by hearing him speak without

* A famous London waxworks.

constraint, and I was surprised at the quickness and politeness that appeared in everything he said, joined to a person perfectly agreeable and the fine hair of the Princess Caroline, his mother.'

When Frederick reached the age of eleven, George I further dignified him with the title of the Duke of Gloucester. Almost at the same time the stingy king told Prince George that he must now contribute some £40,000 a year towards the upkeep of his son's Hanover 'household'. Prince George defiantly refused to make any contribution and obtained legal opinion to strengthen his stand. But the prince promised that as soon as Frederick's education was finished he would gladly pay for his household.

As the Griff approached adolescence his health again caused anxiety. His face remained attractive, but his little body seemed to be lagging behind his age. Periodically he collapsed in a fever. He would also complain of severe glandular pains. Reports of her absent son reached Caroline through the king. It is to the mother's credit that these made her worry and urge that he receive the best of modern medical care. The unfortunate boy, in the fashion of the day, was often encased in tight steel stays to make him look lithe and upright when presiding over the Herrenhausen court as representative of the king-elector. The cruel grip of these stays caused his suffering body such agony that he was allowed to scrap them for a corset of whalebone. The Griff would have most probably overcome his physical weaknesses sooner if he had been spared the palliatives of the latest medical science. Surgeons bled him and thereby courted anaemia. He was put on a strict regimen of asses' milk. This unpleasant beverage was then regarded as a cure for almost every complaint. Asses' milk had an enthusiastic champion in the renowned Dr. John Arbuthnot who had presided at the deathbed of Queen Anne. Arbuthnot even succeeded in persuading the usually stubborn Jonathan Swift copiously to imbibe the milk of the stubborn donkey. As Caroline read reports regarding the ailments of her son she expressed anxiety that these might seriously affect his sexual potency when he reached manhood.

Later, with the king's permission, Caroline dispatched a Dr. Maitland to Hanover to inoculate Frederick against smallpox. The inoculation made the lad so ill that for some days it was feared he might die. Caroline paid Dr. Maitland £1,000 for this smallpox inoculation, a new practice in its experimental stages and denounced by many clergy as sinful and against Holy Writ. At the end of the century Edward Jenner introduced the safer system of vaccination against small-pox, still in defiance of strong opposition.

The Griff returned from sick-bed to the dreary ceremonial of the court and to happier hours of diversion among his friends the grooms, the pages and the other servants. As his strength returned, the Griff became more headstrong and difficult for his tutors to manage or to guide. Jean Hanet, the youth's governor or head tutor, was replaced by another Frenchman, a Monsieur Neibourg, who was in close touch with the Prince and Princess of Wales. The dislike between Frederick and this Neibourg was mutual, the tutor being shock-ed at his behaviour under the influence of his servant friends. When Frederick was aged about fourteen Neibourg visited London and poured out complaints about the youth's beha-viour to Caroline, who, in reply, dismissed it as being merely 'antics of a page'. But the tutor boldly challenged this, insisting that Frederick's antics were 'those of a lackey and a rascal'.

Living in an immoral court in an immoral city, the Griff had, soon after the advent of adolescence, been sexually corrup-ted and at the age of sixteen he had a regular mistress. The name of the woman has not survived the years, but she was known to his mother, who regarded the liaison as natural and normal. She raised no objections. The honour or the shame of corrupting the future Prince of Wales was, according to several records, that of a Madame d'Elitz of the family of Schulenburg, of which 'Maypole' Ermengarde Melusine, mistress of George I, was a member. At one time Madame d'Elitz was the mistress of this George in Hanover before his accession to the British throne. Next she became the paramour of his son George Augustus. Finally Madame d'Elitz was to crown her triumph by seducing Frederick, the grandson. This sexual hat-trick inspired the eighteenth-century wit George Selwyn with one of his most-quoted *bons mots*. In discussing the loves of Madame d'Elitz, a friend remarked, 'There's nothing new under the sun.' 'Or under the grandson,' added Selwyn.

Madame d'Elitz was described by Hervey as a witty woman who in her prime had been very handsome. She 'had had a thousand lovers', and twenty years previously had been divorced by her husband after being caught in bed with another man. When Madame d'Elitz attracted the attention of the Griff she was one of many faded beauties who haunted the Hanover court in declining hopes of new amours but still hungry for them. She occupied a private apartment in the palace provided her by the Griff's father in appreciation for past services. Some years later, however, she was summarily evicted by George Augustus, who was by then King George II. The eviction followed a quarrel between Madame d'Elitz with his mistress the Hanoverian Countess Walmoden, later anglicised as Lady Yarmouth. But when the Griff was pursued and con- quered by the voracious Madame d'Elitz her position in the palace was secure. It is doubtful whether Monsieur Neibourg would even have considered trying to rescue the lad from the embraces of the woman who had also embraced both the father and the grandfather.

The Griff's amorous experiences with a woman old enough to have been his grandmother before he himself had attained the age of sixteen led him on to other adventures, but with younger and more lowly females. He accompanied his footmen and stable friends to their night haunts amid the maze of narrow streets in the old city of Hanover. These were wild and bawdy places in the vulgar German tradition, which still survives in the cafés, bars and pleasure houses of Hamburg and other large cities. The nobility and wealthy of Hanover, its many inter- national visitors who came to revel in the society of the 'German Venice'—all had hordes of servants. As in eighteenth-century London, Hanover had masses of cheap inns and brothels for the gentlemen's gentlemen. These were the places into which the young prince plunged with his working-class friends; places so refreshingly different from the stuffy ceremony and etiquette of the court. Dressed in plain clothes like his humble comrades, he could escape recognition. The Griff revelled in these night adventures. When he moved to London he tried to escape into the night as he had done in Hanover, but was nearly always recognised.

While Frederick, following the example of his grandfather and father, sought relish in the pursuit of illicit sex, discussions about a possible marriage for him were for years in progress behind his back. The girl under consideration as a possible bride was Frederick's cousin Wilhelmina, the Prussian Princess Royal. An intelligent girl, gawky and plain, Wilhelmina was the daughter of his father's sister Queen Sophia Dorothea and King Frederick William I of Prussia. It was Queen Sophia who first suggested that Prussia and England should strengthen their ties through a marriage between the Griff and Wilhelmina. Still more, the queen urged that the Griff's sister Amelia should eventually become the bride of her son Prince Frederick of Prussia. Although George I hated his daughter's husband King Frederick William, he became enthusiastic about her plan for marriage between his Anglo-Hanoverian grandson and grand-daughter to his Prussian grandson and grand-daughter.

King Frederick and his queen first met George I in Hanover to discuss the plan. Simultaneously there were talks between British and Prussian ministers accompanying their monarchs. Later there came a visit by George I and ministers to Berlin, where he offended Wilhelmina by holding a candle close to her face and 'inspecting her like a piece of merchandise'. During a palace banquet lasting more than two hours the icy George I just stared at Wilhelmina but never spoke. However, his ministers Carteret and Townsend conversed with the princess for a long time and pronounced her intelligent and charming.

It was difficult for King George and his ministers to assess the suitability of Princess Amelia and her cousin Prince Frederick to one another. Both were still mere children, Amelia having been born in 1711 and Frederick in 1712. They agreed, however, that the boy Frederick, who was horribly bullied by his tyrannical father, had an attractive presence and and that his future was promising. Their expectations were fulfilled, for he grew up to become known in history as Frederick the Great. The result of the conference between King George and King Frederick in Berlin was the drafting of the Treaty of Charlottenburg. This treaty contained clauses of agreement to the two marriages.

The Treaty of Charlottenburg remained unratified. Nevertheless the Griff, soon aware of the plans, developed deeply romantic feelings for the Princess Wilhelmina he had never seen. He wrote her simple but delightful letters. He sent her little presents. In the traditions of his father, grandfather and other antecedents the Griff continued with his gross physical relationships in court and city. At the same time he worshipped the idea of a perfect marriage with this cousin he increasingly idealised and whose letters in reply to his own he cherished. And within a few years sister Amelia in England learned how she was destined to become the bride of Cousin Frederick of Prussia. Amelia too was delighted and had her own romantic dreams of an idyllic connubial future which was never to come. Apparently it was during Amelia's girlhood that she obtained or was given a small miniature of Frederick. But nothing was known of this until Amelia died at the age of seventy-five, an eccentric and plain spinster. On her body was found a small locket of gold. In this was the old miniature.

In his forced separation from his parents and from England, Frederick could not have found any inspiration in the behaviour there of his grandfather and father. It was cruel and foolish that the Griff should have been left behind for so many years in Hanover, but at least he was spared the pain of becoming involved in their inane quarrels. The king and the Prince of Wales got on tolerably well together for a short time after their migration to England in 1714. But the king was soon becoming indignantly jealous at the popularity of his son and daughter-in-law Caroline in London society. On a handsome income of £100,000 a year granted by the government they were able to entertain lavishly and to attract more affectionate attention than did the cold king and his fat and lean Hanover mistresses. The king liked to surround himself with German servants and to make no political decisions without consulting his three non-English advisers. These were Baron von Bothmer, Andreas Gottlieb von Bernstorff and Jean de Robethon, a Huguenot refugee. The Prince and Princess of Wales also won popularity by employing many English servants and by taking advice from English ministers. The king felt humiliated because his son would accompany him to cabinet meetings in order to act as an interpreter between himself and the ministers. Finally the king decided not to preside at cabinet meetings any more.

When King George went to Hanover for six months in 1716 he was almost overwhelmed by fears and suspicions that his son was scheming with his ministers. Such fears, jealousy and mischievous tales pouring into his ear resulted in his dismissal of one minister, Lord Townsend, and the temporary resignation of another, the great Sir Robert Walpole. Relations between father and son reached their most lucidrous point when after the birth of a baby boy to Caroline the christening was held in her bedroom. The king insisted that the Duke of Newcastle (then Lord Chamberlain), who was detested by the Prince of Wales, should be a godfather. After the ceremony the prince shook his fist in the duke's face. In thick German accents he called the duke 'a rascal', adding words which Newcastle believed to be a challenge to a duel. The duke reported this to the king, who thereupon had his son arrested. Next day the baby was snatched from Caroline's arms and was removed, together with her three small daughters Anne, Caroline and Amelia. The king took custody of them and expelled the parents. The Prince and Princess of Wales, bereft of their children, bought a house in Leicester Square and a country lodge in Richmond. The baby, sickly at birth, died soon afterwards while in the care of the dowager Countess Portland. Naturally rumours arose among the king's enemies that the tiny prince had been murdered.

The quarrel continued, with the king doing all possible to persecute his son the more. Caroline's personal servant and dresser was Mrs. Henrietta Howard, later the Countess of Suffolk. Mrs. Howard was also the Prince of Wales' mistress, apparently with Caroline's complete acquiescence. Mr. Howard, the husband, lived at St. James's Palace as Head Groom to the Bedchamber of the king. And when the king learned of his son's relationship with Mrs. Howard he commanded Mr. Howard to go to Leicester House, cause a disturbance and demand that his wife be returned to him. When the quarrel between king and prince was patched up in 1720 the three children were still held by the grandfather under the care of Lady Portland. In the following year Caroline gave birth to another boy and was allowed to keep him. The boy was named William Augustus. His parents thought still less about their son and heir over the water as they and the nation celebrated the arrival of William Augustus, who was later, as Duke of Cumberland, to steal the limelight from his elder brother as a military commander.

In 1725 Frederick's eighteenth birthday, ignored in England, was celebrated in the court of Hanover with a grand ball. He was now allowed to appoint his own household, his 'governor' Monsieur Neibourg retiring into the background, full of dislike for his former charge. Frederick was also given an annual allowance of 8,000 crowns. His health was now very good. He had become increasingly interested in the arts, particularly music and French literature. At the same time he maintained a gay devil-may-care attitude towards life. He had developed a new passion—for cards and the gaming table. He still wrote to Princess Wilhelmina and became increasingly impatient to meet and to marry her.

Another year passed and the living skeleton in the cupboard of George I ceased to move. Sophia Dorothea, his divorced wife, died at the age of sixty, thus ending thirty-two years as a prisoner in the castle of Ahlden. In those thirty-two years she had never seen her former husband nor her two children George and Sophia. Her only reminder of them were two small portraits painted in their childhood. George I had ignored her written pleas that they be allowed to visit her. In London the Prince of Wales dared several times to speak sympathetically of his imprisoned mother to the king, who became red with anger and resentment at such impertinence. Of course, Frederick and his grandmother never met, but it was said that he inherited much of her youthful gaiety.

George I was not indifferent when news reached him of Sophia Dorothea's death. He was terrified. A superstitious man, he had once been told by a fortune-teller that when his divorced wife died his own death would follow within the next twelve months. Sophia Dorothea died on the 13th November 1726, cursing, it was said, the man who had been her husband. Early in June 1727 the king was still alive, but was suffering the tortures of a grisly premonition. He was leaving home for Osnabrück in Germany to visit his brother Bishop Ernest Augustus, Duke of York.

'On the eve of the king's departure', recorded Horace Walpole, 'he took leave of his son and the Princess of Wales and with tears, telling them he should never see them more. It was certainly his own approaching fate that melted him, not the thought of quitting for ever the two persons he hated.' Walpole also told how the king 'in a tender mood promised the Duchess of Kendal' (the Maypole) 'that if she survived him, and if it were possible for the departed to return to this world, he would make her a visit.'

The Duchess of Kendal was a companion of the king on his trip. When the two with their attendants crossed the North Sea to Holland on the 3rd of June he had, it seemed, lost his deathly forebodings. The king and his mistress drove in easy stages across Holland spending nights at the houses of friends. On the 9th of June they enjoyed a huge dinner at the home of Count de Twillet in Delden. Early on the following morning the king and some of his party went ahead towards Germany.

His mistress was to follow later and they would be reunited at the palace of the bishop.

While chatting in the moving coach with two Hanoverian officials named Hindenburg and Fabrie, the king suddenly collapsed. He retained consciousness but was unable to speak. In sign language he indicated that he wanted to be taken on to Osnabrück. On reaching the bishop's palace he became unconscious and died the following day.

Three days later the son of the dead king and his wife Caroline were having their customary afternoon nap in their bedroom at Richmond lodge when they were awakened and told they were now king and queen. The messenger was Sir Robert Walpole, chief minister of the late monarch. Sir Robert had ridden horseback at speed from London, forcing himself into the bedroom against the protests of servants. George II, as he now was, at that time regarded Sir Robert as an enemy and received him coldly. Then the new king and queen, dressing hurriedly, drove to London, where at their home, Leicester House, they received the congratulations of their friends in a jovial party-like atmosphere.

The people at large were unable to weep for George I or even given the satisfaction of watching the pomp and pageantry of a royal funeral. For the body of George I was never brought back to England. First it was put into storage in the vaults of the bishop's palace at Osnabrück while London and Hanover haggled over its final destination. Finally, two months later, it was interred for good in Hanover in a ceremony by night which seemed too furtive to be worthy of a king-elector.

The genuine sorrow of George's beloved Ermengarde Melusine, Duchess of Kendal, would have compensated for the cynical indifference at his death displayed by many in London who had pretended to be his friends. Back in England, the duchess remembered the promise of her George that, if possible, he would visit her after death. And Horace Walpole wrote that the duchess so keenly anticipated fulfilment of this promise 'that a large raven, or some black fowl, flying into one of the windows of her villa at Isleworth, she was persuaded it was the soul of her departed monarch so accoutred, and received and treated it with respect and tenderness of duty, till the royal bird or she took their last flight'. What of George's second German mistress, fat Charlotte Sophia von Kielmansegge, whom the Duchess of Kendal had outrivalled? She was spared the grief of bereavement, having herself died in 1725 to be remembered in England as the Countess Darlington.

When Frederick was told of the death of his grandfather he collapsed and lay in bed sorrowing. And, well aware of the hatred which had existed between the king and his father, Frederick had the courage to write of his great grief to his eldest sister Anne, who, incidentally, he had not seen for thirteen years.

'I am sure', his letter told Anne, 'that you share the grief I have felt since the death of our dear grandfather. I should be lacking in filial duty of the most ungrateful of men if it had not caused me great sorrow, for he treated me with especial affection and friendship. I was so overcome by sadness when they told me the news, I could not leave my bed for two days and fainted twice. My only consolation in this sad affliction is the knowledge of my dear parents' goodness. I flatter myself that I shall always conduct myself in a manner deserving of their esteem and friendship for me. I pray you dear sister, as you are by them, to remember me often to Their Majesties.'

Some biographers have questioned the sincerity of Frederick's letter. They have inferred that the Griff, then aged twenty, had been incapable of feeling very sorry at the death of the grandfather who had never failed to show him kindness on his visits to Hanover. The natural charm of the Griff had, it seems, often melted the ice of George's temperament. George had admired the poise and confidence which his grandson showed, from childhood upwards, as his representative at the many ceremonies of the Hanover court. The king-elector always praised Frederick. There is no record of his ever reproving his grandson, even for those antics in the old city with his servant companions. Certainly there is every reason to believe that the Griff was broken-hearted when his grandfather died. He who was grateful for the grandfather's affection was later to suffer from a father's hatred. Still unaware that the new king and queen wanted to prevent his coming to England as Prince of Wales, Frederick, in his letter to Anne, was doubtless sincere in his belief that they were good, and also that he would prove worthy of the friendship which mistakenly he believed they bore for him.

'Frederick is the dearest of my children', Caroline wrote to her friend the Duchess of Wolfenbüttel in 1727. Simultaneously she and the new king were quietly doing their best to delay the Griff's move to England and even to prevent him from becoming the accepted heir to the British throne. Despite Caroline's protestations of affection for the Griff, it would seem that to herself and husband he had become no more significant than the signature on the dutiful letters he had written to them over the years. On the death of George I they made no move to go to the continent to see him or to summons him to them. All their affections were now, it would seem, focussed on the plump infant Prince William, born to Caroline in 1721. The gurgling William almost miraculously captured the hearts and attention of parents ordinarily so indifferent to babies. The infant became Caroline's biggest diversion outside cards, political scheming, philosophy and theology. The methodical George II, whose intercourse with mistresses was rigidly regulated by the clock, now always found time to jab and to admire little William. On reaching the age of four the boy had been conscripted by his army-obsessed father into the crack 2nd Regiment of Foot Guards. In a tailor-made uniform and with miniature weapons also made to measure the child was placed on sentry duty at his parents' home, Leicester House, while onlookers cooed with loyal and sentimental delight. At the age of four William was also awarded the Order of the Bath, with the dukedom of Cumberland following when he was five.

Efforts to rob Frederick of his hereditary rights in Great Britain were made by the Prince and Princess of Wales even in 1725 when he became eighteen and while King George I was still alive. The diary of June 24th of that year of the Lord Chancellor Peter King stated that 'The Prince of Wales and his wife were for excluding Prince Frederick from the throne of England, but that after the king and prince, he should be Elector of Hanover, and Prince William his brother King of Great Britain; but that the king said it was unjust to do it without Prince Frederick's consent, who was now of an age to judge for himself, and so this matter now stood.' Robert Walpole, as chief minister to George I, warned him to bring Frederick to England during his reign. Otherwise, added Walpole, Frederick might never be able to come to England at all.

As the months followed the death of George I, Frederick awaited in vain for the call to England to take his rightful place in his father's court as Prince of Wales. Queen Caroline's 'dearest child' was forgotten as she worked and schemed to strengthen her influence over her husband the king and over the nation. 'The darling pleasure of her soul was power', wrote Lord Hervey of Caroline, who succeeded in having Robert Walpole retained as prime minister although he had been hated by her husband, Walpole had pleased Caroline, who in turn influenced the king, by a huge increase in the civil list. Then in October 1727 came the lavish coronation in Westminster Abbey, with the monarch's eldest son uninvited and still languishing unhappily in Hanover. His little brother William Duke of Cumberland was the darling of the coronation celebrations. And Queen Caroline's three train-bearers were his sisters Princesses Anne, Amelia and Caroline. They walked behind a mother who sweated profusely and breathed hard. For Caroline's body and gown were weighed down by nearly two and a half million pounds worth of gems, the big proportion of them hired for the day.

3

At Last to England

In 1728 the Griff reached the age of twenty-one. His character was formed to remain little changed for the rest of his life. One distinct feature about the adult Griff was his unpredictability, although, when faced with a problem, he could always be expected to do something quickly. What, however, this something might be could never be predicted. It was invariably a novel surprise which astonished the many and infuriated the few.

The great problem facing the Griff at the start of 1728 was why his parents, king and queen since June of the previous year, had not sent him that invitation to come to England. A secondary problem was how to advance his romantic wish to become the husband of his cousin Princess Wilhelmina of Prussia. The Griff was aware that his father was against the plan of his late grandfather for his marriage to Wilhelmina and for the marriage of Amelia to Prince Frederick of Prussia. Far from sharing the desire of George I for closer relations with Prussia and its royal family, George II at that time abhorred the whole scheme. It seemed to the Griff that the Treaty of Charlottenburg would never be ratified.

Accordingly the Griff evolved a plot which might win him his desired bride and thereby cause such a stir that the people of Great Britain, romantically moved, would demand to know why he was still barred from her soil by his father. Yes, he would secretly journey to Berlin, where, with the connivance of his aunt Queen Sophia of Prussia, he would quietly marry her daughter Wilhelmina. His parents would know nothing until he and Wilhelmina, one of the most eligible princesses in Europe, were man and wife. After this *fait accompli* Prime Minister Walpole would insist upon their majesties bringing them to London, where they would live happily ever after. Indeed, for the king to dare to ban him together with the Princess Wilhelmina would constitute a diplomatic insult that would outrage Prussia and other German states.

Frederick's aide-de-camp Lamotte disappeared from his side in the Herrenhausen palace to be driven towards Prussia. With a few intimate friends Frederick discussed how he himself, when the anticipated call came, could leave the palace, reach Berlin and be married before his absence was discovered. On arrival in Berlin aide-de-camp Lamotte got into touch with courtiers close to Queen Sophia. Frederick, he told them, wanted to marry Princess Wilhelmina, although his father (Sophia's brother) was against this alliance for which his grandfather had so earnestly wished. Would their majesties of Prussia agree to a marriage? If so, Prince Frederick would secretly leave Hanover for Berlin at the earliest for the wedding ceremony.

When Sastot, Queen Sophia's chamberlain, whispered to her this message she was delighted. She had long favoured a marriage between her daughter and Frederick. Moreover, it would please her to annoy her brother George II, whom she heartily disliked. The Prussian queen was a talkative tactless woman. In her excitement she foolishly told British ambassador du Bourgeay something of Frederick's suggestion for a secret wedding. The honest ambassador shocked the queen by replying that he was duty-bound to report this to his government. Within a few hours a messenger left the British ambassador in Berlin with a dispatch from du Bourgeay to Walpole in London. Meanwhile, with growing confidence in the success of his mission, Lamotte had obtained assurances from the mother that Wilhelmina had agreed to marry Frederick. At the time Lamotte was unaware that the princess had needed much persuasion. Despite her exchanges of letters with Frederick, she shrank from the idea of becoming his wife. At this stage the queen had not yet mentioned any detail of this marriage plot to her fiery husband King Frederick William. She was stifling her loquacity until he was in a suitable mood.

Walpole read the dispatch from Berlin and quickly informed the king, who received details of Frederick's marriage plot with consternation and anger. Since he was then so deeply opposed to closer relations with Prussia, the Griff in his scheming was impudently challenging not only his wishes but also carefully planned English diplomatic policies. Moreover, George, a man of many hatreds, held the Prussian royal family in detestation. Walpole used the Griff's plot as an example of the folly of keeping him in Hanover instead of bringing him to England where he would be under some surveillance. In the past Walpole had repeatedly urged the king to let Frederick settle in London. At last both George and Caroline reluctantly consented. They would have to feign a welcome for their eldest son—a stranger for fourteen years—who would, alas, take precedence over their dear little Willie, Duke of Cumberland.

The Griff's plot proved to be a double rocket. While one half exploded in London, the other half exploded in Berlin with a resounding bang. King Frederick learned for the first time about the plan for the secret wedding of his daughter. Whether this intimation came to him through his bumbling wife or through diplomatic channels is not known. And the news also spread among the Prussian public. There were rumours that Frederick had already been seen in Berlin in ineffective disguise. King Frederick was furious, realising that any revival of the marriage plans in the dead draft of the Treaty of Charlottenburg could only result in a humiliating snub to himself and Prussia from his brother-in-law George II. Frederick, already notorious for the ill-treatment of his children, punished Wilhelmina with a beating. In his uncontrollable rage he also thrashed Frederick, his son and heir. In later years Wilhelmina expressed her pleasure that a marriage between herself and Frederick never took place.

The Griff's great marriage scheme was his first important venture in his personal policy of complete unpredictability and astonishing surprise. And the venture cannot be dismissed as a failure. True that he failed to win Wilhelmina as his bride, but his venture succeeded in persuading his father to open the doors of England to him. Indeed, under some pressure from Walpole, the king was soon insisting that his eldest son be fetched from Hanover at the earliest and installed under observation in London. It was felt that, left any more to his own devices in Hanover, the Griff might get up to more mischief to the harm of Great Britain and the embarrassment of her monarch. Moreover, George II was already disturbed by rumours that members of the opposition party were organising a petition asking that Frederick be allowed to come to London to enjoy his rights as heir to the throne.

Daily, king's messengers travelled between London and the electorate. To the lively Griff the communications they brought were usually dreary. They were full of his majesty's wishes regarding Hanoverian foreign policy, internal development and official appointments. Messengers would also from time to time deliver dutiful conventional letters written to the Griff by his sisters. And almost daily the Griff had to receive titled and wealthy personages and their wives from England, anxious to observe and to glitter for a while in the receptions and balls of the Herrenhausen palace. The furore over the sensation of the prince's marriage plot was subsiding. Now he was in the midst of Hanover's winter social season. He was presiding at a succession of banquets, dances and receptions. Between these he was also spending many hours at card and gaming tables, adding to his debts which had already reached huge proportions.

It was during one of the biggest palace balls of the season that a Colonel de Launay and Marquis de la Forêt were announced as personal emissaries of his majesty the king. Frederick slipped away from the ball to receive their message. This was that the king commanded him to make the necessary preparations to leave with the colonel and marquis for residence in England without taking a formal and public farewell of the court and people of Hanover. There is a traditional story that

Frederick and the two departed for England that very night. Actually, however, weeks elapsed before they quietly set out on the journey. This was early in December 1728.

The journey was an ordeal for the Griff who had never before been beyond the frontiers of the Hanover electorate and who had always lived in an atmosphere of warmth and luxury. Because of the absurd secrecy surrounding the journey he was provided with no mounted military escorts, and inadequate plans had been made for suitable rest and guidance across Germany and Holland in wild and wintry weather of terrible intensity. The prince and his party in carriages overloaded with his luggage were dragged by frightened horses along highways made invisible by snow and ice. The story of the prince's perils were recorded in the diary of the Earl of Egmont from the account told him by one of the party. On one occasion drivers and passengers believed they were on a safe road when the coach ahead of Frederick's sank into the water and ice of what proved to be a treacherous marsh. Further on, in Holland, the horses and coaches with their passengers were in danger of sliding from a dyke into a canal. Then the packet boat in which the prince was to cross the North Sea was prevented by ice from reaching the quayside at Helvoetsluys. The prince and party were rowed in a small boat through crackling ice to the vessel.

The Griff, generally regarded as soft and pampered, endured the journey across both land and water with surprising fortitude. While on the turbulent North Sea he gaily planned suddenly to appear before his parents at St. James's Palace while they were still unaware that he had even left the continent. He asked that on his arrival no message about him should be sent ahead to London, so that he could, faithful to his policy of unpredictability, take the king and queen by surprise. When the ship docked, however, on December 7th a too zealous naval officer ashore immediately dispatched an express messenger to London with the news that Prince Frederick was come.

Despite the message of this dutiful officer nobody in palace and government circles seemed to care that Frederick had

arrived. Somehow Frederick and his attendants reached
Whitechapel, ignored because they were unrecognised. The
prince, who must have been exhausted after his tempestuous
journey across land and sea, could have at least taken a rest in
one of that village's inns. Instead he hailed a hackney coach
like any ordinary Englishman and gave St. James's Palace as
his destination. A half-hour's night drive through London's
smelly and unlit streets, and the Griff was at last at the massive
but unpretentious-looking St. James's Palace. No ceremonious
welcome awaited him. He was shown up a private staircase
leading only to the apartments of the mother he had not seen
for fourteen years and whom he could scarcely remember.

At last he stood before the queen, with her strong but
kindly face and noticeably ample bosom. Soon also he was bowing low before the fussy, red-faced little king. The Griff, with
humble and reverent deportment before their majesties, made
such charming little speeches that both were suddenly, if only
temporarily, pleased to have such a son. The young man was
as pleasant in person as in manner. His nose was a little too
sharp, his eyes a little too outstanding—but his smile was
attractive. He was beautifully dressed. In those days men's legs
attracted special attention. The Griff's legs in their silk stockings
had a feminine shapeliness. Soon the Griff was also meeting
his sisters—proud, musical Anne, aged nineteen; Amelia,
aged seventeen, vivacious and talkative; Caroline, aged fifteen,
quiet and shy. And for the first time the Griff saw his brother
the seven-year-old William, and two more fairly recent
sisters Mary, aged five, and Louisa, aged four.

Of course, Frederick was soon to receive words of welcome
together with the sharpest scrutiny from the most powerful
man in Great Britain. This was Sir Robert Walpole, first Lord
of the Treasury and Prime Minister. The two could hardly
have been less alike. Frederick's appearance and demeanour
seemed feminine as he focussed his charm on this political
genius who was also the coarse, hard-swearing, hard-drinking
Norfolk squire. Through Walpole's efforts the once alien
House of Hanover was now strongly entrenched as the ruler

of Great Britain. Through Walpole's economic policies the nation was on her way to unprecedented expansion and wealth. Walpole had dominated George I, and now, through the influence of Caroline, he guided and advised George II. Indeed, it was Walpole who had persuaded the king to bring his eldest son at last to England. Now the hard alcoholic face of Walpole faced the more sensitive but weaker face of the prince. Surveying Frederick with his sharp brown eyes, Walpole would have wondered whether he could control and dominate him also. As time passed, Frederick, while refusing to be led by Walpole, became much interested in him as an outstanding example of an eighteenth-century country gentleman turned politician. Possessing Houghton Hall, one of the finest country homes in England, Walpole found his greatest pleasures in hunting foxes and women. He enjoyed low company perhaps more than high company. 'Walpole', said Samuel Johnson, 'always talked bawdy at his table because in that all could join.' In London he would read the reports of his gamekeepers before government papers and dispatches. Nevertheless, when necessary he could display great learning and cultural interests which he would have hotly repudiated while 'talking bawdy' to his bucolic guests at Houghton Hall in Norfolk.

On his move from Hanover to London the Griff was soon meeting many kinds of Britons. The young German who had never been beyond the electorate was quick to understand and to become on friendly terms with them. But he showed the greatest enthusiasm not for individuals but for the fabulous city of London itself, so much larger and of so much more variety than little Hanover. At twenty-one the Griff was in the prime of youth, without moral inhibitions, charming, hungry for new adventures, novel sensations. He had always, it seemed, money to spend and squander; borrowed from others when he ran out of his own. Now before the Griff was London, his oyster; the London which, as Johnson told Boswell, possessed 'all that life can afford'.

It would be difficult to understand the behaviour of the

immigrant prince without picturing the London of the first half of the eighteenth century. At the time of his arrival it was the boom city of the Western world. With a population estimated at nearly half a million, London was still smaller than Paris, but soon would be bounding ahead, the growing wealth of Great Britain making it the magnet of Europe. The London of the Griff had everything, from the art and beauty of the highest culture to the shame and hideousness of the most terrible forms of crime, vice and poverty.

London was a feast of art, music and literature, of an exciting and elaborate social life, of fine mansions, graceful and trim gardens. The music and opera were particularly outstanding. Musicians, composers and singers flocked to London from all parts of Europe. Perhaps the most distinguished of the composers was George Frederick Handel. He had lived there since 1711 and had become a naturalised Englishman in 1726. The theatre was rising to the greatness it attained later in the century, although some playhouses also discreetly accommodated brothels. London had everything to offer to the Griff in his partial addiction to high living. The nobility dwelt in splendid mansions and entertained magnificently. The wealthy were waited upon by hordes of servants and retainers. Indeed, one in every five of the population of the capital was said to be in domestic service. The need for more servants annually attracted an average of 5,000 youths and girls to the capital from the countryside. A great gulf was fixed between the nobility and its servants who were too often regarded as repulsively inferior creatures. The Marquis of Aberdeen, indeed, insisted upon his housemaids covering their common hands in white kid gloves when they made his bed. Gaming was a big but insidious pastime of society. In this the Griff was to obtain both pleasure and pain and to pile up prodigious debts. Then everywhere in London were beautiful women eager for love affairs with royalty. But as a gentleman's city there were in Pall Mall and St. James's Street, so near to the palace, exclusive coffee houses and taverns for leisure and talk secure from feminine intrusion.

While the coarse hands of servants might be concealed in white kid gloves, nothing could conceal the vulgar side of London. It was too painfully apparent. In Hanover, with his friends the pages and stable boys, the Griff, playing truant from the Herrenhausen palace, became familiar with the maladorous old city and its low life. The Griff could not venture far in London without encountering worse conditions. Even the main streets of the city had open sewers or none at all. They were unpaved and unlighted. Suddenly the wayfarer would stumble from thoroughfares of reasonable respectability into dreadful and dangerous slums such as in Drury Lane and St. Giles. The Thames crowded with boats, including luxurious private barges, was the pride of Londoners. Yet this river was green and brown from the sewage or other filth running into it, and the scented handkerchiefs held to the noses by sensitive folk could not neutralise the stink. Yet from the waters of the Thames were daily taken millions of gallons for drinking and washing.

The common folk of London were fired by cheap gin obtainable from street barrows, barbers, tobacconists and tailors. In some streets of the town one shop out of four had gin for sale. The favourite pastimes of these cockneys were also fiery. These included open-air cock-fights, bull- and bear-baiting, watching prisoners being hanged on the Tyburn gallows and semi-nude prostitutes being given the lash at Bridewell. Other popular sights included races between young women wearing only shifts or bloomers, and poking sticks at the caged lunatics in the Bethlehem Hospital at Moorfields. There was natural beauty in St. James's Park which, to the surprise of the visiting Abbé Prevost, 'was open to all ranks'. Other open spaces in London included Lincoln's Inn Fields and the lawns of Gray's Inn. Like most of the streets of the capital, these were night and day haunted by prostitutes.

The Griff found London gripped in an era of permissiveness, compared by moralists with the condition of ancient Rome before the fall. They interpreted the permissiveness to be a certain omen of the impending decline and collapse of England.

When the Griff settled in London the Society for the Reformation of Manners, founded three years previously, was valiantly trying to tame its wildness. The society employed a regiment of informers 'to report sabbath breakers, houses of bawdry and disorder, whores, nightwalkers and cursings'. But these efforts produced no reform.

Such was the London found by Frederick. However, there were many indications that he adored it. He would have agreed with his friend (and later enemy) Lord Hervey who 'couldn't imagine what people mean when they sigh over the degeneracy of the age and the badness of the world'. Hervey found them 'delightful' and boasted that 'I had rather live in these times than in any times or country I ever read of'.

For a short time after his arrival in England the Griff had to avoid the clandestine pleasures of the town to be acclaimed at celebrations planned for him, without great enthusiasm, by his parents. He made his début in the court at a great ball in St. James's Palace where he was cynosure of the eyes of the nobility of the land. The lords and ladies stared, many of the latter through their fashionable bejewelled lorgnettes. They saw Frederick, smiling and entirely at ease, the gold lace on his dress coat glittering like sunbeams. The general impression made by the Griff might be that expressed by Lady Bristol: 'He is the most agreeable young man it is possible to imagine without being the least handsome. His person is little but well-made and genteel; a liveliness in his eyes that is undescribable and the most obliging address that can be conceived.'

The great ball continued in its magnificence until nearly midnight. Letters left to posterity by Lord Hervey challenge our romantic imaginings of such exalted eighteenth-century occasions by comments pertaining to the olfactory. He described an evening at court as 'a bore' with 'dancing, sweating and stinking in abundance'. On the other hand, society of the time was challenging its party perspiration with powerful liquid weapons. Ladies and gentlemen soaked themselves in the heavy scents of Cordova water, aqua Mellis and spirit of Ambergis. At midnight with the end of the formal ball departed the older nobility, the doddering lords and ladies, the faded dowagers. The young people left behind retired for some minutes and returned prepared for the masquerade that lasted all night. The St. James's Palace masquerade was an inheritance from the electors of Hanover who earlier had adopted the masquerade from their sojourns in Venice. Faithful to this tradition, the men wore grotesque and often frightening masks; the women hid their faces behind small masks of black or mauve velvet. The masks of these court masquerades invariably stifled human modesty as well as disguising human features. Often there were brawls and more often there was conduct of a flagrantly erotic nature. In the words of Lord Egmont (written in January 1729): 'These masquerades are the corruption of our youth and a scandal to the nation, and it were well to be wished the king would not encourage them. The bishops have addressed in a body against them and exposed them in their sermons, but all to no purpose.'

The Griff revelled in this, the first of many rowdy and unrestrained masquerades in which he joined in London. Indeed, the humid light of a London morning had arrived before he removed his disguise to snatch a short rest in the wing of the palace where he now had apartments. While London was such a novelty to the Griff he could ill spare time for sleep. Not content with moving only in royal and noble circles, he wanted to see a lot more of the capital and to make the acquaintance of the common people. Completely without any class consciousness, he could mingle and talk with these without the slightest hint of patronage or condescension. This is not surprising when his long and close association with the servants and stable workers of the Herrenhausen palace is recalled. Closely observing Frederick in these early days in London was Reichenbach, the Prussian ambassador to the court of St. James's. His dispatches to a curious King Frederick William described the enormous popularity which the Griff was winning in London through his natural democratic ways.

In a sightseeing tour which included the Tower of London and Somerset House Frederick amazed and delighted

Londoners by breaking away from his attendants and plunging into the crowds to shake hands and exchange sallies. Today in the 1970s a 'royal walkabout', as it is called, is regarded as something quite novel. 'Royal walkabouts' were, however, originated by the Griff early in the eighteenth century. In this trip to the Tower, Somerset House and the City the prince was again and again mobbed by the crowds. The prince on his part received the adoration of the multitude with unconcealed delight. 'Nothing has pleased me so much in my life as those huzzas,' he remarked in his precise but heavily German-accented English. As the days passed, the desire of the people to see this heir to the throne, who had come so belatedly from Hanover, grew still greater. Crowds would hover near St. James's Palace to obtain a glimpse of him in his comings and goings. He had always a smile and a wave for the throng as he passed by. Meanwhile, in addition to printed reports of the Griff's popularity, there appeared for sale in the streets scurrilous broadsheets purporting to describe the immoral past of the prince in Hanover. Whether true or false, it seems that the attribution to the young man of such human failings only increased the affection of the public towards him.

The remarkable success of this young man of twenty-one during his first days in a strange land he had never previously seen, deserved the gratitude, pride and admiration of his father. George II, however, felt no such sentiments. On the contrary he was much displeased. The self-confident young Griff was driving him from the national spotlight. All kinds of people were finding the Griff attractive and charming. The curse of the Hanoverians—inane hatred of father for son—was now visited upon George II. He who had been hated by his father George I was now beginning to loathe his own son and heir.

George II had regarded the Griff with suspicion from the very day he had landed in England. He had in their first meetings been pleased with the young man's filial deference and courtesy, and had even confided in Walpole, 'I think this is not a son I need be much afraid of.' Nevertheless the congenital Hanoverian jealousy lay in wait. The king created his son

Prince of Wales. He 'welcomed' him to membership of the Privy Council. Yet these gestures were made only after efforts of persuasion from Sir Robert Walpole and other ministers. On the death of George I, George II was allowed by the government to retain the £100,000 a year he had received as Prince of Wales. Although his own income was now nearly £900,000 a year, he declined to surrender all of the £100,000 to the Griff. The king argued that so much money would be bad for a young man who had in Hanover run up huge debts which were still owing. Thus the king decided to give his son £2,000 monthly. Added to this would be the revenues of the Duchy of Cornwall. It was estimated that the Griff would be receiving only half what his father had as Prince of Wales.

The new Prince of Wales was in what to him was a strange country among strange people, the strangest of whom seemed to be his own father. He badly needed a wise and trustworthy friend who could guide his footsteps. His mother Caroline had wisdom; but where he was concerned she was bowing to the selfish whims and wishes of his father. Walpole had proved a faithful guide first to George I and now to the present king. Walpole could have helped the prince; but Walpole was not going to imperil his relationship with the father by showing too much friendship for the son. Frederick was seeking the appropriate friend and adviser, familiar with English ways when, towards the end of 1729, John Lord Hervey returned from a long stay on the continent. The two renewed an acquaintance of some thirteen years previously when the young Hervey on his grand tour met the boy Frederick in Hanover. Now in London these two unusual personalities got on so well that the Griff believed he saw in Hervey the wise and staunch friend he needed so badly.

John Lord Hervey, son of the 1st Earl of Bristol, was Member of Parliament for Bury St. Edmunds. More significant, he had been a gentleman of the bedchamber to George II when he was Prince of Wales. While in that office he had become a friend of Caroline. Hervey, aged thirty-three in

1729, was married to Molly Lepell, a young woman of exceptional beauty who had been a maid of honour to Caroline. Hervey was a delicate man and subject to epileptic fits. It was in the course of an illness that in July 1728 Hervey went to Spa in Belgium for treatment, accompanied by his beloved friend Stephen Fox, later the 1st Earl of Ilchester, of Redlynch, Somerset. In exchanges of letters with Fox, Hervey addressed him endearments comparable with those of a lover to his mistress. Of handsome features, Hervey had an effeminate appearance because of his attempts to conceal an unhealthy pallor with colourful cosmetics. No coward, he fought a duel with the statesman William Pulteney. Among the many scurrillous appellations of Pulteney for Hervey were, 'Pretty Mr. Fairlove', 'Pretty little Master Miss' and 'Delicate hermaphrodite'. Others sneered that there were not two but three sexes—'Males, females and Lord Hervey.'

Hervey is best remembered for his brilliant, acid and heavily biased *Memoirs of the Reign of George II.* He was also evilly immortalised in the pitiless lines written by Alexander Pope after the two had quarrelled. In these Pope calls Hervey by the name of Sporus, the castrated boy 'mistress' of Nero. Extracts:

> *Let Sporus tremble—What! That thing of silk?*
> *Sporus! That mere white curd of ass's milk?*
> *Satire or sense, alas! can Sporus feel?*
> *Who breaks a butterfly upon a wheel?*
> *Yet let me flap this bug with gilded wings,*
> *This painted child of dirt that stinks and stings!*
>
> *Amphibious thing! that acting either part,*
> *The trifling head or the corrupted heart,*
> *Fop at the toilet, flatterer at the board,*
> *Now trips a lady, and now struts a lord.*

No lady in Lord Hervey's body tripped into the life of the Griff, whose amorous motivations were unfailingly wholly directed with dedication towards females, from young girls to mature matrons. And whatever suspicions regarding Hervey's friendship with Stephen Fox and the flagrant insinuations of both Pope and Pulteney, Lord Hervey consorted normally with his wife, who bore him eight children. With the Griff he also showed an active interest in other women. It was rivalry over a woman whom each desired that eventually destroyed their friendship.

As 1729 drew to its close, Frederick could congratulate himself that his first full year in England had been a success— with one lamentable exception. This exception was his failure to retain the affection and goodwill of his father. Friendship shown by the king for his heir had in jealousy been quickly withdrawn. But now the Griff had the friendship of Lord Hervey, who, so close to Queen Caroline and the court, would surely influence them in his favour. The outstanding triumph of this Prince of Wales from Germany was that he had effortlessly strolled into the hearts of the common people of England. He had become 'the people's prince', moving here and there without fuss or pomp. He would go shopping in London on foot, exchange jokes and sallies with admiring crowds, hail shabby hackney carriages. He gave royalty, which had been so remote from the working folk of London, a new significance. By descending from the common to the sordid, however, he foolishly placed himself in grave danger.

The Griff stole secretly from the palace at night to rove in St. James's Park, in the darkness a haunt of prostitutes and toughs. A report of one such expedition reached the Earl of Egmont, surprising and paining this pious peer, who was prominent in court circles. John Cooper, the servant of Peter Wentworth, a royal page, had through the semi-darkness recognised the Prince of Wales stealing alone into the park, not through the usual entrance, but the palace stables. The Griff, among the bushes and the trees, picked up a woman. Soon she was running away from him. In her possession were the Griff's watch, to which were attached his royal seals; two guineas and a gold medal. The Griff sought the help of a Grenadier guardsman, asking him to find the thieving slattern, to take from her the watch and the seals and then to let her go. She could keep the money, added the Griff, since the watch and the seals were the only articles he valued. The guardsman set out in pursuit, but the woman vanished into the night. The watch and the seals did not remain long in her possession. Next morning an astonished pedestrian found them lying on the ground in the Mall. They were safely returned to the Griff. The prostitute or her confederates probably discarded them there on realising they belonged to the Prince of Wales and that such a theft could result in death on the Tyburn gallows.

Alas, the good Earl of Egmont was soon again to become worried by the Prince of Wales, who for a night was so disgracefully deprived of his official seals.

4

'Fat Ill-shaped Dwarf'

Friendship with the influential Lord Hervey did not bring to Frederick the status in the hierarchy of Great Britain that he so earnestly desired. Hervey treated and admired the Griff as a cultured young man with literary, artistic and musical interests. He also eagerly shared his friend's fondness for dalliance with women. Yet apparently he refused to take seriously the wish of the prince officially to serve the nation for whose common people he had quickly formed a real affection. Certainly such an escapade as that in St. James's Park would not encourage faith in the prince as an earnest responsible person. Yet he had, as we shall see, a serious side and splendid propensities which might develop if only they were encouraged. Yet Hervey, with his influence with Queen Caroline, Sir Robert Walpole and others, failed to support the more noble ambitions of the Griff.

The Griff had tried to be accepted as one of them by his parents and three eldest sisters who regarded him with mistrust and jealousy. He entered into their private family life, a routine of tedious sameness. On those evenings when there were no 'Drawing Rooms' or other public receptions the queen invariably insisted that the diversion should be card games such as basset, cribbage or commerce. The queen presided at one table with the eldest girl the Princess Royal (Anne). She liked the Griff to preside at another table, and often little brother the Duke of Cumberland was there also. The king might wander off to enjoy the company of his mistress Mrs. Howard, although in the evenings he often preferred 'talking bawdy' with feather-brained family governess Lady Deloraine in the apartment of his daughters. The Griff, too,

59

would also have preferred another diversion than the family card games. He loved cards played seriously for high stakes, but not as an empty pastime.

When the king had tired of 'talking bawdy' with the governess he would usually join the rest of the family after cards. The Griff and his father, however, could find little in common. The king's intellectual and artistic interests were strictly limited. Like the Griff, he enjoyed music, but as for the literary, he never read books. Indeed, he objected to books so much that he never liked the clever studious queen to flaunt them in his presence. She had to do her reading in secret in her private sitting room. Then even a discussion between the king and his son on England would have been unhappy; for whereas the Griff loved England, George hated her. This hatred, growing with the years, finally exploded into the famous outburst: 'No English cook can dress a dinner; no English player can act; no English coachman can drive: no Englishwoman knows how to come into a room; no English-woman knows how to dress herself.'

In these early years of his English domicile the Griff got on reasonably well with the queen despite the dreariness of her perpetual family card parties. Caroline, like the Griff, had culture. They shared an interest in philosophy and religion. While the Griff saw the approach to religion through the emotions rather than through reason, Caroline's method of approach was rational. She was an enthusiast for the Latitu-dinarianism of John Tillotson, the seventeenth-century arch-bishop, with its respect for ethical and moral precepts but indifference to doctrine and liturgies. The Griff was in later years to become moved even by the emotional, irrational preaching of Methodist George Whitefield. While, however, the mother was willing to speak long to her eldest son on eternity, her lips were sealed in his presence on matters of state. King, queen and their advisers would confide none of these to the heir to the throne, just as in the following century Queen Victoria withheld such information from the future King Edward VII.

Disappointing also was the Griff's relationship with sisters Anne, Amelia and Caroline. Anne, proud and high-spirited, had an independence of outlook and pronounced opinions which were soon to come into collision with Frederick. Each was devoted to music, but their individual views on what constituted good music differed. And because the Griff so often had outbursts of boyish pranks and tricks, she mistook him for a fool. For a time they had a musical partnership, Anne playing the harpsichord and her brother the 'cello or fiddle. Mutual music-making, however, failed to calm a mutual animosity. The Griff and witty, talkative Amelia seemed close friends for a short period, for they both enjoyed gossip with much cynical and irreverent comment. But when the Griff learned that she was repeating to others confidences which he had entrusted to her their relationship became strained. Sister Caroline, quiet and tactful, usually succeeded in keeping on peaceful terms with the Griff, but they were never close. In rows between the Griff and his other sisters Caroline endeavoured to maintain a benevolent neutrality, most of the benevolence being reserved for Anne and Amelia.

At the approach of May 1729 it was announced that King George would be leaving for three months in the electorate of Hanover, his first visit there since he and Caroline had departed with George I for England in 1714. It seemed that the Prince of Wales would at last be accorded official recognition and responsibility by being appointed regent during his father's absence. The Griff was willing and eager to become his father's representative in London as in boyhood he had been the living symbol of King-Elector George I in Hanover. Then came the announcement that the regent would be Queen Caroline. The king was not going to allow his son, so popular with the British people, to be accorded this eminent position where he might influence the government and attract lustre to his own name and reputation. Besides, Queen Caroline, with her lust for power, desired to see herself as regent. The Griff suffered this snub from his parents with comparative grace. Stubbornly and sadly they would never take him seriously. This attitude doubtless helped to drive him on to new follies, indiscretions and extravagances.

There was the marriage plot hatched by old Sarah, Duchess of Marlborough. This began when the Griff was so short of money that he asked one of his most trustworthy attendants to try to borrow some. This attendant approached Sarah. She refused a loan to the Griff, but instead offered him her lovely grand-daughter Lady Diana Spencer together with a dowry for £100,000. There is evidence of this double offer, but other details of the story are circumstantial. The Griff, it is said, accepted the offer. He had several meetings with Lady Diana and heartily approved of her. A secret wedding was arranged in the chapel of Windsor Lodge, one of the duchess's country houses. The plot, runs the story, was punctured by Sir Robert Walpole, following a report from a paid informer. The duchess was warned that the king would not tolerate such a marriage.

However, at about the same time the Griff was reviving his youthful dreams of a marriage with Princess Wilhelmina of Prussia. By now British policy towards Prussia and its royal house had changed. George II was now willing for his son to marry Wilhelmina, but only if King Frederick William also gave his own son Frederick in marriage to Amelia as had years ago been agreed between the Prussian monarch and King George I. Colonel Sir Charles Hotham was sent as special British envoy to Berlin to discuss this revived scheme. And the Griff pursued this envoy with letters by messengers begging him to do his utmost to win Wilhelmina on his behalf. 'Please dear Hotham', said one letter, 'get my marriage settled. My impatience increases daily and I am foolishly in love.' Hotham's mission failed because of the refusal of King Frederick to accept what today might be described as a package deal. Wilhelmina could wed the Prince of Wales, he said, but he wouldn't permit his son Crown Prince Frederick to become husband of Amelia. Hotham, on his king's instructions, insisted that it must be the two marriages or none at all. Fiery King Frederick lost his temper and insulted Hotham who beat a hasty retreat back to London and a disappointed Griff. In 1731 Wilhelmina became permanently out of his reach by marrying the Margrave of Bayreuth.

The Griff did not lack feminine consolation for the final collapse of the Anglo-Prussian marriage plan. His roving eyes had been drawn to a Miss La Tour, the daughter of an oboe player in the orchestra of a London theatre. Father La Tour would not surrender the girl for nothing. The Griff had to purchase her for a 'fee simple' of £1,500. He set her up in a house adjoining that of her father. Among later acquisitions of the Griff was a girl known only in history as 'an apothecary's daughter of Kingston'. In his diary Lord Egmont quoted evidence of one of the prince's entourage that 'he was not nice in his choice' of mistresses and that 'he talked more of feats this way then he acts'. Apparently like his father the Griff enjoyed boasting of his sexual prowess. Nevertheless he certainly possessed more discrimination in his choices than George II, of whom it was said: 'No woman comes amiss of him if she were but very willing and very fat.'

Meanwhile Monsieur Neibourg, who in Hanover had been Frederick's 'governor' and chief tutor, took his leave of Queen Caroline. This disagreeable Frenchman, who had hated his former charge so much, had for some reason followed him to England. Now he departed for good with final stabs in the young man's back. He told the queen that since he wouldn't be seeing her again he must 'discharge his conscience' by speaking out about her elder son. Neibourg added: 'He has the most vicious nature and the most false heart that ever man had, nor are his vices the vices of a gentleman but the mean base tricks of a knavish footman.'

Comments on the prince's character made by others in the same period differ from those of his former tutor. These comments praise Frederick for his kindness, generosity and humanity. The young man maintained his mistresses and pursued other women. He gambled madly. But these were common habits among young men of his age and class in the period in which he lived. At that time, indeed, there were even bishops who kept mistresses and sired bastards. Dr. Haiter, Archdeacon of York and chaplain to King George II, was the illegitimate son of the then reigning Archbishop of York. Similarly gaming for high stakes was a pastime that gripped highly respected statesmen, professional men, their wives and sons. Augustus Schutz, Master of Robes to George II, commented upon the great but undiscriminating generosity of the Griff who 'often wants to do a well-placed kindness by giving to unworthy objects'. Then Schutz described him as 'extremely dutiful to his parents, who do not return it in love, and seem to neglect him by letting him do as he will, but they keep him short of money'. Others testified that anyone in want would never ask the help of Frederick in vain. He was a compassionate man, always sincerely touched by the suffering of others. He was a strong advocate for prison reform, for the betterment of conditions among the poor. Towards sick friends he was solicitous and attentive. After Lord Hervey had suffered an epileptic attack he sat long at his bedside quietly consoling him.

Augustus Schutz was among many to comment adversely upon a 'childishness' that would at intervals overwhelm the Griff. This led to foolish talk and often to even more foolish actions. This 'childishness' or rather rebellious boyishness was often directed uncomfortably towards pompous, important people. In a modern phrase, although so much a child of the establishment the Griff was too often offensively anti-establishment. Unconscious of his high station he also revelled in practical jokes and elaborate hoaxes. When George II had left for Hanover, the Griff and Queen Caroline were invited to dinner by the fussy Duke of Newcastle. There the Griff challenged all formality by making everybody drink bumpers to his mother's health until she laughingly broke up the dinner. Next the Griff called for fiddles for an impromptu dance. Later the queen was joining the prince in baiting the old Duke of Grafton who was notorious for his meanness. They mischievously hinted for an invitation to stay with Grafton at his hunting lodge in Richmond. The duke made the excuse that this was unfit to receive them. Thereupon the Griff said he would bring tents and pitch them in the garden. The Griff induced intoxication in the Duke of Newcastle's guests by insisting that they down bumpers in the queen's honour. However, he certainly would not have drunk as much himself. Rarities in the hard-drinking eighteenth century, the Griff touched alcohol only occasionally while his mother did not drink at all.

Ambition intermingled with boyish mischief led the Griff, with Hervey's collaboration, to foist a hurriedly written five-act comedy upon the London public under the name of a non-existent 'Captain Bodin'. The Griff and Hervey wrote the play together, then had it delivered to Wilks, the actor-manager at Drury Lane Theatre. Wilks read the first three acts with boredom. He then cynically commented: 'If the last two acts which I have not seen are exceedingly better than the first three I have seen, then the play might last one night.' Nevertheless secret pressure from Hervey's court cronies persuaded the theatre's owners to overrule Wilks and to insist upon the play being presented. The unhappy Wilks remained in ignorance that 'Captain Bodin' was really the Prince of Wales and Lord Hervey.

In fear that Wilks's judgement might be correct, a detachment of rough men concealing cudgels and also soldiers were engaged to sit vigilantly in the audience. The acting had not proceeded far when there was an uproar. There were protests and catcalls from many who did not like the play. These were eventually subdued by the cudgel-men and the soldiers. Nevertheless an heroic theatre-goer named Powell arose and cried: 'The highest power on earth cannot force the freeborn subjects of England to approve of such nonsense.' On the second night another audience, also protesting, had the money for their tickets refunded. Nevertheless the play staggered on for a few more nights. On one of these a brave Prince of Wales was in the audience.

The Griff and Hervey drew increasingly closer in friendship, to the discomfiture of Stephen Fox with whom he had been emotionally so close. In his letters to Stephen, Hervey would frequently make affectionate little mentions of Frederick. Hervey had recently been appointed Vice-Chamberlain to the Royal Household. This seemed much to the advantage of the Griff as Hervey would doubtless often be speaking to the king and queen in his favour. The Griff was godfather at the christening of the third son of Hervey and his lovely wife Molly. Then the Griff became ill at Hampton Court and was overwhelmed by mysterious convulsions. In sore distress his bosom friend dashed off letters to Stephen Fox with the latest on the beloved patient's progress. Finally the prince recovered, giving expensive presents to all those who had helped to nurse and sustain him. 'The prince', wrote Hervey, 'does these things from goodness of heart and a natural disposition and a desire to give pleasure.' Yet only a few years later the same Hervey was to write of Frederick as 'the prince who never forgot an injury or remembered an obligation'.

The affection of Lord Hervey for the Griff turned to hatred towards the end of 1731 and early in 1732. The cause of the rift was a young woman. She was the Honourable Anne Vane, a daughter of Lord Barnard and a maid of honour to the queen. Short and dumpy, Anne was described as plain by some of her contemporaries and as pretty by others. Lord Egmont in his diary saw Anne as 'a fat ill-shaped dwarf' and 'without sense or wit'. To Horace Walpole 'she had no other charms than being a maid of honour who was willing to cease to be so at the first opportunity'. Anne, whatever her looks and disposition, was miscast as a maid because of tendencies which to orthodox moralists seemed heretically nonconformist. No sooner did Anne achieve her maidenly status in Queen Caroline's entourage than she formed an improper relationship with the then Vice-Chamberlain Lord Harrington who was twenty-seven years her senior. Harrington had promised to marry Anne, but according again to Egmont's diary 'he forsook her having gained his ends without it'.

It was then that Lord Hervey and Anne formed a liaison. Hervey and Frederick were so friendly at the time that there is no doubt that the latter was well aware of this relationship, although some biographers have suggested that he was ignorant of it. However, in addition to his intimacy with Hervey, the Griff would have learned from other friends at court of the 'maid' whose affairs were notorious and subject to much gossip. Not long after the withdrawal of their play from the Drury Lane Theatre, Hervey bid the Griff *au revoir* and left London for visits to friends in the country. It was during Hervey's absence that the Griff decided he would enjoy getting to know Anne better. He besieged her and conquered, doubtless meeting with only token resistance. This was in the age of permissiveness and, after all, Frederick was Prince of Wales. It was unlikely that he regarded his pleasures with the notorious Anne as a disloyalty to his friend Hervey. The prince who as a boy in Hanover was a pupil of Madame d'Elitz, the woman 'of a thousand lovers', could hardly think it unfair that Anne should welcome just one more to her bed.

But when Hervey returned to London he learned of the Griff's conduct with his mistress and was appalled. And Anne in her exultation at the attentions of the Griff now completely rejected Hervey. Moreover, Hervey was told that both Griff and Anne were associating with wealthy and ambitious Mr. George Bubb Dodington. This Dodington was trying to usurp the place of Hervey as the Griff's best friend. Those humorists who claimed there were three sexes ('men, women and Herveys') could now have added truthfully that 'Hell knows no fury like a Hervey scorned'. Suddenly in his letters to Stephen Fox Hervey abandoned praise of the Prince of Wales for damnation. He described the prince as 'false', 'foolish', 'wicked', 'silly'. At the same time Hervey, in his feminine manner, revealed himself as miserable and brokenhearted. Clearly it was the loss of the Griff he deplored, rather than the loss of the bed-soiled Anne. Yet he could not bring himself to forgive the Griff and forget his affair with an unworthy woman, so much less admirable and attractive than Molly, his own faithful wife.

In his grief, fury and exasperation Lord Hervey became a

confirmed enemy of the Griff and did all possible to harm him. He reported to Queen Caroline the relationship between the maid of honour and her son. Caroline presumed to be shocked and angry. This was a hypocritical posture to be adopted by one who not merely tolerated but also encouraged the sexual adventures of her husband with other women. She knew well of his methodical adultery with her dresser Mrs. Howard. She had heard with merriment from the king himself of his libidinous pastimes with other women while in Hanover. Yet the tale-telling of her beloved Lord Hervey against the Griff aroused her venom and spite. At the time of Hervey's mischief-making Anne Vane had written to the queen requesting leave from the court for several months 'in order to visit my grandfather'. In reply Caroline sent a withering message to her maid of honour telling her she could leave the court for good.

When the Griff learned of the queen's displeasure and of her snub to Anne his prompt reaction was much in keeping with his character and policy of surprise. He immediately decided to elevate the status of his new mistress and to insist that she be treated as a great lady. He purchased a fine house for her in Grosvenor Street. He had it furnished and decorated in his impeccable taste. He also presented Anne with a magnificent service of plate. At the same time he promised her an annual income of £3,000, which at today's monetary values would have had a purchasing power exceeding £30,000. There, in Grosvenor Street, Anne settled as a kind of miniature queen. The Griff made it clear to all high-born persons that to retain his friendship they must pay respectful calls upon Anne who was now becoming known as 'Mrs. Vane'.

The Griff discovered a rebel in his campaign for the social elevation of Anne. This was Colonel Schutz, a member of his household and brother of Augustus Schutz. The colonel, a man of high moral principles, failed to call upon 'Mrs. Vane'. Confronted by an angry Griff for such lack of respect, Schutz tried to defend himself. Becoming even angrier, the Griff said that since he had done Mrs. Vane such an honour by making her his mistress, his servants ought to hold her in great respect. Colonel Schutz said: 'If your royal highness commands me to wait on her, then I must go.' The prince retaliated by remarking that on such a matter his servants shouldn't wait to be commanded. Still reluctant, Colonel Schutz was soon 'waiting upon' Anne at her house.

Smouldering with rage at the situation, Lord Hervey suddenly took fire and dashed off an hysterical letter to Anne. He gave it to his friend Bussy Mansel, a Member of Parliament, and asked him to hand it personally to Anne immediately. The letter upbraided her for the harm she had done him. It threatened that unless she changed her attitude he would reveal details of her murky past life to the prince and thus ruin her standing with him. Anne read this letter, went into hysterics and hurled it at Mansel. Mansel then lost his temper because Hervey had deceived him with the story that the letter contained only the recommendation of a midwife to Anne. Mansel told Anne he would kill Hervey for this deception. Anne took this murder threat so seriously that she was quick to report the whole incident to the Griff, who reported it to St. James's Palace. And on this occasion the king and queen and also Sir Robert Walpole took sides against Hervey and expressed their displeasure at the foolish letter he had sent to Anne.

The campaign by Hervey to win back Anne was later to be revived. Meanwhile stories of the Prince of Wales's new mistress and the struggles around her were spreading throughout London. In court and society Anne had often been given the nickname of Vanella. Now in the gossip of the taverns and coffee houses, and in the mischievous and salacious pamphlets hawked from Grub Street, she was invariably called 'the beautiful Vanella'. The prince was said to be pouring out money to Vanella in a growing passion for her, and that his debts had reached a staggering size. There was evidence of financial embarrassment in instructions from the Griff to his treasurer for cancellation of a standing order for the annual distribution of £1,200 of his income to charities. No more was being heard of the two mistresses acquired earlier by the Griff.

Apparently they received their redundancy pay and then moved into an honourable retirement.

Soon after the acquisition of Anne Vane, the Griff, further defying the rules of solvency, had embarked upon another extravagance. He decided to have his own splendid royal barge, a vessel which would in every way surpass the monarchal barge of his father. George II was still excluding him from participation in the nation's statecraft and government. Although a little more generous than in the past, the king still allowed him far less than he should be receiving as Prince of Wales. But the Griff decided that at least on the river he would outdo his father in sheer grandeur and thereby give another stir to the ever-simmering kingly jealousy.

Elaborate private barges, with their liveried oarsmen, moving up and down the Thames, were the status symbols of the rich and great. They were used by monarchs for enjoying themselves and for showing off before the vulgar mob watching a safe distance away on the river banks. George I had not long arrived in England from Hanover when he was being rowed from Whitehall to Chelsea in a luxurious barge. Just behind followed a City company's barge with an orchestra of fifty entertaining the king with a new symphony specially composed for the trip by Handel. George II also enjoyed being rowed on the Thames with music following close behind. The only feature likely to diminish the pleasure of such excursions was the strong smell of the river's polluted waters.

To ensure that his barge should in every way be harmonious and lovely, the Griff engaged as his consultant and designer William Kent, one of the greatest artistic geniuses of the Georgian age. Kent was a superb architect; he was a master of landscaping; of interior and exterior decoration; of ornamentation and design; and even of portrait painting. In co-operation with a naval architect and shipwrights, Kent and the prince produced what is still often called 'the most beautiful boat in the world'. Slender, graceful and sixty-three feet long, her exterior was adorned with mermaids, seashells, golden feathers, lions, dolphins. The stateroom of the barge shone with gilt and had elaborate decorative designs in the ceiling.

In the spring of 1732 the barge was launched. She was rowed by twenty-four watermen. They were, says a contemporary account, arrayed 'in scarlet coats with blue sleeves richly laced with gold lace in imitation of fishes' scales, blue breeches, stockings and velvet caps braided in like manner, with gold in the peaks, with his highness's crest in embroidery and a silver badge on their left breasts'. At the tiller was the prince's bargemaster, in equally decorative dress. For some time the barge was kept out of sight of the king because it was felt that if he came upon it suddenly he might explode with anger at his son's extravagance, besides feeling jealous at her superiority to his own. But when George went again to Hanover later in 1732 the Griff invited his mother and sisters to accompany him on a trip from Chelsea to Somerset House in the barge, which was now flaunting his personal flag adorned with the three Prince of Wales feathers. The party was followed by a band of musicians. Crowds ran to the river banks to wave and cheer.

On a later occasion a race was organised between the barge of the Prince of Wales and that of the king. Each craft had the same number of oarsmen. To the Griff's delight his own barge won. Nevertheless he was very modest about this success, telling Lord Egmont that he felt his barge 'too fine' for a person like himself. Diplomatically Egmont replied that 'fine sights please the people, and it is good-natured to entertain them in this way'. In the case of Frederick, Egmont was right. The common people of London, accustomed to seeing their popular prince riding in hackney cabs and even moving through their filthy streets on foot, were pleased to see him at last enjoying some splendour which they felt he had earned and deserved.

The cost of constructing 'the most beautiful boat in the world' was announced as a mere thousand pounds, but there is no doubt but that her expensive ornamentation and fittings with many kinds of incidental expenses would have added thousands more to the bill. The barge was even in use during the reign of Queen Victoria when, unfortunately, the exquisitely adorned saloon ceiling was painted over with Victoria's own arms. Now the barge rests in retirement in the National Maritime Museum at Greenwich.

The year 1732 was to Frederick one of two important acquisitions. He built the barge. He also leased a house in the pretty village of Kew, seven miles south-west of London. The Griff had been denied the right of occupying an official residence of his own in the capital itself. The king said he could not afford such a home for his heir. Besides, by keeping the Griff in apartments at St. James's Palace he could quickly be given details of the comings and goings of the latter's visitors. For members of the opposition party to the regime of George and Robert Walpole were already courting the Prince of Wales in the hope he might become their leader and rallying point. However, the king raised no objections to the Griff leasing this house at Kew which was only two miles from Richmond Lodge where he and Caroline often spent week-ends.

The Griff, however, while anxious for a modest country place, was not an enthusiast for the traditional rural Britain, the Britain of beefy roistering hunting men. He was not envious of Hervey's visits to Sir Robert Walpole at Houghton Hall where his friend 'had to sit down to dinner in a snug little party of about thirty odd, up to the chin in beef, venison, geese, turkeys, etc., and generally over the chin in claret, strong beer and punch'. The Griff didn't relish the rural England of the first half of the eighteenth century described to Francis Place by the old Rev. Robert Knipe when 'fox hunting, drinking, bawling out obscene songs and whoring was the common delight of the leading gentry'. The Griff rarely drank, he was not an enthusiastic hunter or singer of dirty songs. Of all those activities named by Knipe as constituting 'the common delight', the Griff experienced pleasure in only one.

The countryside ideal of the Griff was clean and tidy in the artificial tradition of much pastoral poetry. He sought a civilised country life in sweet and orderly surroundings. He was a gardener, not a farmer. Kew, so near London, was a safe distance away from the bucolic savagery of the shires. It was a small well-behaved village with a church clean and new, built as recently as 1713. Kew House was the name of the Griff's residence which had sometimes been known as the White House. Nearby was a larger building called the Dutch House, owned by the king but only occupied occasionally by the elder princesses. Kew House was a modest residence with eleven acres of gardens laid out by Lord Capel in the previous century. In the later occupation of Capel's grand-niece Lady Elizabeth Molyneux and her husband the garden had somewhat deteriorated. As soon as the Griff had obtained Kew House he called in his friend William Kent for help and advice. Together they drew up plans for the grounds to be re-landscaped. At the same time the Griff eagerly went ahead in making lists of flowers, herbs, bushes and trees with which his gardens should be planted. He had long been a student of botany, and he decided to try to grow at Kew many rare plants from abroad. In many cases his experiments proved successful. From his efforts, indeed, evolved the Royal Botanical Gardens at Kew, with its world-famous and unique collection of rare plants. But the eleven acres of gardens so tenderly cultivated by Frederick have been increased to nearly 300 acres.

One of the last intimate meetings Lord Hervey had with the prince before their final break over Anne Vane was at Kew House. The Griff had not been long in occupation there and was excitedly going ahead with developments which included the building of a Chinese summer house with paintings illustrating the life and teachings of Confucius. In a letter Hervey told how in the main house the Griff had 'made two charming pretty rooms, and is going to do a lot more'. But Hervey's host didn't do any work that day. They 'played at ninepins all day and did not dine till five o'clock'. Dinner was usually between two and three.

5

'Bubb is His Name'

The place of Lord Hervey in the life of the Griff became well and truly taken by George Bubb Dodington, politician, wit, eccentric and *bon vivant*. Hervey had feared this would happen when he learned that the fat Dodington had been seen about town with the prince. One day the prince, Dodington and Anne Vane had visited the apartments of Lady Deloraine, the *risqué* governess to the daughters of the king and queen. Accordingly this sudden alliance between the Griff and the devious Dodington became the talk of palace and town. The alliance was interpreted as the start of a more powerful political opposition to the king and Sir Robert Walpole. This might develop into the 'prince's party' to the embarrassment of the Walpole administration.

The Griff collected some strange friends during his brief but controversial life. Of all such friends George Bubb Dodington was the strangest. In no other age but the eighteenth century could this mixture of wisdom and folly, wickedness and piety, vulgarity and propriety have obtained acceptance in public life. Richard Cumberland rightly described Dodington as 'one of the most extraordinary men of his time'. Short and very fat, Dodington had a snub nose and protruding eyes. His mother came from an aristocratic West Country family, the Dodingtons of Dodington. She had scandalised her relatives by marrying common Jeremias Bubb, Irish chemist and adventurer who sat in the House of Common four years without distinction. Born in 1691, their son George started his career as a diplomat. He did valuable work for two years as special British envoy in Spain. Then in 1720 he lost an uncle, George

74

Dodington, who left him an enormous fortune. He became M.P. for Bridgwater in 1722, and two years later a Lord of the Treasury. Dodington's wealth, and his estates in the West Country, gave him considerable political power, several constituencies being under his patronage and influence.

Dodington was clever, witty and an astute debater. He was also a cynic who often put his own personal interests above the England he publicly professed to adore and to serve. His philosophy was well expressed in his own verse:

> Love thy country, wish it well—
> Not with too intense a care;
> 'Tis enough that when it fell
> Thou its ruin didst not share.

While a generous patron of literature and art, Dodington was in his own person a vulgarian and a show-off who lived with ostentation rather than with elegance. As soon as the death of his Uncle George made him so rich, he spent £140,000 on the completion of a mansion in Eastbury, Dorset. Later he had houses in Pall Mall and Hammersmith which competed in pretension and ill taste with his Eastbury home, where the walls of some rooms were covered in red and flowered velvet together with tawdry gold-laced satin. In his Hammersmith villa, named La Trappe, the ceilings were covered with painted frescoes and the walls with gobelin tapestries. On the first floor was a sculpture gallery consisting mostly of massive nudes on a floor inlaid with thick marble. There were fears that the weight of this monstrous sculpture might one day cause the floor to collapse and to precipitate the nudes into the rooms below. 'Some people tell me this room should be on the ground floor,' Dodington remarked to a distinguished guest. 'Be easy, Mr. Dodington,' was the reply. 'It will soon be there.'

Dodington's bedrooms in all three homes were in keeping with his love for the oddly spectacular. The bedroom in La Trappe was dominated by a colour motif of bright purple. Its bed, with a coverlet of purple and gold, was surmounted by a big canopy of peacock feathers. The Eastbury bedroom of Dodington had a weird-looking carpet in gold and silver embroidery, which, according to Horace Walpole, 'too gloriously betrayed its derivation from coat, waistcoat and breeches by testimony of pockets, buttonholes and loops, etc.'

Known widely by the nickname of 'Noll Bluff', he drove about London in a tremendous coach glittering with gold paint. This was drawn 'by six, fat unwieldy horses, short-docked and of colossal dignity'. Dodington dressed with ostentation in a style which in London was out of fashion and better suited to the reign of Queen Anne. In later years, as Lord Melcombe, he suffered a sartorial mishap which caused attendants in a solemn court ceremony suddenly to burst into merriment. This was when Dodington, dressed in an embroidered jacket with lilac waistcoat and breeches, bent low to kiss the hand of the queen. For then 'his breeches forgot their duty, and broke loose from their moorings in a very indecorous and uncourtly manner'.

Vulgar and undiscerning both in his own dress and in the adornment of his mansions, Dodington was equally vulgar and undiscerning in the expression of his romantic passions. He was secretly married, but had a favourite mistress in a coloured woman named Mrs. Sawbridge. For a time he had a liaison with disreputable and grasping Fanny Murray, who, in the course of her long career, was at separate times the mistress of the rake Jack Spencer, the Earl of Sandwich and Beau Nash. Fanny placed such a high value on herself that when given a £20 note by Sir Robert Atkins, she contemptuously slapped it between two slices of bread and ate it. Dodington also became a close friend of notorious Sir Francis Dashwood, participating in his orgies at Medmenham Abbey with girls dressed as nuns. Notwithstanding his vices, Dodington was a religious man, as many passages in his diaries have proved. He had a kindly and sympathetic nature and adored children.

Since Dodington had so many faces to show to the world it is not surprising that the Griff became interested or even fascinated by more than one of them. The two became acquainted at an opportune time for each. The Griff, bitter at his father's indifference to him, wanted support in his plans to fight for his full rights as heir to the throne. Dodington, on the other hand, had become disillusioned by Sir Robert Walpole, whom he had been serving well, and with the king. Dodington wanted his social ambitions to become fulfilled by the gift of a peerage which might make him seem worthier of his wealth and gold coach. He had hinted hard for this honour, but there had been no response. So he was ready to pay court to the Prince of Wales. From early in their friendship the young man was pressing Dodington to take up in parliament his case for a bigger allowance and more responsibilities of state. But Dodington, an astute politician, suggested that such moves should be delayed until a more opportune time. Meanwhile Dodington preferred to turn other faces towards the Griff, the face of the generous friend and that of the wild, hilarious playboy.

Not content with having only a home in the country, the Griff was now intent upon having a house of his own in London also. He found close proximity to his parents and sisters increasingly hard to endure. To them he was still the troublesome cuckoo, unwelcome in their nest. He shared some of his mother's intellectual interests. Yet with his father he could find nothing in common. They shunned each other in St. James's Palace. And when the king was at Richmond he did not visit his son at nearby Kew. To the king, the passion of the Griff for growing flowers was unmanly. The king preferred the more robust activities of hunting and shooting, but under conditions made specially easy for him. He slaughtered stags driven directly into his path. And to make his majesty's shooting easier, Richmond Park gamekeepers made massive wild turkeys even more massive by a special diet of acorns and barley. The weight of many of these exceeded thirty pounds. While the intrepid marksman waited, dogs chased the turkeys, which with difficulty succeeded in ascending to the lower branches of the trees. Then the king started shooting them down.

In his zeal to keep a wider distance from the king in London, the Griff turned to Dodington as the generous friend. He had become interested in a London mansion, a short walking distance from St. James's Palace. This was Carlton House, close to the house of Dodington in Pall Mall. The Griff decided to defy his father's wishes that he should have no independent London residence. He would own Carlton House, then being offered for sale for £6,000 by the dowager Lady Burlington. The snag was, however, that he did not possess £6,000. His mistress Anne Vane was expensive and his recent gambling losses had been huge. Accordingly the Griff begged a short-term loan of £6,000 from a member of his household staff and handed it over to Lady Burlington. Then he looked about for someone who would lend him this amount for a longer period in order that he might repay the short-term loan. He thought of Dodington and approached him. Dodington handed over £6,000 without security.

The Griff was soon joking among other friends about this transaction, assuring them that he never intended paying back his debt to Dodington. Biographers have used this and other similar remarks made by the prince later after borrowings from Dodington as examples of ingratitude and criminal deception. However, the Griff would often jokingly depict his friend as a simpleton and buffoon whom he loved to cheat. Certainly the Griff had some of the shocking moral weaknesses of the Georgian age, but it would have been against his nature deliberately to defraud anyone who did him a kindly action. It would also have been characteristic of Dodington with his immense wealth to have turned his loans to the prince into gifts.

Having proved himself the generous friend, Dodington was next to attract the prince as the wild playboy. The Griff's erstwhile friend Hervey had once remarked that 'there is no country in the world but England, where so many clowns are heroes, and so many men of quality clowns'. Dodington, who had then turned forty, and the Griff, sixteen years his junior, both loved clowning. Their hours of serious discussion would rove over politics, religion, music and literature. Then suddenly they would turn to mad uninhibited clowning and licence. They playfully wrestled on the ground like schoolboys. There were many practical jokes in which Dodington, as the prince's social inferior, was invariably the victim. Several times Dodington was ingeniously booby-trapped. Once he was rolled in blankets and shoved down a flight of steps by the prince. And then, as their friendship grew still closer, Dodington introduced the Griff to the real underworld of London. This included the low clubs where the rakes were supplied with girls by madams who were known by such searing names as Mother Sulphur and Mrs. Brimstone.

In their intimacy the Griff and Dodington began to lead lives which were almost communal. The garden of Carlton House ran down to that of Dodington's house. An entrance was made from one garden to the other so that each could wander over the other's property at any time. Latchkeys and other keys were also exchanged so that they could enjoy the freedom of one another's houses. Often at night, it was said, the prince would, unseen, slip into his garden and a few moments later be letting himself into Dodington's house through the back door. Then Dodington would dispatch his running footman to the bagnios of such underworld queens as Mother Sulphur or Mrs. Brimstone. Soon afterwards girls would discreetly be admitted into the Dodington mansion. Despite elaborate efforts at secrecy, the alleged night excursions to Pall Mall of 'whores, does and dollymops' became the scandalous gossip of the drawing rooms and card tables of both London and Bath. Scurrilous hints about the lives of both the prince and Dodington also appeared in some of the Grub Street publications. Even years later the cruelly satirical poet Charles Churchill was inspired to write of Bubb Dodington:

Bubb is his name and bubbies doth he chase,
This swollen bullfrog with lascivious face.

Augustus Schutz, of the court of George II, who knew the Griff well, said that while 'the prince can talk gravely according to his company, he is sometimes more childish than becomes

his age'. During this, his first, period of association with
Dodington the child in him seemed to be in control nearly
all the time. Alienation between his parents and himself
seemed complete. The king and queen, resenting his alliance
with Dodington, declined to make any friendly gestures
towards him or to give any assurance regarding his future.
Sir Robert Walpole was himself suggesting that the alienation
had gone too far and might later divide the unity of the nation.
Yet at that time the prince had done no worse than mischievously to listen in parliament to attacks on Walpole's controversial Excise Bill, thus giving the impression that he was a
supporter of the opposition. Rather than pursuing any serious
activity, the Griff was, with Dodington's encouragement,
devoting himself still more to foolish and aimless pursuits.

They 'disguised' themselves with false beards and huge-
brimmed hats and went out to share the pastimes of the common people. The only effect of such absurd masquerade was
to draw attention to themselves. The two in their loose beards
were recognised at Hockley-in-the-Hole at a session of bull-
baiting, an activity more likely to appal than to amuse the
kind-hearted prince. More to his liking and temperament,
he plunged with Dodington into a study of fortune-telling
and occultism. London's leading seers and crystal-gazers were
visited by these two absurdly mysterious figures for long
consultations. The prince, so dissatisfied with his present lot,
gazed into crystal balls in the hope of foreseeing a more
important and useful future for himself. These sessions with
fortune-tellers which the Griff started with Dodington were to
continue for many years until it was said he was given a cruel
prediction which swiftly came true.

Foolish pursuits with Dodington and week-ends of gardening
at Kew did not occupy all the prince's time. There was also
Anne Vane in her expensively furnished house in Grosvenor
Street. The 'fat ill-shaped dwarf' must have exercised great
physical charm to have been maintained at such a standard of
luxury by the prince, for she was notoriously bereft of the
higher mental attributes. Outside the bedroom the Griff

would have found her companionship monotonous. Accordingly, in his undisciplined mood of that time, the Griff could not be content with Anne as she was. Even inside the house he had bought for her he sought new distractions, new excitements. And so one day his large eyes were distracted and suddenly dazzled by his mistress's chambermaid. Soon afterwards she surrendered to his advances.

About a year later Anne, to the great joy of the Griff, gave birth to a baby boy. The Griff gave a hundred guineas to the messenger who brought him the news. At a grand christening the baby was given the name of 'Fitz Frederick of Cornwall'. Lord Baltimore and Anne's brother the Hon. Henry Vane were the godfathers. The godmother was Lady Mansel. If there was joy among the unmarried Anne and her relatives over the arrival of little Fitz Frederick it turned to bitterness in the following month, for news reached them of the birth of a baby to her former chambermaid. Moreover, the Griff had bought this humble mother of his second child one house in London and another in the country. Lord Egmont in his diary recorded that the Griff's faithlessness had 'fretted Mrs. Vane into a consumption'. Egmont scribbled some additional scandalous gossip about the prince. He had 'attempted to gain the favours of Mrs. Bartholdi, the Italian opera singer, and likewise the Duchess of Ancaster's daughter, but both in vain'.

Despite the close friendship with the rich and generous Dodington, the Griff was sinking deeper and deeper into debt. His household treasury was empty. Yet he was still living extravagantly on credit. The king was still allowing the Griff £50,000 a year—half the salary he had enjoyed himself as Prince of Wales. Even Hervey, now so alienated from the prince, was pleading with the queen to influence her husband to improve her son's allowance and to take more interest in him. Caroline flew into a temper, replying that she wished the Griff was as decent with his father as his father was to him. But there were many in high circles who blamed the neglect and dislike of the Griff by his parents for his descent into so much dissipation and folly. By refusing him proper status in the nation and court, they had made him an outsider and an adventurer. But far worse was to come.

Towards the end of 1733 the king informed the Houses of Commons and Lords of the betrothal of his eldest daughter Anne, the Princess Royal, to the twenty-two-year-old William Prince of Orange. Both houses received this news with conventional expressions of delight and congratulations. Actually most members knew next to nothing of this Prince of Orange, who was still in Holland, but there was majority pleasure at the idea of closer relations with the Dutch. Besides, Anne was now twenty-four, an age when a senior princess should have found a husband. Parliament's dutiful joy was followed by a gesture of more value. It presented the betrothed Anne with a marriage jointure of £80,000. There was no precedent in British history of a princess being voted such a large sum on her marriage. Indeed, to stifle any protests against such magnaminity Sir Robert Walpole quietly obtained the £80,000 from a sum of £93,000 which the state had recently been paid for sale of crown lands in the West Indies.

While the loyal masses of England threw their hats into the air and lit bonfires in demonstrations of well-organised joy over the royal romance, the Prince of Wales was sad and angry. He had badly wanted a proper financial grant from parliament. Instead he had to rely on the charitable handouts from his disapproving and mean father. He had longed for marriage and legitimate children. He had wanted the Prussian Wilhelmina as his bride—but his hopes had been dashed. The king had made no effort to find another eligible princess in Wilhelmina's place. As the eldest member of his family, and as heir apparent, he should have been able to marry and to have been given a substantial financial settlement before Princess Anne. These were the thoughts confided by the Griff to his friends and even to his sister herself.

The friendship between the Griff and Anne had been short and fleeting. Anne was a proud and haughty princess who was soon regarding her gay and unconventional elder brother with disdain. She was encouraged in this attitude by her parents, who in their conversation were constantly denigrating the Griff. He and Anne had shared an interest in music. But eventually music caused a bitter quarrel between them. Anne adored Handel, then the darling of the British musical establishment. The prince feigned to despise him. From this disagreement developed the great London opera war, with Anne and Griff on opposing sides, as described in Chapter 6. After the announcement of the betrothal Frederick flew into a temper with Anne. He scolded her for daring to 'be married before me'. After that the two were ignoring each other, although the Griff treated her fiancé with courtesy and kindness.

For Princess Anne to marry this insignificant William of Orange, so unimportant compared with the William of Orange who had ruled England with Mary, was indeed a daring action. This insignificant William was of high birth, indeed a recommendation to the snobbish Anne. But otherwise he had little to recommend him, except for the possession of a kind heart and the willingness of the king to accept him as a son-in-law. Anne had never met William, but she had been forewarned by her father. Wrote Walpole in his memoirs: 'This Mars, who was locked in the arms of this Venus, was a monster so deformed that when the king had chosen him for his son-in-law he could not help in the honesty of his heart and the coarseness of his expression, letting the princess know how hideous a bridegroom she was to expect; and even gave her permission to refuse him: she replied she would marry him if he was a baboon. "Well then," said the king, "there is baboon enough for you."'

One good reason for the acceptance by Anne of William was the shortage in the Europe of that time of eligible protestant princes. If the protestant William were rejected, then no other bridegroom might be obtainable. In the words of the sardonic Lord Hervey: 'Her royal highness's option was not between this prince and any other but between a husband and no husband . . . but whether she would go to bed to this piece of deformity in Holland or die an ancient maid immured in her royal convent at St. James's.'

William Prince of Orange arrived in England early in November 1733 accompanied by a retinue of seventy. He was escorted to apartments at Somerset House. There in the evening large numbers of the nobility gathered to bid him welcome. Since William, in accordance with protocol, was not due to meet the king and queen until the following day, Hervey was sent to Somerset House with their greetings. Another who helped to welcome William on the same evening was Lord Egmont, who found him 'greatly deformed with excessive roundings of the right shoulder', with short waist and long legs 'without calves'. But Egmont thought William had a handsome face and good manners. Hervey thought that his body was 'as bad as possible' but his countenance 'far from disagreeable'. Later Hervey was to describe Orange as 'almost dwarf', with breath 'more offensive than it is possible for those who have not been offended by it to imagine'.

On the day following William's arrival the king sent a coach to transport him from Somerset House to St. James's Palace. But much to the displeasure of the jealousy-obsessed George, crowds mobbed and cheered the Dutchman all the way down the Strand and in Pall Mall. Seemingly blind to the physical defects of the unfortunate dwarf prince, Anne met him with delight and affection. He brought her a present of £30,000 worth of jewels. This caused astonishment because the prince had been regarded as comparatively poor. Soon Anne had an affectionate nickname for her dwarf. It was 'Pepin'. The king treated William with coldness and arrogance, telling his courtiers that his only claim to distinction was that he was marrying into the British royal family. Except for his future wife, only one member of the royal family showed William real courtesy and friendship. This was the Griff, who, repressing his distaste for the coming wedding, took his future brother-in-law on a long sightseeing tour through London.

Then a few days before the date fixed for the wedding William, overwhelmed by excitement, suddenly fell ill and vomited while attending a thanksgiving service at the Dutch Church in Threadneedle Street. Egmont recorded that 'the medicines he takes stay not with him, but pass downwards' and that 'all his nourishment passes away in urine, which is diabetes'. The wedding was postponed while the invalid was trundled over more than 100 miles of bumpy wintry roads to Bath to take the cure. He was so weak at the spa, it was said, that while playing cards he needed an assistant to take them up and down from the table.

The Griff had for months been absenting himself from the various grand receptions held by the king in St. James's Palace. At such affairs he had been too humiliated by the refusal of his father to recognise his presence with even a few polite words. The coldness of the monarch towards his heir had long been noticed and deplored. Bubb Dodington, whose role as serious adviser to the Griff had been so farcical, at last made a useful suggestion. He urged the Griff to end his absences from the court by appearing at the king's great levee on New Year's Day of 1734. Dodington doubtless realised that a reconciliation between the king and his son would be in his own interest also. He would have heard of the displeasure of the king and queen at his influence over their son. The Griff took Dodington's advice. He decided to attend the levee.

John Hedges, the prince's treasurer, babbled to Lord Hervey of the Griff's decision. This resulted in the mischievous Hervey suggesting to the queen that it was a crafty plot on the part of the prince. For the prince, suggested Hervey, ignored again by the king would arouse public dislike for the latter and a wave of sympathy for himself. Thus Hervey suggested that on this occasion the king should deliberately speak to the Griff at the levee. Accordingly, before a host of nobility and gentry in the grand drawing room George condescended to address a few words to his elder son.

On January 20th* was the Griff's twenty-sixth birthday. This had customarily been celebrated with a palace ball. On the day before the birthday the queen made an expensive gift, not

* January 31st by the German calendar.

to the Griff but to his petty-minded enemy Lord Hervey. The gift was a magnificent gold snuff-box. It caused the Griff later to reprove his mother for so honouring a man he had come so deeply to dislike. On the Griff's birthday the king appeared at a morning reception in the palace. However, there was no ball, it being explained that the queen was unwell.

Messengers from Bath soon brought better news of the Prince of Orange. The prince had drunk deep of the unpleasant-tasting mineral waters with the result that he was stronger and doing some sightseeing. He would soon be back in London to await his marriage to Anne. Meanwhile he visited the rude and filthy city of Bristol, where he was puzzled by a stranger who, thrusting his head into the coach, said: 'God bless you, sir, you have many friends here, and God damn you, you have as many enemies.' Back in London the prince and his retinue again made their headquarters at Somerset House. In London also there was some hostility where previously there had been only praise and acclamation. One morning a villain hurled a turnip into the prince's coach, hitting him on the chin.

While Anne remained rapturous over the prince, the king became increasingly difficult. Anne suggested a private wedding to relieve her delicate fiancé of any unnecessary strain. 'It shall be a public wedding,' snapped back the king, 'or not at all.' Then when the king sat down to a formal Sunday dinner he commanded his future son-in-law to join the gentlemen-in-waiting whose duty it was to stand at attention behind his chair throughout the meal. When someone dared to suggest to his majesty that this was hardly the way to treat his royal highness the Prince of Orange, he replied: 'What's the Prince of Orange until he has married my daughter?' Nevertheless the prince escaped the indignity of standing behind the king's chair by pleading he was too weak to undertake such duties.

The wedding at last took place in the Chapel Royal of the palace at seven in the evening of March 15th, 1734. Anne, so fresh-complexioned but marked by smallpox, glittered with a necklace of twenty-two diamonds given to her by the bridegroom. But he glittered also in a lacey suit of gold and silver brocade. A long peruke flowing over his back concealed its deformity. Numbers of peers and peeresses who had been sent invitations to the marriage ceremony failed to appear, as if indicating their contempt for the unpopular king and his haughty daughter. Tickets had been printed for admission to a gallery from which high-born subjects could watch the procession from the chapel to the banqueting hall. But many of these tickets were purloined by palace footmen and sold at three shilling apiece in the coffee houses of the city. Thus into the gallery poured vulgar noisy people, much to the annoyance of King George and Queen Caroline.

The climax of the evening was when the bride and bridegroom were undressed by their attendants and escorted to the large bed where their marriage was to be consummated. Guests poured into the bedchamber to wish them good night. According to Hervey, the appearance of the poor little bridegroom in his nightgown and nightcap 'was as indescribable as the astonished countenances of everybody who beheld him. From the make of his brocaded gown, and the make of his back, he looked behind as if he had no head, and before as if he had no neck and legs.' The next day the queen expressed her horror to Hervey that 'this monster' should be sleeping with her daughter. Princess Anne was, however, blind to the appearance of her bridegroom and deaf to the cruel remarks made about him. Like Titania with Bottom she gazed upon him in ecstasy.

William and his bride spent six more weeks in England before he took her home to Holland. These were weeks of celebration and gaiety during which they were both treated with surprising affection by the ordinary people of London. The gnome-like Dutchman had an easy friendly manner which endeared him to the crowds. When the couple visited the opera they were given a long and loud ovation. This upset the king, who, while received respectfully at opera and theatre, never aroused such demonstrations of affection. The Griff also became pained by the fickleness of the many who had previously reserved all their cheers for him. However, while ignoring the bride, the Griff still had friendly meetings with the bridegroom. Hervey hinted that William had spoken to him disparagingly of the Griff. On the other hand, William, now aware of the past associations of Hervey and Harrington with Anne Vane, had humorously suggested to an indignant Griff that her baby, Fitz Frederick of Cornwall, had been fathered by a triumvirate.

The £80,000 settlement by parliament upon Anne, the king's continued policy of treating him with insulting indifference and the uncertain behaviour of Dodington all helped to produce a state of mind in the Griff which exploded into one of his surprising and unexpected decisions. He dropped Dodington, his seemingly inseparable friend, his Pall Mall neighbour, his companion in boisterous fun and clammy vice; and, of course, his political adviser. The break came with an inexplicable suddenness. One day the fat, snub-nosed man and the prince were almost as one. The next day they were wide apart. On the Griff's orders, workmen were blocking up the gate which had united their two gardens. Locksmiths were fitting new locks on the doors of Carlton House. This was to prevent the now despicable Dodington from making his entrance with the duplicate set of keys which the Griff had given him when they were friends. Next a brigade of workmen were planting trees in the prince's garden. The prince, in his sudden suspicion of Dodington, feared that the latter from his own lawn might watch what went on behind the windows at Carlton House. The trees would now obscure this view.

Dodington had been a witty and generous companion; in conversation he had protested his undying devotion and loyalty to the Griff. At the same time he had expressed his strong disapproval of the prime minister, Sir Robert Walpole. But Dodington was failing to translate these protestations into action. The Griff begged Dodington to take his cause to parliament, to plead that the Prince of Wales be given his own allowance and establishment. He wanted Dodington to organise an effective opposition to the party of Walpole and the king. Dodington nodded his head but did nothing. While always delighted to act as the prince's pander, Dodington still shrank from wholeheartedly becoming his political mouthpiece.

Dodington had dared to flout the will of Walpole by attaching himself to the prince. But still awed at the power and prestige of the prime minister, he had been tortured by second thoughts. Walpole had not satisfied his grand longing to be given a peerage. Perhaps, however, this might come if he did not alienate the prime minister altogether by forming an effective opposition party for the prince. Only one willing to take tremendous chances would at this time dare absolutely to defy the 'great man', as he was called. So many of the lesser great, from dukes to esquires, grovelled for favours before this vulgar twenty-stone prime minister. Dodington had once been such a groveller, even writing and laying before the 'great man' a sheaf of sugary flattering poems extolling his greatness. It was hard for Dodington to make the complete break with Walpole that the Griff demanded. His enormous satin-breeched seat was caught between two stools.

Soon, with Dodington no longer welcome, other important men of political acumen and ambition were coming and going from Carlton House. There were mysterious sessions presided over by the Griff in his cabinet room overlooking the garden. But when, from his own domain, the desolate Dodington gazed that way he could not see those men in the cabinet room because of the newly planted trees.

6

The Griff versus Handel

The man who replaced George Bubb Dodington as chief favourite of the Prince of Wales was George Lyttelton, son of Sir Thomas Lyttelton, a wealthy Worcestershire baronet. This Lyttelton shared Dodington's enthusiasm for politics and poetry, but he had definitely a more refined and sensitive nature. In appearance Lyttelton was indeed Dodington's opposite. His body was tall and skinny, his face looked insufficient for his height; his voice was weak and monotonous. Both Dodington and Lyttelton were religious, but although the former's pious professions did not deter him from a life of vice, the professions of the latter were consistent with a life of virtue and integrity. Lord Chesterfield, friend and admirer of Lyttelton, was shocked by his 'distinguished inattention and awkwardness'. But despite his appearance and unfortunate traits the plain and lanky aristocrat became nationally known as 'the good Lyttelton'.

George Lyttelton is believed to have been introduced to the Griff by Dodington, the man he supplanted. Lyttelton, two years younger than the Griff, plunged into politics after an elongated grand tour abroad. In 1735 he became M.P. for Okehampton and a loyal member of the opposition to the Walpole administration. Soon after meeting the Prince of Wales Lyttelton became one of his equerries and a bosom friend.

Another in the favour of the Griff after the expulsion of Dodington was Philip Dormer Stanhope, fourth Earl of Chesterfield. Unlike 'the good Lyttelton', Chesterfield had a philosophy where goodness played only an infinitesimal part.

He was tricky, devious, ambitious and sexually immoral. At the same time he had a brilliant mind, a capacity to charm and literary ability approaching genius. A close friend of George I and then of George II, he was ambassador at The Hague where he fathered an illegitimate son by a Mademoiselle du Bouchet. Back in London as Lord Steward at the palace he won the hatred of Queen Caroline through his close friendship with the king's mistress Henrietta Howard. This led to a squabble culminating in the dismissal of Chesterfield from his court office and the end of his amity with George II.

In 1733, however, Chesterfield married Petronilla Melusine Countess Walsingham, bastard daughter of George I through his mistress the Maypole, Duchess of Kendal. Soon after this marriage to the countess, who brought him a great fortune, Chesterfield was parading with a new mistress, the beautiful Fanny Shirley. In their indifference to moral standards Chesterfield and the Griff shared an affinity. They were both also students and admirers of French literature. A polished writer himself, Chesterfield is best remembered for his letters to his illegitimate son on how to win friends and influence people through flattery, dissimulation and good manners. The Griff enjoyed the society of the cynical and witty Chesterfield. He also benefited much from Chesterfield's championship of his cause among his peers of the House of Lords. Chesterfield would refer to the upper house as 'the hospital for incurables'.

With less personal influence over the Griff, but rallying about him as figurehead of the opposition, were other interesting and vital personalities. There was opposition leader William Pulteney, an eloquent speaker with charming and winning manners. But Pulteney could also, when stirred, reveal himself as a master of biting sarcasm, a writer of cruelly satirical verse. With the sudden but temporary disappearance of his charm Pulteney could with his pen make terrible innuendoes, as Lord Hervey found out when they quarrelled. Pulteney advised the Griff in his personal affairs with wisdom, urging him to act with forethought and restraint. Another of the Pulteney group, and now drawn towards the Griff, was

William Pitt, later to reach such heights as a statesman and politician. There were also Lord Cobham and George Grenville, who, with Lyttelton, called themselves 'the boy patriots'.

The nervous Dodington had discouraged the Griff against taking any really bold action to end the impasse he had reached in relations with his father. The Griff still yearned for a royal bride; he was still in need of a much greater allowance. The king was the only man with the power to satisfy these desires of his son. Sir Robert Walpole was indubitably the most powerful man in England, yet he could do nothing towards the Griff's advantage without the consent of the monarch. Chesterfield's advice to the prince was to try to end the impasse through a face-to-face confrontation with his father. If the king snubbed his son in such a meeting, then this snub would become ammunition for the opposition in taking up his case in parliament.

The court was in residence at Kensington Palace during the warm summer of 1734 when a member of the staff of the Prince of Wales arrived with a verbal message for the king. It was that the prince desired an audience of his majesty and would appreciate a time and place for this. It was a simple message from a son to a father, but nevertheless it threw George, Caroline and Walpole into a flurry of worry and suspicion. At once it was suspected that the Griff might be coming as a tool of the opposition in some treacherous political plot. Walpole begged the king to keep his temper whatever might happen at the interview.

On the following morning the prince was bowed into the king's closet at Kensington Palace. There sat the king and, to the visitor's surprise, Sir Robert Walpole was present also. Belief that the visit of the prince was part of an opposition plot had remained so strong that Walpole had asked to be at his royal master's side. The Griff, undisturbed by the stares of the formidable Walpole, boldly asked for a marriage to be arranged for him as a marriage had been arranged for sister Anne. The king replied that attempts at finding suitable matches had been made, but they had failed. According to the story passed on to Lord Egmont, the king became angry, accused his son of impertinence and warned he would do nothing for him until his conduct improved. The Griff, on his part, begged to be told the precise causes of his father's displeasure. The king accused him of being rude and undutiful to his mother.

Next Caroline condescended to discuss the crisis with her son, who behaved towards her with becoming tact and respect. She suggested that the Griff should write a letter of apology and submission to the king. Later the Griff produced such a letter, and showing it first to his mother, she suggested alterations that made it extremely submissive. Then the letter was delivered to the king. A reply, coming verbally through Caroline, was briefly that he would judge the sincerity of his son's words by his future actions. There followed in the palace much silly speculation about the authorship of the original letter written by the Griff. Some said this had been prepared by Chesterfield and others that it displayed the guile of Dodington. Incidentally, at that time the prince was not seeing Dodington at all.

The Griff's talk with the king and his amended letter did some good. A better relationship, however tenuous, now existed between him and his difficult parents. Caroline, indeed, became a little sentimental, even admitting that the young man had some good points and expressing her belief that he bore some love towards her. Chesterfield, Lyttelton and other sincere advisers of the Griff were doubtless happy for him when there were indications that the king was at last making some efforts to find his heir a presentable and suitable bride.

One suggestion was the Princess of Denmark who had a plain face and was several years older than the Griff. Another suggestion was the daughter of the Duke of Württemberg-Stuttgart. A portrait of this girl, sent to London, revealed her as petite and pleasing to the eye; but unfortunately she was aged but thirteen. Hopes were then placed on the coming visit of the king to Hanover, where he might encounter some more protestant maidens of illustrious lineage and of greater eligibility.

Meanwhile Princess Anne, homesick for England, made a trip to London. She had a passionate reunion with her parents. Although her brother Frederick was now *persona grata*, or at least tolerated by his parents, his relations with Anne proved no better. Their quarrel over George Frederick Handel and his music was unhealed. For the Griff was still stubbornly supporting London's powerful musical opposition to Handel. And before Anne returned to Holland again she made an appeal to Lord Hervey to do his utmost towards helping Handel and his work.

The flow of this story must briefly run into a tributary while Handel's career in England is reviewed, for in the entire life of the Griff his treatment of Handel stands out as the most discreditable of all his actions. During that life he was profligate and immoral. He might have been called unscrupulous because of his failure to pay his debts. Some of his activities seemed incredibly foolish. All these weaknesses were part of the general permissiveness of his class in the age in which he lived. Yet this conduct with regard to Handel was unforgivable. He set out to destroy the greatest composer then in England as a spiteful whim and with no other object than upsetting his sister Anne, his parents and a host of music-lovers. Musical himself, and later to admit his admiration for Handel's works, the Griff nevertheless inaugurated a movement which brought the composer great mental suffering, humiliation and financial loss.

When Frederick first arrived in England in 1728 Handel had become a musical institution in his adopted country. He had written the *Water Music* for George I and *Zadak the Priest* for George II's coronation. He had as choirmaster to the Duke of Chandos, who had his own private orchestra, written *Esther*, his first oratorio in English, and many anthems. For the company he founded in 1720 he had written more than a dozen operas. He was, moreover, music master to Princess Anne. 'The Great Bear', as Handel was called, was achieving wonders for opera because he had a unique capacity for mastering temperamental Italian singers who flocked to

London, often causing hysterical scenes with their rivals. When, for example, the powerful soprano Cuzzoni said she would refuse to sing one of the Great Bear's songs at her London début he grabbed her in his arms and threatened to throw her out of the window until she complied. Handel also succeeded by threats and discipline in bringing Cuzzoni and her deadly rival Faustina together in the same opera and even to sing a duet until quarrelsome scenes both on the stage and among the audience brought their unfriendly co-operation to confusion.

George II's taste in art was vulgar. He liked suggestive pictures of nude women, the fatter the better. He hated books. He was indifferent to the beauty of nature. Yet he loved good music. He would attend the opera and concerts and listen in a state of enchantment. Of all the living composers he admired Handel most, and for a period made him an allowance of £1,000 a year. Even more enthusiastic about Handel, of course, was Princess Anne. It was Anne who insisted upon the institution of a royal box when, after a previously unsuccessful operatic venture, Handel organised a new company at the King's Theatre with Heidegger its proprietor. The king, queen and Anne, with parties of friends, would attend with regularity. Their presence at these Handel operas and the pleasure they showed became talked about all over London. And also attracted to the King's Theatre were many people who, with little interest in music and singing, wanted to be seen and to be thought fashionable. Handel had willy-nilly become the symbol not only of good music but also of the social ladder.

Always held at a distance by the king, queen and the rest of his family, the Griff was rarely seen in their company at these happy nights at the opera. He liked Handel's compositions, but disliked Handel's growing number of friends and patrons. He saw his father and sister Anne assuming the roles of arbiters of the nation's musical taste. A rebel against convention, the Griff disliked seeing the art of Handel becoming so respectable, and of Handel himself becoming a mere minion of the king. Wickedly and mischievously the Griff resolved to ruin Handel.

Handel's biggest rival was the Italian composer Bononcini. Despite the rivalry, they had for a time co-operated in the management of an opera company. The Griff consulted his friends. Together they decided to establish an opera at the Lincoln's Inn Fields Theatre with Bononcini in charge. The scheme was to force Handel out of business in the Haymarket by staging far more spectacular productions in Lincoln's Inn Fields. Large sums were subscribed by rich friends of the Griff to bring singers from Italy to steal the limelight from those already employed by Handel. More than a good voice was needed for the stage of this new opera. Preference was given to attractive bosomy girls with at least as much appeal to the eyes as to the ears. Bononcini's first season at the Lincoln's Inn Theatre opened in 1733.

As for the Griff, his own popularity could at any time surpass that of his father. Thus when it became known that he was chief patron of this new opera and went there often, large numbers of the younger nobility in particular transferred their musical allegiance from Handel to Bononcini and flocked to Lincoln's Inn Fields. Except, perhaps, for the absence of Handelian music they were not disappointed. Gentlemen were surprised and pleased by the support given the prima donnas by choruses of voluptuous-looking girls, often in suggestive costumes. Moreover, the unconventional atmosphere of the new theatre led to scenes formerly regarded as unbecoming at grand opera. Members of the audience, not satisfied with cheering vocalists they liked, would rudely hoot those they disliked. This led to brawls and fights in the auditorium among the champions of rival singers. No wonder the Griff's opera became the talk of London.

Society called these attempts to ruin Handel 'bear-baiting'. The Big Bear growled his protests and made futile threats while the audiences at his theatre became smaller and smaller. King George, Queen Caroline and Anne (before her marriage) still came faithfully, but sometimes they sat in a theatre that was almost empty. There were nights when the artists on the stage outnumbered the people in the audience. The faithless nobility deserted their king and Handel for the sensation and fun of Lincoln's Inn Fields. 'In a little while,' mourned Anne sarcastically, 'I expect to see half the House of Lords playing in its orchestra there in their robes and coronets.' The princess attacked the Lord Chamberlain, accusing him of using his influence in the rival theatre's favour. This was now advertising itself as the 'Opera of the Nobility'.

The War of Tweedledum and Tweedledee, as it has been called, grew in fury. The temperamental Bononcini, exhausted by battle, shrank into the background. Another Italian, Niccolo Porpora, took over the command of the 'Opera of the Nobility'. In most ignoble forays Porpora enticed away Handel's best vocalists with offers of higher salaries. Large sums of money were flung into the struggle by the Duke of Marlborough, Lord Delaware and other wealthy friends of the Prince of Wales. When Handel's contract with Heidegger expired, representatives of the Lincoln's Inn Fields Opera with speed and cunning took over the lease of the King's Theatre. They audaciously laid claim to £500 of its funds said to have been contributed to Handel by the king. While the dispossessed Handel took his company to the Lincoln's Inn Fields Theatre, Porporas's company strutted the stage of the King's Theatre. Soon afterwards Handel moved on to the new theatre built by Christopher Rich in Covent Garden. There he produced *Alcina* with considerable success.

A big victory in the War of Tweedledum and Tweedledee was won by Porpora when he lured to England his former pupil Carol Farinelli, the Neapolitan regarded as the greatest singer of the day. His appearance proved a triumph for the Griff and a terrible blow to Handel. In gratitude to Farinelli, the Griff, although steeply in debt, showered him with gifts which included diamond knee buckles and a gold snuff-box encrusted with gems. However, the war eventually reached a stalemate through financial exhaustion caused by wild bidding for new stars. In one season the 'Opera of the Nobility' lost £12,000, while Handel's company lost £9,000, considerable sums in those days. But the Griff and his friends had enjoyed their fun. Their opera venture peacefully expired.

Despite the Griff's efforts, Handel survived. However, his health was declining. His nerves and pocket had suffered cruelly from the mischievous and heartless campaign waged against him. But he was to suffer still another misfortune arising from the antipathy of the king and the Prince of Wales for one another.

The king during 1735 paid his third visit to Hanover since his accession to the throne. Again the Prince of Wales was passed over and the queen made regent. The prince, according to the records, did not express his indignation this time. The reason was probably because part of the mission of his father in Germany was to find him a suitable wife. Another girl was being mentioned as a possible bride. She was Princess Augusta of Saxe-Gotha, aged sixteen, and said to be tolerably good-looking. Letters passed between the king and his diplomats in Germany developing a plan that he meet Augusta—by chance, as it were—during his stay in Hanover.

The king departed for Hanover with zest, delighted to escape for a few months from his British subjects whom he so heartily despised. He could also look forward to new romance with new women, the erotic side of his kingship in England having gone stale. He had broken for all time with a mistress of twenty years' standing. This was Henrietta Howard (now the Countess of Suffolk), Mistress of Robes to the queen. The departure from the court of the deaf and ageing Henrietta had pained Caroline because George's almost daily assignations with this woman, although mischievous, kept him out of more dangerous mischief. His break with Henrietta became known as the 'great Court Revolution'. The revolution began when the king demanded of the queen, 'Why will you not let me part with an old deaf woman of whom I am tired?' The redundant Henrietta was handsomely pensioned off and presented by her old lover with a new house at Twickenham.

Henrietta, a widow of several years, later married a Mr. George Berkeley.

Seeing so much of Lyttelton, Chesterfield, Pulteney and other members of the opposition, the Griff temporarily became less wild. Gone was the foolish night life he had enjoyed with Dodington. But by day he would still wander on foot about the streets of London which he had grown to adore. Without rudely mobbing him, the cockneys never failed to show their delight that he was among them. He became the hero of a hundred anecdotes. For example, an old woman had her basket of oranges upset by a passing coach. The Griff, who was walking close by, picked up the oranges for her. He was recognised by a porter, who, waving his hat, cried: 'Hurrah for the prince!' The prince slapped the porter on the back and replied with the cry of 'Hooray for liberty and property!'

The Griff was happy at the prospects of a marriage, and of so many evidences of the affection felt for him by the common people. There was also a new occasion for pleasure in the form of a plain but nevertheless attractive matron aged thirty-five, seven years his senior. She was Jane, daughter of the Earl of Abercorn and third wife of Lord Archibald Hamilton, to whom she had borne ten children. An uncle of the Duke of Hamilton, Lord Archibald, born in 1674, was a highly respected official at the Admiralty.

From dalliance with Anne Vane, with her chambermaid and other girls with sex appeal but no intellect, the Griff rushed with enthusiasm into the arms of this mature and intelligent heroine of ten *accouchements*. He was also made welcome at all times by Lord Archibald Hamilton, just as in a later historic love affair, a namesake, Sir William Hamilton, happily acquiesced to Horatio Nelson's attentions to his wife Emma. The Griff visited his new mistress often at her home. She, returning his calls, would go to Carlton House. Together they would often be seen walking in St. James's Park, talking incessantly. Hervey recorded how at the court drawing-room functions the prince would be seen talking with Lady Archibald Hamilton all the time.

The prince's new addiction to Jane Hamilton, together with
the possibility of an early marriage to a German princess, led
to a crisis in his relationship with Anne Vane. Queen Caroline,
while disapproving of her son's association with Lord Archibald Hamilton's wife, urged that he should break with Anne
and banish her, even though she was the mother of his child.
This time the Griff, usually so defiant of his parents' wishes,
needed no more urging. He decided that Anne should be
separated from him by many miles and, if possible, by the
North Sea or the English Channel.

But a surprising development was to complicate the Griff's
negotiations with Anne for her banishment. She had secretly
revived her passionate association with Lord Hervey,
master of intrigue and enemy of the Griff. Unknown to
Frederick, Anne and Hervey were, in a self-created atmosphere
of melodrama, having meetings in London. These took place
first in an obscure coffee house, next at Anne's town house and
then at the home of Lord and Lady Hervey in St. James's.
For the coffee-house encounters Anne, in a wide-brimmed
floppy hat, would be carried in her sedan chair to St. James's
Park. There she would tell her chairmen that she would leave
them for a long walk for her health. She would slip out of the
park, with hat drawn low to cover most of her face, and walk
to the coffee house where Hervey would be waiting. More
intimate meetings took place between the two in Anne's
Grosvenor Street house while nearly all her servants were
away at the country lodge which the prince had recently
bought for her and their son in Wimbledon. Hervey would
glide through the darkness of London in the middle of the
night. He would knock on the door of Anne Vane's house.
She would open the door herself, disguised in a cloak as a
servant. And when Lady Hervey went on a long trip to the
continent Anne took her place in the arms of Lord Hervey
in their St. James's home.

Meanwhile the Griff made his first move to dispose of Anne
Vane. He decided that instead of seeing Anne himself a verbal
message should be taken to her by his friend and Chief Lord

of the Bedchamber Lord Baltimore. The wealthy Lord Baltimore not only owned the state of Maryland in America but
had also married beneath his rank the daughter of Theodore
Janssen, a very rich businessman. A man of tact and charm,
backed by the self-confidence of great wealth. Baltimore was
soon sitting face to face with Anne in her drawing room.
The Prince of Wales, he told Anne, was anticipating an early
marriage, so it was very necessary he should take leave of her.
It was his royal highness's wish that she should go as soon as
possible to Holland, France or any other place abroad and
remain there for two or three years. If she did this, the prince
would give her an allowance of £1,600 a year for the rest
of her life; but if she refused, all maintenance would end. As
for their son, the little Fitz Frederick of Cornwall, he could
remain in England and the prince would look after his education. In presenting these proposals or commands to Anne,
Lord Baltimore stressed how much better it would be for her
to be out of England when the prince married. Otherwise
she might be hurt by remarks concerning her which malicious
people might make. Baltimore's charm and softly spoken word
cast no spell upon Anne Vane. She interpreted the prince's
message as an ultimatum. She chided Baltimore for daring to
deliver it.

Anne rushed to Lord Hervey in the role of an innocent girl
terribly wronged by the rich and powerful prince who had
used her for his pleasure and then cast her aside. And now this
callous prince was going to tear her baby from her arms and
banish her to a strange land! Hervey, the mischievous and
spiteful, seized this opportunity to harm the Griff. He jumped
at Anne's suggestion that he should compose a letter of protest
to Frederick which she would copy in her own handwriting
and sign. The letter resulted in the Griff's affair with Anne
becoming a national joke. It began with a reproach to the
Griff that he should have thought 'an ambassador (Lord
Baltimore) necessary to go between us' instead of coming
himself verbally to deliver his message to her. The letter
continued:

But that your royal highness should break with me in the most shocking way; that you should not be content to abandon me without banishing me, nor take yourself from me without driving me from every other friend, relation and acquaintance, and depriving me of those comforts at a time when I shall want them most, is sure an aggravation to my bad fortune and unhappy situation which you are as much in the wrong to ask me as I should be myself to comply with. Your royal highness need not be put in mind who I am, nor whence you took me: that I acted not like what I was born, others may reproach me; but if you took me from happiness and brought me to misery, that I might reproach you: that I have long lost your heart I have long seen and long mourned: to gain it, or rather to reward the gift you made me of it, I sacrificed my home, my youth, my character, the world, my family, and everything that a woman can sacrifice to the man that she loves: how little I considered my interest, you must know by my never naming my interest to you when I made this sacrifice, and by trusting to your honour when I showed so little regard, when put in balance with my love, to my own.

I have resigned everything for your sake but my life; and, had you loved me still, I would have risked even that too to please you; but as it is, I cannot think in my state of health of going out of England, far from friends and all physicians, I can trust, and of whom I stand in so much need. My child is the only consolation I have left. I cannot leave him, nor shall anything but death make me quit the country he is in. Your royal highness may do with me what you please; but a prince who is one day to rule this country will sure, for his own sake, never show he will make use of power to distress undeservedly; that one who has put herself without conditions into his hands has the hardest terms imposed upon her, though she never in her life did one action that deserved anything but your favour, your compassion and your friendship; and it is for these reasons I doubt not but your royal highness will on this occasion, for your own sake if not for mine, do everything that will hinder you from being blamed and me from being more miserable than the reflection of what is past must necessarily make one who had known what it was to be happy, and can never expect to taste that font again.

I know how vain it would be to think reproaches could ever regain a heart which kindness could not keep, and for that reason I will add nothing more than to assure your royal highness I shall ever wish you health, prosperity, and happiness, and shall ever be, with unalterable affection, etc.

Receiving Anne's letter, the prince was angry, puzzled and suspicious. This letter, addressed to a Prince of Wales by his mistress, was insulting. Moreover, Anne would not have been capable of writing with such wounding subtlety. Then who was the polished stylist acting as his former mistress's scrivener? In his annoyance and bafflement the Griff showed the letter to his friends, to some of his servants and even to his mother and sisters. Simultaneously Anne Vane shared another copy of the letter among her own friends, proudly pretending that she was its author. Details of the affair spread from court and from Anne's house in Grosvenor Street all over town. Muckraking journalists and versifiers were quickly at work. Their publications were being sold in the streets, taverns and coffee houses. They bore such titles as *Vanella or the Amours of the Court* and *The Forsaken Whore*. The public were divided into two sides—against and for the prince. He was accused of being heartless in his treatment of Anne. On the other hand, among the many who adored Frederick for his gay amoral ways, his break with Anne was seen as merely the end of amorous capers with a woman who was lucky to have enjoyed his attentions at all.

It was at about this stage when sagacious opposition leader William Pulteney, adviser to the Griff, intervened. Fortunately Pulteney had remained on good terms with Anne Vane, so he was able to move between the two and lead them towards a settlement. First the Griff denied having sent the cruel message through Lord Baltimore as alleged in her letter. Second, Lord Baltimore himself denied having delivered such a message. These denials, however false, threatened to make Anne appear to be a scheming liar. It is believed that Pulteney, with Hervey's reluctant acquiescence, was responsible for persuading Anne to write a second letter to the prince, apologising for her first, but without climbing down into complete subservience. And again Hervey wrote a draft of this for Anne to copy. This letter read:

It is so easy to remove the appearance of a fault when one is conscious of not meaning to commit one, that I make no doubt but your royal highness will think me thoroughly justified for writing my last letter when I tell you nothing could have induced me to such an expostulation but the harsh message which I thought I had received by your royal highness's order through Lord Baltimore.

In that confusion, shame and vexation, I wrote just what I felt, but resolved (how ill I might execute my resolution I know not) to urge my own request, and to represent what I thought your ill usage of me, in the most respectful terms that such complaints would admit of. If I said anything I ought not to say or in a manner I ought not to say it, I am heartily sorry, and ask your pardon, and appeal now to your justice to tell me whether I ever did or said anything in my life that was not consistent with what I owed to you, though I am very ready to own I have for your sake done things very inconsistent with what I owed to myself.

That I received such a message by Lord Baltimore is certain; whether he was authorised to deliver it I know not; it is certain, too, that all the messages I ever sent by him were answers to others, and not any that came originally from me. It is hard your royal highness will not allow me an opportunity to clear myself; but deal with me as you please, I shall ever pray for your happiness and prosperity, even whilst I reflect it at least to your love, if not to your hate, that I owe the loss of my own. I am, with the greatest respect and truth, etc.

The Griff found this letter far more satisfactory than the last. His indignation with Anne subsided. He finally accepted the advice that on no account must his former mistress be allowed to assume the crown of martyrdom by being exiled abroad and without her child. A new agreement was made which gave Anne full possession of the child, and £1,600 a year and occupation of the Grosvenor Street house for the rest of her life. Anne Vane was delighted with this settlement. But tragedy was soon to overtake her and her little son.

Anne Vane had not long been put safely out of the way when Queen Caroline heard from the king that he had met Princess Augusta of Saxe-Gotha and found her suited to become the bride of the Griff. At the time of this carefully arranged 'chance meeting' between George and his future daughter-in-law Augusta was aged but sixteen. The queen told the Griff that the possibility of his early marriage was now very real. But there could be no more details or progress until the king returned to London from Hanover in the autumn. True that the king frequently wrote thirty-page letters to his wife, but these were almost wholly devoted to his private pleasures. Over many pages the fifty-two-year-old husband described in detail to his wife his adulteries with a new mistress he had found in Hanover. She was thirty-five-year-old Madame Amelia Sophia von Walmoden. A member of a family that had produced several distinguished courtesans, Amelia was grand-niece of the disreputable Countess Platen. George was renewing his old relationship with the veteran Madame d'Elitz when his attentions became distracted by the plump charms of Madam Walmoden. As a result the two women quarrelled. Siding with the newcomer, the ungrateful king expelled from her apartments in the Herrenhausen palace this veteran who during her long career had also slept with his father George I and debauched his son Frederick. Caroline was reputed to enjoy the indecent confessions of her lustful ageing husband who so much preferred playing the Don Juan to doing his duty as king. Anyhow, in his absence she was such an efficient regent that Prime Minister Walpole and others were relieved to have the ill-tempered and fussy monarch out of the way. It was also noticeable how much better Frederick got on with his mother when his father was absent.

The period of peace in the English court ended in October 1735 when the king returned from Hanover. His conversation was full of reminiscences of his fun and raptures in the Herrenhausen palace with Amelia Walmoden and others. In his luggage he had brought pictures of Amelia and other females who had joined the revels. He insisted upon hanging this eighteenth-century version of 'pin-ups' in Caroline's dressing room. He would, with the aid of a candle, examine them and loquaciously revive memories of his pleasures, much to the boredom of the queen and her ladies. The king and Amelia Walmoden exchanged long letters. He was proud when she wrote and told him that as a result of their association she had become pregnant. Immediately George decided he would return to Hanover and the arms of Amelia as soon as he could decently again leave his kingdom.

The Griff was told that now the Princess Augusta was definitely his. All that was needed before the marriage was a series of ceremonial gestures. The king would have to obtain formal consent of the Griff to 'demand the hand' of Augusta on his behalf. An envoy would have to be sent to the court of Saxe-Coburg with that demand. The Griff had begged his father to find him a suitable bride; but now that she had been chosen he was tortured by second thoughts. There were evidences that he still felt pangs for the loss of the Prussian Princess Wilhelmina whom he had so much wanted to marry. Then he had now developed such a happy companionship with the mature Jane Hamilton. Although he had dropped Anne Vane without qualms, he could never face a parting between himself and Jane. Anyhow, he longed to have more knowledge of Augusta than merely her picture and the description given by his father. Accordingly he ordered a member of his household named Cresset to travel to Saxe-Coburg without delay to meet Princess Augusta to assess her looks and her temperament. Cresset returned to Frederick with a favourable report.

Early in November the king sent Lord Chancellor Talbot and four other members of the Privy Council to see Frederick. Talbot formally told him of his majesty's willingness to demand for him the hand of Augusta. In the words of his enemy Hervey, 'the prince made answer with great decency, duty and propriety, that whoever his majesty thought a proper match for his son would be agreeable to him'. But it seemed there could never be any dealings between the king and the Griff without new rows, new misunderstandings. The Griff had a meeting with the Prussian ambassador Count von Borcke. A letter written after this by the ambassador to King Frederick William was intercepted by one of Walpole's legion of spies and informers. It quoted the prince as saying that the marriage with Augusta was being forced upon him against his will; also that he disapproved of England's policy towards Prussia. On receiving a report from Walpole of this alleged conversation both king and queen were furious. However, it is quite possible that von Borcke grossly twisted and exaggerated some lightly spoken words of the prince. It would have been characteristic of the Griff to joke that he was at last being dragged kicking and struggling to the altar.

In the New Year of 1736 the Griff waited patiently while officials charged by the king with completing plans for the marriage dillied and dallied in studies and arguments on precedences and procedures. No 'demand for her hand' had yet been made to the willing Princess Augusta. Meanwhile the Griff had his almost daily meetings with Lady Archibald Hamilton. He was also amusing himself by writing in French a satire on his parents. Then one day in February he was told of the sudden death by convulsions of little Fitz Frederick, his son by Anne Vane. All his usual zest and gaiety turned to forlorn sadness. Never before, said his mother and sisters, had they seen him suffer so deeply.

When Anne Vane was granted the Grosvenor Street house and an income for life in the final settlement with Griff, she boasted to Hervey of her happiness. But at the same time the 'fat ill-shaped dwarf' was moving into an illness which her London physicians could not cure. They could only classify it as 'cholics and general decay'. Since in the 1730s the mineral waters and the damp air of Bath were regarded as the supreme healers, Anne was sent there. She left her son in London under the care of her brother the Hon. Henry Vane, later Lord Darlington. It was in the home of Vane and his wife that Fitz Frederick suffered his fatal convulsions. The Griff walked behind the coffin of the boy in a burial service at Westminster Abbey where in the register he was candidly described as 'natural son of the Prince of Wales by Anne Vane, daughter of Gilbert Lord Barnard'. An account of Fitz Frederick's funeral had not long reached Anne Vane when she also was dead.

7

The Wedding

In 1735 King George had been absent from his British
realm for five months enjoying himself in Hanover
with his new-discovered mistress Amelia Walmoden. The
king's agreement with the queen and Walpole was that he
should go to Hanover once every three years. It was felt that
for him to absent himself from England more often than that
would arouse criticism from members of the opposition and
from masses of his subjects. Yet early in 1736 George was
whispering to friends his intention of returning to Hanover
as soon as possible rather than waiting until 1738 in observance
of his agreement with Caroline and the prime minister.
Walpole was much disturbed when he learned of the king's
rebellious plans. He realised that by deserting England again
so soon the king would anger his British subjects and set
many malicious tongues wagging. Details of his passionate
affair with Amelia Walmoden had already got into print in
London.

Walpole even suggested to Queen Caroline that this Hanover
courtesan be brought over to England as a replacement for
Lady Suffolk. The wise queen and prime minister looked upon
the monarch as on a spoiled boy crying for his new toy.
Caroline adored him and was tolerant in allowing him to
have his unsavoury fun. Nevertheless suggestions for Amelia
Walmoden's domicile in England were abandoned. There
were good reasons to believe that Caroline, despite her love
for George, was not averse to having him out of the way.

The queen loved to wield power as regent. She liked also
to mingle more often with religious, literary and artistic

friends whom her husband, the Philistine Royal, abhorred. Intellectual bishops, a species for which the king had special contempt, increasingly dominated Caroline's interest. While the height of enjoyment for the king was to toy with a brainless mistress, the queen found delight in matching her wits against those of clever theologians. The Clerk of Her Majesty's Closet was Joseph Butler, later author of the renowned *Analogy of Religion*. A frequent companion was Thomas Sherlock, then Bishop of Salisbury and later of London. She used also to spend hours in discussion with Sherlock's theological enemy Benjamin Hoadley, Bishop of Winchester and controversial Latitudinarian and rationalist. The king objected particularly to Hoadley, complaining of his 'nasty stinking breath', his 'silly laugh' and 'nasty rotten teeth'.

Discussions in court and parliamentary circles on 'what the king was going to do', together with the queen's intense involvement in intellectual activities, seemed in February 1736 to have pushed plans for the marriage of the Prince of Wales to Augusta into the background. Nevertheless, special committees continued with their seemingly interminable talk over a nuptial ceremony for which no date had been set. Lord Delaware, Treasurer of the King's Household, had been appointed as the special envoy who should travel to Saxe-Coburg to 'demand' Augusta's hand and to escort her to England. The grim-faced and lanky Delaware was, however, kept waiting in London while the officials talked on. Meanwhile, perplexed by the delays, the Griff continued to find consolation in Lady Archibald Hamilton.

Suddenly the king struck. Dropping all pretences of secrecy, he boldly announced that he would leave for Hanover as soon as he had prorogued parliament in May. And he added threateningly that unless the marriage of the Griff and Augusta hadn't taken place by then, it would have to be postponed until the winter. Otherwise he would not be present. The king was not going to have his reunion with his pregnant mistress delayed by the wedding of his elder son. The threats had an immediate effect. Practical plans for the wedding at last went ahead. The forty-year-old Lord Delaware left for Saxe-Coburg with orders to bring back the Princess Augusta who had just turned seventeen. He was welcomed by Augusta's brother the duke, who duly 'granted her hand' to the Prince of Wales. There was a farewell banquet and ball. A few days later Augusta kissed good-bye to her brother and mother. With the ungainly Lord Delaware the brave girl was driven towards The Hague on the first stage of the journey to the country and future husband she had never seen. She knew not a word of English either. But Augusta's mother had assured her that this would not matter, since George I and George II, as Hanover-born kings, would have insisted upon all their British subjects learning German. On the journey to The Hague, Augusta was accompanied by a very special chaperone. The chaperone was the person most beloved by the princess, old Madame Rixleiven, her governess. Earlier confidential reports to London had named Madame Rixleiven as wielding too much influence over Augusta. Accordingly Augusta had been told that her governess would not be welcome in England. Once The Hague was reached, the two would have to part, Madame Rixleiven returning to Saxe-Coburg.

When the party arrived at The Hague the princess was placed under the chaperonage of Lady Irwin while the old governess departed in tears. Lady Irwin, daughter of the Earl of Carlisle, had been sent by the king and queen from London to meet Augusta as her first lady-in-waiting and advise her how to behave on arrival in England and afterwards. The queen, as Lady Irwin reported in a letter to Lord Carlisle, 'desired me in the strongest terms to recommend to the princess to avoid jealousy and to be easy in regard to amours, which she said had been her conduct. and had consequently procured her happy state she had enjoyed for so many years'. Apparently Caroline, close friend of so many Christian bishops, was advising Augusta to tolerate any unfaithfulness on the part of Frederick.

On Easter Sunday, April 25th, the Prince of Wales had gone to church to the Holy Communion service. As he knelt in his pew a message was pushed into his hands. This told him of the arrival of the Princess Augusta at Greenwich. He remained in church until the end of the service. But within an hour afterwards he was on his way to Greenwich and his princess. His dream of many years was at last materialising. He was to have a legitimate wife. They would have their own home, children and the peace and joys of family life. His years had been crowded with what the Georgians called 'amours'. And all the females who had favoured him had been second-hand, tarnished—Madame d'Elitz, the whores of Hanover, the thieving trollop in St. James's Park, Miss La Tour, the apothecary's daughter, Anne Vane, Anne Vane's chambermaid, the wenches of Mother Sulphur and Mrs. Brimstone, Lady Archibald Hamilton. . . . Now he was to become the husband of a seventeen-year-old princess, virgin, innocent. To meet this girl he was making this one of the most exciting days of his life. He had been assured by Cresset that Augusta was handsome, that her disposition was simple but pleasing. On his way to Greenwich the Griff must surely have prayed that these things were true.

Augusta had landed with Lord Delaware and Lady Irwin after a rough voyage from Helvoetsluys which had lasted for twenty-four hours. Sir John Jennings, governor of Greenwich Hospital, had greeted the princess on the quayside and escorted her to the nearby royal palace where he had apartments. Presented to her there were two more ladies-in-waiting appointed by the queen—Lady Torrington and the Countess Effingham. During that Easter Sunday afternoon Frederick arrived and saw his future wife for the first time. She was fair-haired, blue-eyed and in appearance seemed younger than her seventeen years. About the same height as Frederick but slight in figure, she had a sweet but shy smile. Although no classical beauty, Augusta's features had a pleasing symmetry. Her complexion had a youthful freshness, but her cheeks bore the marks—so common in those days—of smallpox.

The Griff was inexpressibly touched by this girl who had left her home and all those she loved to come to England and to him. Words could not show his appreciation or impress upon her his resolve to protect her and to preserve her happiness. He could only convey his thoughts and feelings to her through affectionate embraces. During this first meeting between the Griff and Augusta, Lady Irwin briefly interrupted their privacy to serve them with tea. Later this lady-in-waiting was to write 'how vastly pleased' the prince seemed with his princess and how 'he embraced her ten times while I was in the room'. And after that 'with great civility' the Griff kissed Lady Irwin and thanked her for the care she had taken of Augusta on the journey from The Hague. During the evening a vast crowd had gathered outside the palace calling for Frederick and Augusta. The balcony doors opened and the couple appeared, smiling and waving. It was after midnight when Frederick bade Augusta farewell and returned exultant to London.

This had, of course, been the greatest day in Princess Augusta's young life. Any fears she may have had about Frederick had vanished. He had shown such obvious pleasure in her person and in her company. He was warm in nature and kind. They had talked together without strain or nervousness, as if they had known each other for many years. Yet there were two reasons why this, her great day, could not have been perfect. The first reason was that King George and Queen Caroline had made no affectionate welcoming gesture to the girl who in two days would be the bride of their elder son. They had simply sent to her a curt message. This 'presented the compliments of their majesties who hoped the Princess Augusta was well'. The princess had been too short a time in England to be aware of the jealous nature of her future father-in-law. She did not realise how he detested any publicity which might draw friendly public sentiments towards his elder son.

The second reason why the perfection of Augusta's first day in England had been prevented was the absence in Greenwich Palace of any relative or close friend from her Saxe-Coburg home. Her mother had not been able to come.

Her adored old governess Madame Rixleiven had been allowed
to accompany her to The Hague and then no farther. Augusta's
three new English ladies-in-waiting were kind, but she could
not unburden her heart to them as she would have to Madame
Rixleiven. Because Augusta knew no English and was even
imperfect in French, it was difficult for her to communicate
easily and clearly with Lady Irwin and the others. But Augusta
did have one companion from Saxe-Coburg who had not been
torn from her side. This was a large jointed doll, the favourite
plaything of her childhood. Now in her big bedroom in
Greenwich Palace the doll did give her the feeling that someone
from home was still close to her.

While the king and queen still contented themselves with
'hoping that Augusta was well', the Griff had hurriedly made
plans to honour her. Monday the 26th April was the day
before the wedding. Augusta had much to do in preparation.
But because of the insistence of the Griff much of such preparation had to be left to others. For on this Monday morning
he was back at Greenwich from London aboard his pride,
that lovely barge that had been built for him in 1732. The
Griff proudly escorted his fiancée aboard this, the queen of
the Thames, its fresh gold paint glittering in the spring sunshine. As the barge's twenty-four oarsmen propelled her into
midstream, a procession of private barges and other river-craft
formed. In front of the Prince of Wales's barge was another
filled with musicians complete with a conductor. The procession started. The orchestra played. Warships fired salutes.
There were loud cheers from those in the escorting craft and
also from crowds now gathered on the river bank. Frederick
and Augusta rose and waved. When the barge reached the
Tower of London the couple disembarked. In a banqueting
hall at the Tower they ate their dinner. In the custom of the
day a crowd of fortunate Londoners were admitted to watch
them eat from a respectful distance.

The Griff took Augusta back to Greenwich Palace. She now
loved and trusted him sufficiently to ask him a favour. This
was that Madame Rixleiven should be allowed to join her in

England. The Griff readily gave his consent, although the order to bar the old governess had originally been made by his father. The Griff said he would send some of his servants at once to Saxe-Coburg to attend Madame Rixleiven on her journey. The princess, still in the company of her big jointed German doll, went to bed happier. On the morrow she would be meeting the king and queen. Perhaps they would then receive her as a beloved daughter. This, together with marriage to Frederick, would complete her happiness.

The Griff had begged his father that the highest honours should be paid to Augusta on her drive from Greenwich to St. James's on Tuesday, her wedding day. He had hoped that his bride would be given an impressive military escort and that she would take a roundabout route through the City so that many thousands of Londoners could welcome her. The king would not agree. He said that Augusta must come without any fuss and with a minimum of pomp and ceremony. He begrudged the delight which Augusta was giving his son. The Griff had told his mother: 'If I had myself to look all Europe over I should have pitched my choice upon Augusta.' His old longing for Wilhelmina had vanished with Augusta's coming.

One of the king's coaches picked up Princess Augusta at Greenwich Palace on the morning of her wedding day. The coach, with a small escort, took her as far as Lambeth. There she was whisked into a royal barge and rowed to Whitehall, where in an extraordinary arrangement there awaited the king's sedan chair. The princess was carried in this through St. James's Park, seen at last at close quarters by some hundreds of people. Progress through the park was slow. On reaching St. James's Palace she was an hour behind the time at which the punctual king had expected her. If there had not been such complicated travel arrangements the princess could have come all the way from palace to palace by coach. She would have been seen by many thousands of Londoners and an adequate escort of mounted guards would have prevented any delays.

The princess was greeted by the Griff at the foot of the

steps which led from the palace to its back garden. The palace was thronged with richly dressed people present for the pre-wedding reception being given by the king. They were agog to stare at this unsophisticated maiden from an obscure German duchy, to assess her and to measure her embarrassment at suddenly being thrown into the company of such exalted people. Gathered in the great drawing room of the palace were the king, queen and entire court. The king was fuming at the late arrival of his future daughter-in-law. By his standards of morality unpunctuality was an almost unpardonable sin. In this unhappy atmosphere the doors of the stuffy drawing room were thrown open by the tall liveried footmen. There stood the Griff with Augusta. He was holding her hand. She was wearing a dress of rich brocade and many diamonds. The Griff, with her hand still in his, led her the length of the room, past the staring nobility and the greatest of Great Britain to the throne-like gilt chairs in which the king and queen sat.

As they rose, Augusta flung herself on the floor before the king in an exaggerated but nevertheless graceful curtsy. She got up and again descended very low to the floor before the queen. These were gestures of humblest respect and deference. When Augusta was erect again the king and the queen affec-tionately kissed her. Everybody agreed that Augusta's per-formance had been magnificent. The king was delighted that she had in her first appearance before him given such proof of her reverence for his greatness. Augusta had atoned for and been forgiven for the unpunctuality of her arrival.

The general opinion regarding the seventeen-year-old girl from Saxe-Coburg was that she was moderately pretty but of great charm. Some, however, saw Augusta in another light. To Caroline she was 'far from beautiful, has a wretched figure pretty eyes and a good mouth. She is as anxious as a good child to please. Her hair is almost the same shade as the Duchess of Devonshire's but rather more of a sheep's colour.' Lord Hervey, with his painted face, stood close to Caroline during Augusta's prostrations. The princess, he wrote, was rather tall, 'and had health and youth enough in her face, joined to a very modest and good-natured face, to make her countenance not disagreeable; but her person, from being very ill-made, a good deal awry, her arms long, and her motions awkward, had, in spite of all the finery of jewels and brocade, an ordinary air, which no trappings could cover or exalt'. Lord Egmont, also a witness of the scene, wrote that Augusta was about the same height as Frederick. He added: 'She is much pitted with smallpox, and had a great colour from the heat of the day and the hurry and surprise she was in. But she has a peculiar affability of behaviour and a very great sweetness of countenance, mixed with innocence, cheerfulness and sense.' Egmont was impressed by 'the great profusion of clothes' worn in the drawing room by the men as well as by the women. He commented that the decorative new suit worn by the Duke of Montague had cost £400.

At about 2.30 p.m. the reception ended. There were plans for a friendly family dinner in the Griff's apartments where the Princesses Amelia and Caroline and the young Prince William Duke of Cumberland might get to know their future sister-in-law. But this meal was marred by a squabble even before it had begun. The meals of members of the royal family were governed by the strict regulations of precedence, procedure and etiquette which had been observed at the old court in Hanover. These had been largely copied from the French court. Since this was his wedding day the Griff had planned, in honour of Augusta, to be given the dining-table deference which was his due as Prince of Wales. Thus at the top of the table was placed a chair with arms from which he might preside. Around the table were placed so-called 'stools'—chairs without arms. Learning of her brother's seating arrangements Amelia lost her temper and refused to enter the dining room. Sister Caroline found her pouting in its ante-chamber. A report of the quarrel was rushed to the king. As usual, he opposed the Griff's wishes. Although the Prince of Wales happened to be his eldest, ruled his father, all his children were nevertheless equal and must therefore all be given identical chairs with arms. The king also commanded that the servants should not kneel only to Frederick while serving the wine but to his sisters and young brother as well. The meal took place, but the princesses withdrew before the serving of the coffee. One of the servants detailed to wait upon Augusta was apparently going to pour the coffee for all at the table. The sisters feared he might do this in a manner suggesting that they were inferior in rank to the girl who within a few hours would be Princess of Wales.

To Augusta the ordeals of this wedding day had been hard. There had been the tiresome journey from Greenwich to St. James's Palace, with jumps from one form of conveyance to another. Worse, there had been the ordeal of that long walk up the centre of the great drawing room to the king and queen, with so many goggling foreign eyes watching her progress and examining her looks. There was the ordeal of the almost acrobatic curtsy of obeisance to George and Caroline. Lastly there had been the dreadful dinner in the Griff's palace apartments, starting with the quarrel and ending with the princesses' sulky retirement before the coffee was served. Now, in the evening, there was the wedding. The bride must have yearned for the presence of Madame Rixleiven or, indeed, any familiar face from Saxe-Coburg. It wasn't even possible for her big jointed doll to be close to her at the wedding.

The marriage took place at 9 p.m. in the chapel of the palace among a horde of richly dressed guests who irreverently treated the ceremony as they would a performance in a theatre. Augusta, struggling to keep her self-possession, walked to the altar on the arm of the plump fifteen-year-old William Duke of Cumberland. She wore a gown of red velvet lavishly trimmed with ermine. Upon her fair hair was a diamond coronet. Walking behind Augusta in attendance were four young women, all in gowns of silver. The bride was given away by the king whose costume rivalled hers in sheer splendour. It was of gold brocade with embroidery of silver. It had buttons encrusted with diamonds. Caroline was in a yellow silk dress weighed down with gems. The bridegroom in his robes as

Prince of Wales was attired in comparative modesty compared
with his father and some of the male guests.

The chapel looked more like a theatre than a place of
worship. In order that as many as possible could be accommodated for the wedding, the pews had been removed and
replaced by rising tiers of seats. The walls of the building were
hidden in tapestry and theatrical hangings of red velvet and
looped gold lace. A gallery for musicians had been constructed
close to the organ above the altar. And to the fore of a large
choir of men and boys were the king's favourite choristers,
known only by their surnames—Gates, Abbott, Lee and
Bird.

The bride, bridegroom and party were hardly in formation
in the chancel when the music poured from the orchestra and
the choir began to sing. Their anthem was *Sing unto God*.
It had never been heard before. Those sensitive to music
recognised this as a new composition by Handel. Because this
anthem was so new and obviously too little rehearsed, the
adult choristers and a boy soloist spoiled its charm by hesitation
and indefinite notes. Handel had indeed written *Sing unto
God* specially for the wedding of the young man who had
treated him so ill; and Handel was soon to suffer tragically
for this grand gesture of forgiveness.

Augusta, who had endured so much for so long, was reaching breaking point during the marriage ceremony performed
by Dr. Edmund Gibson, Bishop of London, with the
assistance of Dr. Henry Egerton, Bishop of Hereford. The time
was approaching when the Griff would place the wedding
ring on the bride's finger. The queen whispered to Augusta
to remove her long gloves. Augusta did this, but in a frenzy
of fright she did not know what to do with them. She tried
to push the gloves into the hands of the queen, who told her
to give them to Lord Effingham, who was standing nearby.
In the words of the queen in a letter to Anne, Princess of
Orange, 'I told her I would make a sign when she should
kneel. She clutched my skirt and said, "For heaven's sake,
please don't leave me." But the Griff bawled in her ear,

making her repeat the marriage sentences. She did not want
to let go of my skirt.'

The marriage had been performed. To the triumphal trum-
petings of the organ, bride, bridegroom, their overdressed
parents and other members of the family moved in procession
from the chapel. They walked to the king's apartments for
talk and exchanges of congratulations and kisses until the time
of the traditional gargantuan nuptial supper. It was during
this hour of temporary retirement from the masses of guests
when the Griff made a touching and forgiving gesture to his
father and mother. Kneeling at their feet with his bride, he
asked their blessing. The King pronounced his benediction
in a kindly voice. Then suddenly the bride was sick. It seemed
that her whole body was revolting against the strain it had
endured throughout that day.

This embarrassing vomiting episode had no lasting effects
upon Augusta. Indeed it seemingly acted as a catharsis, an
outlet for her terrors and pent-up emotions. At the great
supper Augusta had apparently completely recovered her
poise and self-confidence, charming all those grand ladies and
gentlemen, who, bowing and curtsying before her, offered
their flowery congratulations. The king also conducted himself
well, despite the stresses of his son's wedding day. Apparently
he had not made a single outburst of his customary temper
or fussiness; for the queen commented later that he 'behaved
like an angel'.

The decorum of the supper was marred by an unregal
exhibition of misbehaviour by the bridegroom. The dessert
was being served. The Griff ate several glasses of jelly, which
in those days was believed to have strongly invigorating and
aphrodisiac qualities. And every time he took a jelly he turned
towards some of his servants, laughing and winking. It was
as if he were back in his boyhood at Hanover in bawdy jests
with his friends the pages and the stable lads. Doubtless the
servants would have thought such conduct by the Prince of
Wales to be hilarious. Numbers of high-born guests might
have found it funny too. Yet the display was unlikely to

amuse the grave Dr. Gibson, Bishop of London, author of the profound work *Codex juris ecclesiastici Anglicani*, Dr. Egerton, Bishop of Hereford, and other clerical dignitaries present at the supper.

The feast over, there was still another ceremony before bride and bridegroom could be left in peace. This was the ceremony of seeing them to bed. Augusta temporarily retired to be undressed by the queen and some court ladies. The queen was shocked by the simplicity of her daughter-in-law's underwear. 'Her undress was so miserable', she wrote later, 'that it made me go quite grey.' The queen and her assistants decked Augusta in a nightgown of fine silk. Meanwhile elsewhere high members of the nobility were undressing the Griff. He was honoured by the appearance of the king, who personally pulled over his head the undershirt to his silver-adorned nightgown. The Griff's head was crowned with a tall starched lace nightcap. Bride and bridegroom then joined one another in bed. Next, members of the court and distinguished guests filed through the bedroom to bid the couple good night and to wish them well.

The Griff and Augusta had to be up and about early next day in order to attend a court reception at which hundreds of guests would be kissing their hands. Despite the ordeals of the previous day the princess seemed calm, confident and poised. The queen and Lord Hervey, with their Peeping Tom minds, expressed surprise at the fresh appearance of the bride after the first night of her honeymoon. They surmised that 'she had slept very sound'. And 'her majesty did not forget to descant at the same time on the glasses of jelly and the nightcap, saying the one made her sick, and the other, if it had not been her son, would have made her laugh'. The queen regarded her daughter-in-law with affectionate contempt. To her, Augusta was sweet, but insipid, ill-educated and stupid. History proved Caroline to be wrong.

The crowd at the court reception on this, the day after the wedding, was described by Lord Egmont as 'intolerable'. Several hours had passed before the hands of the patient

Prince and Princess of Wales had been kissed by the hundreds who were there. They praised the charm of the couple and the graceful manner in which the prince received compliments. Lord Egmont described how in 'the greatest confusion imaginable' of the reception he wished the prince 'a thousand happy years. He replied: "I give you a thousand thanks." ' The prince and princess had planned to dine in the royal manner with some of the public being admitted to the dining room to watch them. But when the king heard of these intentions he commanded that 'nobody shall see them dine!' The Griff was perilously arousing his father's jealousy.

On the same day in parliament the Griff's adviser, opposition leader William Pulteney, moved a congratulatory address to the king on the marriage of his son. Other members of the opposition and admirers of Frederick seized the opportunity provided to express their apparent support of the address, while at the same time speaking far more highly of the Prince of Wales than of the king. Three of Frederick's friends spoke in succession. These were George Lyttelton, George Grenville and William Pitt, then a cornet of Lord Cobham's Horse. Each hinted mischievously that the romance of Frederick and Augusta had developed without much encouragement from the king. Each attributed the resulting marriage to the will and initiative of the Prince of Wales backed by the wishes and goodwill of the British people. The three speakers poured fulsome praise not only upon the prince but also on Augusta with the ducal family of Saxe-Coburg. This was William Pitt's maiden speech in the House of Commons. While the speech purported to praise the king, it obliquely made him the subject of subtle but biting satire, causing Walpole to vow later that 'We must muzzle this terrible cornet of the Horse.'

The enthusiasm of the common people over the bride and bridegroom added to the embarrassment of the resentful king. There were stirringly emotional scenes while the couple drove through London. Their chaise sometimes halted while the Griff thanked the people for their attention or picked upon an individual for an exchange of compliments and quips. On the Friday evening of the gay wedding week the Griff and Augusta went to the opera where the long ovation given them delayed the start of the performance. It had been understood that the king and queen would accompany the couple and preparations had been made to receive them. However, George and Caroline stayed away. People sneered that this was because of George's fear that he and Caroline might receive fewer cheers than Frederick and Augusta.

The week also ended with a magnificent banquet given by the Griff to the Lord Mayor and aldermen of London. The Griff's close friend and courtier Lord Baltimore presided on his behalf at this dinner. Absurd and snobbish court rules prevented a Prince of Wales from presiding personally over and eating at a public dinner with subjects who were not even members of the nobility. For the Griff to have flouted such traditions by attending his own dinner would have quickly resulted in a grave crisis with his father. As it was, the affair was a huge success and won still greater affection for the Griff among the citizens of London.

Growing jealousy made the king spiteful. He was angry that Handel should have written a special anthem in honour of the wedding of the Griff and Augusta. George reasoned that the proper person to be the recipient of Handel's dedications was himself, the monarch, and not the heir apparent. So George decided that Handel should be punished. He thereupon ordered cessation of the special allowance of £1,000 a year paid to Handel. To add to the composer's tragedy, the prince had sent him no word of thanks for the dedication of the new anthem. This was due either to forgetfulness or to still smouldering ill-feeling concerning the man that the rival opera had failed to destroy. However, in a few weeks the Griff sent for Handel. There was a reconciliation after which the Griff consistently praised Handel's works. Nevertheless the shock of the hostile treatment, first by the Prince of Wales and then by the king, contributed much to the deterioration of his health until in 1737 he suffered a stroke which paralysed his right arm and affected his mind. He then went abroad. But a later chapter will tell how he returned to England with recovered health to win back the affection and esteem of the king through more musical triumphs.

The conduct of another offender continued to rankle with George. He was 'that puppy' William Pitt. In the House of Commons this low-ranking army officer, aged but twenty-eight, had dared to talk about his monarch with irony and sarcasm. George decided that such *lèse-majesté* could not go unpunished. Accordingly Cornet Pitt, M.P., of Lord Cobham's Horse, soon received notification of his dismissal from the Army.

George longed to be off to Hanover, but he worried what his son and Augusta might be up to while he was away. If the Griff moved about without surveillance he would, feared the king, strengthen his position with the opposition party. And he might, by moving freely among the public, still more increase his popularity. Members of the opposition were agitating that, in the absence of the king, the Prince of Wales should at last be allowed to act as regent. However, the king announced that once more that position would be held by the queen. The king, moreover, said that until his return to England Frederick and Augusta should live in the royal palace in the pretty village of Kensington and not enter nearby London at all. On realisation that such an order of exile might be difficult to enforce, the king suggested that the couple should always reside in the same household wherever the queen happened to be. If Caroline went to Hampton Court, then they should go there too. When she went to the lodge at Richmond the Griff and Augusta should accompany her. Apparently George feared that by asserting a right to an entirely separate household the Griff and Augusta might form a separate and rival court to St. James's.

At last the king went away. The Griff and Augusta maintained their separate home in apartments at St. James's Palace, but spent much time with the queen at Kensington Palace. And soon in almost constant attendance on the Princess of Wales was Lady Archibald Hamilton as her Lady of the Bed-

chamber, Privy Purse and Mistress of the Robes. These appointments were confirmed only after a fierce tussle. Caroline had
protested that the whole world would be shocked by a woman
commonly regarded as her son's mistress holding such appointments. But Augusta insisted that she must have Lady Archibald.
Finally the king in Germany was asked to adjudicate. He
decided that Lady Archibald could remain with his daughter-
in-law. Lord Hervey wrote that the Griff had deceived Augusta
regarding his past relationship with Lady Archibald. It is more
likely that she was aware of it, but had acquiesced, as had
Caroline in the case of Lady Suffolk and other women.
Anyhow, the friendship between Lady Archibald and the
Griff remained warm. At the same time Augusta and this
mother of ten children became close friends.

London's adulation of the Prince of Wales reached new
heights on November 16th, 1736, when he was presented with
the freedom of the city. The mayor with twenty aldermen
and several members of the council arrived at St. James's
Palace bearing the parchment of freedom in a decorated gold
box weighing forty ounces. The Griff, in a tactful start to his
speech of thanks, said he realised that the gift of the freedom
was really a mark of respect to his father the king rather than
a tribute to himself, and he thanked them for this. He went on
to emphasise the importance of trade to the power and prosperity of Great Britain. He vowed always to do all possible
to promote the prestige and commerce of London. And he
rejoiced in the liberty that existed in Great Britain. It was, for
those days, a vital, modern and original speech to come from
the mouth of a Hanoverian royalty.

The presentation was followed by a giant banquet at
Carlton House attended by the mayor, aldermen, council and
a host of the city's businessmen and tradesmen. Apparently
many attended without invitation, for soon there was not
even standing room in the mansion. Thereupon many were
invited to move to St. James's Palace, where additional food
was quickly prepared and scores of bottles of wine brought
up from the cellars. It was estimated that more than 1,000 of

London's citizens feasted and drank that night at the expense of the prince. Details of the prince's hospitality spread next day throughout London. According to Egmont, 'the city was exceedingly pleased and people said to one another, "Now we have a Prince of Wales of our own." ' On the other hand, Caroline was much displeased. She asked Lord Hervey for details of the banquet. 'My God,' exclaimed the queen, 'popularity always makes me sick!' Then she added that her son's popularity 'makes me vomit'. She protested that the presentation of the freedom and the banquet should not have happened in the king's absence and without his prior permission.

Queen Caroline, clinging to the old rigid traditions of European royalty, had good reason for alarm. The Griff had a complete absence of any sense of rank or class. This absence, together with his easy affable manners, was starting a revolution which would have profound effects on English social history. At the start of the reign of George II royalty, the nobility and landowning aristocracy formed one class. Business, commerce and trade were segregated in another. Except for the few whose great wealth bought them a higher position on the social ladder, those engaged in 'trade' were despised by royalty and the ruling classes. But when the Prince of Wales refused to differentiatè and to treat an ironmaster the same as a duke, the separate social factions began to draw closer. The prince also made the lowest people realise that royalty could possess the same humanity, warmth and sense of fun as the working man. He could in his walks about London exchange jokes with street hawkers. He could, as was seen at his wedding reception, fool hilariously with the servants.

8

Defeat for the Griff

Sir Robert Walpole and others were predicting late in
1736 that as soon as George II was back in England a
big confrontation between him and the Griff was certain.
Marriage seemed to have given the Griff strength of will and
purpose. It might also have increased his capacity for mischief.
He was still seeing much of Jane Hamilton. Nevertheless he
and Augusta were very close. Their marriage was an undoubted
success. Caroline may have dismissed her daughter-in-law as
stupid and ineffectual. Certainly Augusta had some strange
pastimes—such as dressing and undressing her big jointed doll
in front of the amused servants. On the other hand, with adult
firmness she resisted attempts of the queen to influence her,
although for a time they saw much of each other. Madame
Rixleiven, Augusta's old governess, had arrived. Perhaps this
added to her self-confidence. She was also quickly mastering
the English language. Soon she would be speaking English
with less German accent than that of the king and queen.

The Griff had shown toughness in refusing to attend meetings of the Regency Council presided over by his mother.
Since he had not been appointed regent he would have nothing
to do with the council. When they sat down for business he
simply would not be there. Later would come apologies
and excuses from the Griff, pretending that his absence had
been unavoidable. But a still greater indication of the Griff's
true sentiments towards his parents followed the appearance
in bookshops of a little satire called *L'Histoire du Prince Titi*,
of anonymous authorship. This was written in French, but
later there appeared a translation in English. The book—

presented in the form of a fairy-tale—was recognised and denounced as a scurrilous attack on King George and Queen Caroline. There was widespread agreement that its author was the Prince of Wales. This was the satire which the Griff was described as writing in Chapter 6. The prince had written it in French, inspired by the satires in guise of fairy-tales of the Paris author Charles Perrault. Then the book had been translated for the Griff by American-born James Ralph, who was later to do more work for him as a political journalist.

The Griff's story was slight. It lagged far behind Charles Perrault in style. *L'Histoire du Prince Titi* told of a King Guinea and a Queen Tripe. They had an elder son named Titi. King Guinea was so mean and so miserly that he wore on his robes not ermine but the fur of white rabbit. While King Guinea hated and persecuted Titi, he adored and spoiled a younger son who was nasty and repulsive. Titi fell in love with a Princess Bibi. The king and queen hated Bibi, so Titi was disinherited. But the king's subjects who adored Titi arose in rebellion in protest. The revolt was successful. Titi and his parents were reconciled and everybody lived happily ever after.

This clumsy little work quickly attracted attention as soon as its chief characters were identified as George, Caroline, Frederick, Augusta and William Duke of Cumberland. A rush for the book, however, was soon halted. On the order of the Prime Minister officials went from bookshop to bookshop, buying up all the copies. For some time critics would start questioning whether, after all, Frederick had been the author of the satire. But when Ralph died in 1762 a copy of *L'Histoire du Prince Titi* was found hidden in a box among his possessions. This was in the handwriting of Frederick.

The king had left England for Hanover in May soon after the Griff's marriage. He was not on English soil again until the following January. His long absence abroad added greatly to his unpopularity. While the common people of England were applauding the Prince of Wales they were denouncing his father, for many details of the king's adventures in Hanover had become common gossip and had even appeared in print.

Portion of the Herrenhausen Palace, Hanover, birthplace of the Royal Griffin. Here, between the ages of seven and twenty-one, Frederick represented his grandfather, the Elector of Hanover, when the latter had moved to England as George I

Eighteenth-century scene being re-enacted in the baroque garden of the Herrenhausen Palace, where the Royal Griffin played as a boy

*Above. Frederick's barge
—often called 'the most
beautiful boat in the
world'—now in the
National Maritime
Museum, Greenwich,
and left, interior of
barge's saloon*

Far left. Frederick Prince of Wales with sisters Anne, Princess Royal (sitting on left); Princess Caroline (standing left); and Princess Amelia (sitting right). Painting by Philip Mercier, 1733

Left. Frederick Prince of Wales. Painting by Philip Mercier

Augusta Princess of Wales, wife of Frederick. Painted in 1736 by Charles Philips

George II, father of Frederick Prince of Wales. Painting from studio of C. Jervas

Queen Caroline, wife of George II and Frederick's mother. From studio of C. Jervas

*Sir Robert Walpole
(later the Earl of
Orford), the Prime
Minister, close ally of
King George II and
Queen Caroline in their
quarrels with Frederick.
Painting by Jean
Baptiste Van Loo*

*William Duke of
Cumberland, younger
brother of Frederick and
favourite of their father
George II. Painting by
Sir Joshua Reynolds*

George Bubb Dodington,
later Lord Melcombe,
boon companion of
Frederick. From a
contemporary engraving

Prince George, eldest son
of Frederick who on his
death became Prince of
Wales and who, from
1760 to 1820, ruled
England as George III.
Anonymous engraving
after Wilson

*Philip Dormer Stanhope,
4th Earl of Chesterfield,
courtier, wit and letter-
writer. Political adviser
to Frederick. Painting by
William Hoare*

*John Lord Hervey,
court favourite of Queen
Caroline. He was first
a warm friend and later a
bitter enemy of her son,
Frederick. Painting from
studio of Jean Baptiste
Van Loo*

James Thomson, the poet, for many years a friend of Frederick. His masque Alfred, written in collaboration with the poet David Mallet and containing Rule Britannia, was performed for the first time at Cliveden. Painting after J. Patoun

Thomas Arne, composer and friend of Handel. He wrote the music for Rule Britannia and also the arrangement for God Save the King which became the National Anthem. Picture based on drawing by F. Bartolozzi

Madame Walmoden gave birth to a baby boy of which the king was apparently the father. A sickly infant, he soon died. Again Madame Walmoden was having a passionate affair with the king. There were stories how Madame Walmoden produced a husband who demanded £50,000 from the king to give her up; and how shortly afterwards the king surprised both in bed. Next there was the story of a plot of Madame d'Elitz to ruin Madame Walmoden's reputation with the king by having a ladder placed by night up to her window, as if she were receiving another lover. Horrified by such tales, Egmont wrote in his diary that 'the citizens of London cry out that their trade is ruined by his majesty's going and long stay, and that he spends the English money abroad. Last week one of them in the presence of a friend of mine damned him, saying, "If he will have a whore, why doesn't he take an English one and stay. There are a lot of them to be had here cheaper."'

In the city of London were daily heard new jokes about the fifty-three-year-old king and his Hanoverian mistress. A notice was pasted up at the Royal Exchange reading:

It is reported that his Hanoverian majesty designs to visit his British dominions for three months in the spring.

An old and blind horse was found wandering in the street, a shabby saddle and a pillion on its back. On the animal's forehead was this notice:

Let nobody stop me—I am the King's Hanover equipage going to fetch his majesty and his whore to England.

There were certainly moves to let the king bring his 'whore' to England. Queen Caroline, often so tolerant of her husband's infidelities, was pained that Madame Walmoden should have caused him to linger so long in Hanover. First in her letters to George she revealed her displeasure. But later, under the influence of Walpole, she told him to bring Madame Walmoden and that the old apartments of his former mistress Lady Suffolk would be made in readiness for her. But unexpectedly Madame Waldomen herself said she preferred to remain in Hanover. Her decision was wise. Had she dared to come at that time, the public would have given her a terrible reception.

Queen Caroline suffered an alarming experience of the growing public disrespect for the crown when she was one afternoon driving into London from Kensington Palace. A mob surrounded her carriage crying, 'No gin, no king!', a slogan of the campaign against a recent Act controlling gin-drinking. The queen, keeping calm, begged the crowd to be patient until the next session of parliament 'when both will be back again'. Her carriage was then allowed to proceed.

Even the seas seemed to have become angry with the king. After a great ball and supper at Hanover on 6th December 1736 George kissed Madame Walmoden good-bye and, with a large new portrait of his mistress, left for Helvoetsluys, Holland, to board his yacht for England. A fierce storm arose in the North Sea, so the king was advised to postpone his departure. The storm lasted four days. In England it was be-lieved the king had sailed, despite the tempestuous weather. When his yacht failed to arrive it was feared he had been shipwrecked and had perished. If this were confirmed, then, of course, Frederick would have to be proclaimed king. Frederick behaved with restraint and dignity and showed anxiety for his father's safety, but his admirers and members of the opposition could not but hope that the unpopular King George was to be succeeded. Walpole was anxious, not only for the king's safety but for his own future if the Griff came to the throne. It was during this critical period that he uttered to Hervey the denunciation which has in history had such a detrimental effect on Frederick's reputation:

'What will be the prince's case? A poor, weak, lying, dishonest, contemptible wretch, that nobody loves, that nobody believes, that nobody will trust, and that will trust everybody by turns and that everybody by turns, will impose upon, betray mislead and plunder. And what then will become of this divided family, and this divided country, is too melancholy a prospect for one to admit conjecture to paint it.'

Walpole said these terrible words in a coach while taking Hervey to dinner at his home.

On the morning after Hervey's dinner with Walpole a

message reached London from Harwich that distress guns had been heard at sea. There were increased fears that the royal yacht had sunk. Plans were being made for a search. However, later a ship arrived from Helvoetsluys. It brought a letter to Caroline from the king to tell her he had never sailed. The gale ceased, and once again it was believed in London that the king was on his way. Soon a new tempest arose. A few days later several mastless ships reached England, their officers expressing fears that the royal yacht had foundered. However, it was later learned that after setting out from Holland with the king aboard, she had returned to port. After more alternations of anxiety and elation in England the king eventually crossed the North Sea and landed safely on January 15th, 1737, after waiting at Helvoetsluys for five weeks. It was puzzling why during that time he had never troubled to visit The Hague a short distance away to see his daughter Anne Princess of Orange. She was very ill. It was reported that in order to save her life during a difficult childbirth the doctor had been forced to squeeze her baby so tight that it died.

The king must have realised how unpopular he had become when he was driven through the city of London to St. James's Palace at the end of his long, much-delayed journey from Hanover. This was in the early afternoon when hundreds were on the streets or in the eating houses for their dinner. Usually so polite and respectful at the passing of the monarch, these Londoners did not, as was customary, remove their hats. At one point on the route the king was hissed by the crowd, causing Egmont to describe the scene as 'an insolence that I do not remember in British history'. The atmosphere was brighter when the king reached his palace. Despite the ill-feeling caused by Madame Walmoden, George and Caroline had an affectionate reunion. Even the Griff was there to greet and to exchange kisses with his father. But the pleasure of Caroline at her husband's return was marred by his insistence that a new picture be placed opposite their double bed. This was the portrait of Madame Walmoden which he had brought from Hanover.

Unfortunately for the king, all London seemed still to be extolling the Prince of Wales whose recent activities were being told, re-told and embroidered upon. It was related how on the recent Lord Mayor's Day the prince had stood like any common citizen in a crowd watching the procession pass. On being recognised among the rough shoving crowd, he had been hoisted on to the stand of the Company of Saddlers. There were dramatic stories how at a big all-night fire in the Temple the prince arrived and, indifferent to personal danger, led in the quenching of the flames. Then on the very day of the king's return from Hanover, Londoners heard that the prince had sent £500 to the Lord Mayor for the relief of any freemen of London in prison.

The Griff, true to his policy of surprise by sudden, unexpected actions had a painful shock in store for the king. He was, through his parliamentary advisers and friends, going to raise the question of his allowance in the House of Commons and the House of Lords. He was still receiving £50,000 a year. This, as has already been stressed, was half the income enjoyed by George as Prince of Wales. Moreover, the £50,000 did not come directly from the government but through the king, who had the power to stop or reduce it at any time. Then the king, ignoring the precedent of similar cases, had failed to settle any money on Augusta as Princess of Wales. It was not as if the funds received by the king from the civil list and other sources were too meagre for him to afford more for his elder son. George received between £800,000 and £900,000 a year, and Caroline £100,000 a year—huge sums in those days.

The king had not been long home when the tempest burst over the Griff's demands for more money. The king was ill in bed with two complaints—a bad cough and piles. Pain and discomfort had put him into such a temper that he even exploded with rage when one of his gentlemen-in-waiting politely expressed the wish that he was getting better. The king's worries increased the more when Lord Hervey revealed through the queen some details of the Griff's machinations. Henry Fox (brother of Hervey's beloved friend Stephen Fox) had told him that the Griff and his friends were secretly soliciting the support of influential M.P.s and peers in his scheme to have the question of his income raised in parliament. The second Duke of Marlborough was among those busy canvassing on behalf of the prince.

Despite the continued irritation of his haemorrhoids, the king learned details of the Griff's plot with comparative self-control. But if Lord Hervey is to be believed, both the queen and her daughter Princess Caroline flared into burning denunciations of the Griff. They 'wished a hundred times a day the prince might drop dead from apoplexy'. The queen 'cursed the hour of his birth', and described him as 'the lowest stinking coward in the world'. On seeing from her dressing room her eldest son crossing a palace courtyard, Caroline said to Hervey: 'Look there he goes—that wretch! that villain! I wish the ground would open up and sink the monster to the lowest hole in hell. You stare at me: but I can assure you if my wishes and prayers had any effect, and that the maledictions of a mother signified anything, his days would not be very happy or very many.'

In the days that followed, the Griff personally approached every influential acquaintance who might help to bring his cause to victory in parliament. He had buried his pride and wooed the fat George Bubb Dodington, once his adviser and closest crony. Dodington, whose political patron was now the Duke of Argyll, refused the prince's plea for support. Dodington added that he could not endorse any parliamentary interference with the king's financial decisions. He warned that a battle between king and Prince of Wales, waged in parliament, would disrupt national unity and break the British people into two bitter factions. While some of the advisers of the Griff gleefully encouraged him in his belligerent plans, William Pulteney, leader of the opposition, urged caution and moderation. He would have preferred a settlement of the dispute outside the House of Commons.

Into the storm over the Griff stepped the prime minister. Walpole could not conceal his anxiety. He warned that if the

Griff's cause were taken up in parliament he might win. The opposition party might present this case so effectively that they could rally a majority which would overwhelm the prestige of himself and the king. What might happen then, if the Prince of Wales were shown to have higher standing and influence with the public than the monarch? Moreover this family dispute, so totally separating the parents from their heir, might even lead to the destruction of the Hanoverian monarchy. The Prime Minister had to admit that the Griff had a strong case. As it was, his income of £50,000 a year was dependent upon the discretion and whim of the king. It was not fully established, fully guaranteed. And then nothing had been done about a jointure for Princess Augusta.

In the court and king's party there were wavering and vacillation as the day of the debate on the allowance drew near in February 1737. Some who had discussed the crisis with the Griff secretly reported to Walpole that he was stubborn in his resolution that his case must be aired in parliament. The young man so often described as weak was revealing surprising strength. On a cold, dank morning preceding the day of the planned debate Walpole decided that a last-moment effort must be made to avoid it. He quickly developed a plan for the king to send a message to the Prince of Wales promising a jointure for Augusta and also guaranteeing absolutely the annual allowance to him of £50,000. Reluctantly king and queen assented to a message which despite its devious statements and pretentious style, looked very much like a partial surrender to the Griff, although it still refused him his £100,000 a year. The message was prepared. The Lord Chamberlain and Lord Steward hurried to the Prince's apartments to ask him to receive members of the Cabinet Council who had a message to deliver to him from the king.

Soon afterwards the delegation arrived, headed by Lord Hardwicke, who had just been appointed Lord Chancellor. Others in the impressive array included the Dukes of Richmond, Newcastle and Argyll; also Lords Harrington, Pembroke and Scarborough. While the whole delegation stood before the prince, Lord Hardwicke read this message:

His majesty had commanded us to acquaint your royal highness in his name that, upon your royal highness's marriage, he immediately took upon his royal consideration the settling of a proper jointure upon the Princess of Wales; but his sudden going abroad, and his late indisposition since his return, had hitherto retarded the execution of these gracious intentions; from which short delay his majesty did not apprehend any inconvenience could arise, especially since no application had in any manner been made to him upon this subject by your royal highness; and that his majesty hath now given orders for settling a jointure upon the Princess of Wales, as far as he is enabled by law, suitable to her high rank and dignity, which he will, in proper time, lay before parliament, in order to be rendered certain and effectual for the benefit of her royal highness.

The king has further commended us to acquaint your royal highness that, although your royal highness has not thought fit, by any application to his majesty, to desire that your allowance of fifty thousand pounds per annum, which is now paid you by monthly payments, at the choice of your royal highness, preferably to quarterly payments, might, by his majesty's further grace and favour, be rendered less precarious, his majesty, to prevent the bad consequences which he apprehends may follow from the undutiful measures which his majesty is informed your royal highness has been advised to pursue, will grant to your royal highness, for his majesty's life, the said fifty thousand pounds per annum, to be issuing out of his majesty's civil list revenues, over and above your royal highness's revenues arising from the Duchy of Cornwall; which his majesty thinks a very competent allowance, considering his numerous issue, and the great expense which do and must necessarily attend the honourable provision for his whole family.

The 'poor weak wretch', as Walpole called the Griff, showed surprising resolution when the Lord Chancellor read this message, almost surrounded by his illustrious fellow councillors. The prince's mind, working quickly, saw that it meant very little. No sum was named as Augusta's jointure. There was to be no increase on the £50,000-pound-a-year allowance for himself. The prince did not even dignify the

written message to him with a written answer. Instead he
made a verbal reply, which heavily weighted with dutiful
compliments, regretted that there could be no immediate
settlement since the matter was now out of his hands.

Lord Chancellor Hardwicke and other members of the
Cabinet Council withdrew for some minutes to write down as
accurately as possible the statement just made by the prince.
When all were about to return to the king's apartments the
Griff drew Lord Hardwicke aside. He said how sorry he was
over the break with his father. Then he added how he wanted
to make it clear that, despite what was said in the king's
message, he had indeed made representations about his inadequate allowance through the queen. Lord Hardwicke, who
left his own record of this incident, regarded the prince with
affection and was deeply touched. Nevertheless Hardwicke
told him that any remarks he had to make on the subject
should be made to the entire Cabinet Council and not to him
alone. This was the report taken back to the waiting king
and queen by the Lord Chancellor and his colleagues:

*'That his royal highness desired the Lords to lay him, with all
humility, at his majesty's feet, and to assure his majesty that he had,
and ever would retain, the utmost duty for his royal person; this his
royal highness was very thankful for any instance of his majesty's
goodness to him or the princess, and particularly for his majesty's
intention of settling a jointure upon her royal highness; but that as to
the message, the affair was now out of his hands, and therefore he
could give no answer to it.*

*'After which his royal highness used many dutiful expressions
towards his majesty; and then added: "Indeed, my Lords, it is in
other hands: I am sorry for it": or to that effect.*

*'His royal highness concluded with earnestly desiring the Lords to
represent his answer to his majesty in the most respectful and dutiful
manner.'*

Neither the king nor queen were mollified by their son's
desire to be so 'respectful and dutiful'. They were filled with
wrath. They blamed Sir Robert Walpole for persuading them
into sending a message which had brought such a polite but

painful snub from the Griff. Hardwicke reported the Griff's claim that he had asked the queen to speak to the king about his need for an allowance increase. The queen told Hardwicke that this 'most hardened of liars' had never done this. It was true that when single he used to complain to her about his debts, expenses and poverty; but since his marriage he had never talked in that way.

The next day the allowance question was to be opened in parliament. Walpole, George and Caroline realised that now nothing could prevent this. All three were fearful of what the results would be. A substantial majority in the Griff's favour was feared. Frantically Walpole and his friends canvassed members of parliament for promises of support. Even at such short notice two were found who would vote for the king's side in exchange for bribes. Thus the king paid out £500 to one M.P. and £400 to another.

Opposition leader William Pulteney had unsuccessfully urged caution and moderation on the Prince of Wales. Pulteney would have preferred the squabble to have been kept out of parliament. But the will of the prince had prevailed. Thus on the decisive day it was Pulteney who rose in the House of Commons to ask support for an address to the king for settlement on the prince of £100,000 a year. Pulteney appealed that the king should treat Frederick and Augusta as generously as he and Caroline were treated when they were Prince and Princess of Wales. Pulteney claimed that this debate had greater importance than any in the nation's history. In the past the independence of the heir apparent had been protected by the grant of an established income; and it was only fair that this practice should continue. Pulteney stressed that George II was receiving a larger income than any previous British monarch. Parliament had treated him so generously on the understanding that his eldest son would have an adequate and guaranteed allowance.

In opposing the motion Sir Robert Walpole challenged the right of parliament to tell the king how he should conduct his expenditure from the civil list which was his for life and without any conditions. At the same time Walpole went into ponderous and complicated details regarding the king's finances and responsibilities. This was in an endeavour to prove that he was treating the Prince of Wales generously. Several of Frederick's friends and members of the opposition party spoke strongly in favour of the prince's case. Two members of his household staff, John Hedges and Lord Baltimore, contended that Frederick had repeatedly and without results begged the queen to put before the king his need for a larger allowance. •

The opposition seemed to have the stronger case. But when late that night the time came for the division, the results were 234 for the king's party and 204 for the opposition. Many like Dodington felt sorry for Frederick, but they voted for national unity. They saw the peril to this unity if they supported the campaign of the heir apparent to overrule the authority of the monarch. But two of this majority of thirty were, of course, motivated only by the monarch's £900 worth of bribes.

Frederick had never anticipated a triumph from a similar motion introduced by Lord Carteret in the House of Lords, However, there the defeat of the opposition was by an over-whelming 103 votes to 40. Carteret was always delighted to oppose any cause favoured by Walpole. But this time his speech caused far greater offence to Queen Caroline than to the prime minister. In a complicated argument concerning precedents in the payment of royal allowances Carteret compared Caroline's case with that of the wife of Edward III and the mistress of the Black Prince. Caroline believed Carteret had dragged her name into the debate in a spirit of personal malice. But later the scheming Carteret saw the queen. He vowed he had always wanted to serve her but that Walpole had kept him from her, thus casting him into the opposition camp of her eldest son. He vainly begged the privilege of mending the breach between Caroline and the Griff.

George and Caroline were exultant at their crushing defeats of the Griff in the Houses of Commons and Lords. The king felt there should be severe punishment for the son who he said had behaved 'like a silly puppy and undutiful, insolent rascal'. The king suggested that his promise of a jointure to Augusta and a secured income for 'the silly puppy' could now be forgotten. And another sound punishment would be for him to be expelled in disgrace from St. James's Palace. But Walpole argued that such a 'disgrace' might turn into a triumph for the offender. An expulsion from the palace would make a martyr of the Griff who, with the support of more sympathisers, might organise his own court to rival that of St. James's. A griffin at large might become a griffin rampant. Thus on Walpole's advice it was decided he should remain under his parents' roof, but be completely ignored, even when participating in the ceremonies of the court. Accordingly these punitive tactics started. Sometimes the king and the Griff dined at the same table. Often the prince, according to royal protocol, led the queen by hand into the great drawing room of the palace for receptions. At these and other ceremonial occasions neither king nor queen were seen to address a word to the prince, and when faced by the prince they gave him no look of recognition.

When possible the vindictive king also took reprisals against those who had supported Pulteney and Carteret in the debates on the prince's allowance. Sir George Oxenden, who dared to vote in the Commons in favour of the prince, was dismissed from his office as a Lord of the Treasury. At the same time poison tongues, set wagging by the palace, spread stories of Oxenden's alleged debaucheries outside parliament. In disgrace also was Lord Archibald Hamilton, who had thought it judicious to stay out of the House of Commons at the time of the vote on the allowance. Because of his failure to support the king, and because of his wife's position in the prince's household, Sir Archibald was some time later to lose his post at the Admiralty. The prince then made him his cofferer in compensation.

The Griff took his parliamentary defeat and the parental ostracism with apparent indifference. At the palace receptions he still held his powdered head high and poured wit and goodwill on all those who would speak to him. And apart from the court he was proud of the few who had defied the power and prestige of Walpole and king to stand by him. 'The good Lyttelton' was made the Griff's secretary in appreciation of his loyalty. William Pitt, who had made another speech enraging the king's party, was rewarded with the post of Groom of the Prince's Bedchamber.

The Griff was also thinking more about his wife than about the recent lost battle over the allowance. For Augusta was pregnant. Their first child would be born in the coming summer. They were keeping this news from the king and queen. Caroline, who indulged almost as much in sexual speculation as in religious speculation, was fond of discussing with Lord Hervey whether or not the Griff was impotent. This seemed a foolish speculation in view of her son's many mistresses from adolescence to the present. She would cast doubts on his fatherhood of the late son of the late Anne Vane. She would with Hervey indulge in morbid conjectures on her son's reproductive organs. These conversations were still progressing while the baby was moving inside Augusta. The Griff would have been unaware of his mother's engrossing interest in his most intimate functions. However, his relations with the king and queen were so strained that it seemed unwise for the present to convey anything to them regarding Augusta's pregnancy.

Meanwhile there had been a surprising change in the household of Princess Augusta. Her former governess Madame Rixleiven suddenly returned for good to Saxe-Coburg. According to Hervey, the Griff and others were disturbed by the influence that Madame Rixleiven had upon Augusta. She was said to have persuaded the princess to take Holy Communion in London's Lutheran Church instead of in the Church of England 'as by law established'. And according also to Hervey, Madame Rixleiven upset the Griff by talking too freely also 'on conjugal points'. The fact was, however, that Augusta had so swiftly become part of the life and society of England that the ancient governess from Saxe-Coburg had become an embarrassing anachronism. She was unable to help and advise the princess in the sophisticated world of London as could such women as Lady Archibald Hamilton and Lady Irwin. Only one personality from Augusta's Saxe-Coburg remained close to her now. This was the big jointed doll, soon to have its position usurped by a living baby.

Now that his parents held him at such a distance, the Griff had also more time for diversions with his friend George Lyttelton. These diversions were much more wholesome than those Dodington had encouraged while he was first favourite of the Griff. Although Dodington was himself a patron of artists and writers, he had preferred to entertain the Griff with the coarse and sensual pleasures of the town. Lyttelton, on the other hand, refined and aesthetic, introduced the Griff to interesting poets and other writers. While the Griff would in sudden outbursts rush into the company of low, immoral people, he was showing an increasing preference for those of culture and decency. He rejoiced in his gardens at Kew and loved to mingle with those rough but discriminating workers who were making its borders and shrubberies so lovely. At the same time he increasingly valued the friendship of poets and other writers. King George II talked contemptuously of what he pronounced as 'boetry' and never read a book, whereas his eldest son adored poetry and read voraciously. And as was proved by *L'Histoire du Prince Titi* and snatches of songs or verse left behind by Frederick, he tried to write himself—but unsuccessfully.

The Griff came to know and admire the great Alexander Pope, who had a house at Twickenham across the river from Kew. Once, indeed, the Griff accused Pope of disliking princes. When Pope responded with 'I beg your pardon', the Griff followed up with, 'Well, you don't love kings then.' 'Sir,' replied Pope, 'I own I love a lion best before his claws are grown.' Their acquaintanceship did not develop into friendship until 1740 when Pope, then aged fifty-two, dined with the Griff at Kew House. The Griff talked so much that Pope found himself falling asleep. Sometimes at their meetings the two discussed poetry, but more often the topic was gardening, their great mutual interest. One day the younger man surprised the elder with gifts of the busts of Shakespeare and three other poets for his library.

Most members of the literary clique of the Griff and Lyttelton were younger men than Pope. A leading member was bulky heavy-eyed James Thomson, born in 1700 and the renowned author of *The Seasons*. Thomson was regarded as a daring poetical innovator, for in *The Seasons* he abandoned the conventional artificial forms of English rustic verse for a natural romantic treatment of the countryside. The same poem aroused protests because of the abhorrence and derision it expressed regarding the sports of hunting and shooting. Country gentlemen regarded such sentiments, coming from a mere poet, as unprecedented insolence. Lyttelton, as Thomson's patron and closest friend, helped him to shorten the long and rather tedious poem *Liberty* which was dedicated to the Griff. In his dedication Thomson hailed Frederick as 'prince and patriot united'. Thomson praised his possession of 'an overflowing benevolence, generosity and candour of heart, joined to an enlightened zeal for liberty' in his belief that on liberty 'depends the happiness and glory of both kings and people'. In 1738 Frederick granted Thomson a pension of £100 a year.

Poet and miscellaneous writer David Mallet joined the coterie of the Griff in 1736 at the age of thirty-one, on the introduction of his friend Thomson. Poet David Hammond, friend of both Lyttelton and Chesterfield, was one of the coterie most liked by the prince. He became a member of the prince's household staff. There were also dramatist Edward Moore, and poet Mark Akenside, who was in 1737 starting his composition of his *Pleasures of the Imagination*.

Lyttelton and these lively young writers brought many carefree but intellectually stimulating hours to the Griff as, in 1737, the months moved on towards the birth of his child and another volcanic disturbance with his father the king.

9

The Royal Eviction

The late spring and early summer of 1737 were as
tranquil for the king as they were for the Griff in this
welcome interval between one family row and another. He and
the queen spent much of this in the seclusion of the White
Lodge at Richmond with four of their five daughters and court
favourites. But this time George was not shooting so many
fat turkeys from the tree branches of Richmond Park. These
had a rival for his attentions in the person of Mary Lady
Deloraine, the family governess. As related in Chapter 4, the
king had at St. James's Palace made an evening habit of visiting
his daughters' apartments to 'talk bawdy' with Lady Deloraine,
described by Horace Walpole as 'a pretty idiot'. Walpole
attributed to Lady Deloraine 'most of the vices of her own
sex, and the additional one of ours, drinking'. Loose talk had
inevitably led to loose behaviour. Lady Deloraine was now
serving as the king's mistress.

No one in the cynical sophisticated circles of the court
objected much to the king's misbehaviour with Lady Deloraine. It was said that the queen approved because his dalliance
with this mature governess, then aged thirty-seven, would
discourage him from another desertion of England to see his
beloved Madame Walmoden again in Hanover. The opinion
of the prime minister was that because of security risks George
'might have taken something less mischievous than that lying
bitch. But since it is only the king, I think it is of no great
significance.' The fact was that Sir Robert Walpole entrusted
more state secrets to Caroline than he did to George. He
summed up the attributes of the king's new mistress in nine

words: 'A weak head, a pretty face, a lying tongue.' Meanwhile Lady Deloraine would chatter to anybody who would listen about her liaison with the king, insisting that she had surrendered to him only after a long siege. She even described to Princess Caroline the king's amorous passion, inviting her opinion on how it could be controlled. The princess replied that Lady Deloraine would have had more experience at that kind of thing than herself, for Lady Deloraine had had two husbands and many lovers. Truly a career woman, Lady Deloraine, while serving as mistress to the king, continued to supervise the education and upbringing of his two younger daughters, the princesses Mary, aged fourteen, and Louisa, aged thirteen.

Early in July the court, having left Richmond, was now established in Hampton Court Palace, so much more spacious than the White Lodge. Queen Caroline was suffering from bouts of what was then diagnosed as gout. Nevertheless she was finding contentment and peace in the fascinating high panelled rooms of the palace and in its Dutch gardens. But Caroline had got rid of a wide area of topiary, replacing it with chaste lawns. She still had time to speculate whether or not the Griff was capable of procreation. She had assured Hervey that if these powers were absent, her son was quite capable of smuggling an infant into Augusta's bedroom and then pretending it was theirs.

Then a letter from Frederick, delivered to the queen on July 5th, threw her into a state of excitement and into more speculation. Writing from his house at Kew, Frederick told her that the physician Dr. John Hollings and midwife Mrs. Cannons had confirmed that Augusta was pregnant. It was a very formal letter, written in French, without any details but nevertheless assuring her majesty that he remained her 'very humble, very obedient son and servant'. The king received a similar letter. Both he and the queen remained absurdly suspicious. He ordered that the baby should be born at Hampton Court where everything would be under the close surveillance and supervision of the queen. Apparently this would be easier at Hampton Court than at St. James's Palace where the prince and princess had their own private apartments and household. The king would also have disliked the idea of the baby being born in London because of the popularity of his son and daughter-in-law. A birth in St. James's Palace would result in crowds converging there to demonstrate and to cheer the prince and princess. But Hampton Court was in the countryside and of difficult access from London.

But when would the birth take place? The queen met her daughter-in-law and offered her congratulations. The queen asked Augusta for the date on which her baby was expected. Augusta, like an ignorant schoolgirl being questioned by her teacher, replied that she didn't know. On receiving the congratulations of Sir Robert Walpole, the Griff talked vaguely about the baby arriving in three months' time in October. Anyhow, the Griff and Augusta were commanded to move into Hampton Court. The sharp and suspicious Hervey had hinted prophetically that the Griff might even remove Augusta elsewhere to have her baby outside parental observation and jurisdiction. But the queen had vowed: 'At her labour I positively will be, let her lie-in where she will; for she cannot be brought to bed as quick as one can blow one's nose and I will be sure it is her child.'

The couple thus moved into the hostile and unsavoury circle in Hampton Court Palace. It was an uncomfortable, disturbing atmosphere for the eighteen-year-old pregnant Augusta as well as for the Griff. There were the king and queen, hating and ignoring their son and regarding their daughter-in-law as weak and inferior. There was the effeminate Hervey encouraging the queen's morbid speculations over the most intimate details of her son's sexual powers. There was the obscene language of the paradoxical intellectual queen with her interests ranging from sublime philosophy to filth. And in addition there were the two unfriendly elder princesses Amelia and Caroline together with the poisonous Lady Deloraine with her mischievous influence over the lascivious fifty-four-year-old king. No wonder that the prospect of their first baby being born in this household filled the Griff and Augusta with distaste. It is true that there was a wild, immoral side to the prince's nature. Nevertheless there was, in his own household, a sense of beauty and idealism unknown in the household of George and Caroline. Augusta was a quiet lady-like character, a girl of instinctive good breeding, as the records left by many who knew her have testified. Such facts must have strongly influenced the husband's desire to get his wife out of Hampton Court before the baby was born, even if this meant defiance of the commands of the king.

The prince and princess had arrived at Hampton Court as if prepared for a long stay. The princess had brought her Mistress of the Robes Lady Archibald Hamilton, with two of her dressers, Mrs. Paine and Mrs. Clavering. The prince had brought two of his favourite equerries, William Townsend and Thomas Bloodworth. There was Vried, his *valet de chambre*, who, incidentally, was a qualified surgeon and male midwife. Also in the prince's party was his witty, unconventional friend French dancing master Philip Desnoyers. This Desnoyers would have relieved the boredom of both the Griff and Augusta in the hostile household of Hampton Court. Moreover, Desnoyers was unlikely to offend the king and queen because he was popular with them too. Hervey thought Desnoyers was a tricky customer who played to both sides and 'spied' for the king as well as for the prince. However, his deep affection for the Griff was often proved.

It was Sunday, the 31st July. In the morning there had been the customary service in the chapel. In the afternoon Augusta had dined with the king and queen, looking remarkably slim even if, as many believed, her pregnancy was only in its sixth month. In the evening of this Sunday members of this card-obsessed household went their separate ways. The king was somewhere downstairs playing cards, probably with Lady Deloraine. Upstairs in one of the drawing rooms the queen presided at one table for the card game of quadrille with her ladies-in-waiting. Princess Caroline and Lord Hervey were engrossed in a game of cribbage. At still another table Princess

Amelia and friends played commerce. All were so deeply concentrated on their cards that their much disliked Griff and his Augusta were entirely absent from their minds.

But nearby on a staircase of the palace an extraordinary scene was being enacted. There was Augusta, with Philip Desnoyers holding one of her arms and Thomas Bloodworth the other. Behind was the Griff, supervising his wife's escape from Hampton Court. Hovering near were Lady Archibald Hamilton and William Townsend. These two were protesting at the folly of trying to get the princess from the palace at this moment. For Augusta had entered the pains of labour. These had overwhelmed her earlier in the evening. Immediately the Griff had been seized by the impulse to get her out of this place at any cost, away from the king and queen. He had quickly ordered his coach and horses to be prepared and to stand by in the palace courtyard in preparation for the escape.

It is probable that when Augusta's labour pains began she had agreed to leave with her husband for St. James's Palace for the birth of her child, free from the presence of her mother-in-law. But the pains preceding this, her first childbirth, became more intense until the water broke. In her agony Augusta now begged to remain at Hampton Court. The prince's reply was 'Courage! Courage!' 'What nonsense!' he said at her protests, adding: 'It will soon be over.' During this scene a messenger, despatched by the Griff, was riding to Chiswick to the country home of Lord Wilmington, Lord President of the Council. He carried a request to the Lord President to leave at once for St. James's Palace to witness the royal birth.

Amazing, but the king, queen, princesses and others, intent on their card games, had heard nothing of this disturbance a short distance away in the palace. The Griff asked the few servants who were about to say nothing to the king or queen about this precipitate departure of himself and Augusta. She was helped into the large coach, followed by the Griff. Also inside the coach were Lady Archibald Hamilton, Mrs. Paine and Mrs. Clavering. At the back were Bloodworth, Vried and others. The coachman was ordered to take the party to

London at the greatest speed. When at 10 p.m. the coach rolled into the courtyard of St. James's Palace, Augusta was in a distressing condition. The birth had started.

Since neither the king nor the Prince of Wales were in residence, the palace was ill-prepared for the reception of this party from Hampton Court, let alone for an *accouchement*. Many servants, including the Mistress of the Royal Linen, were away. The furniture was smothered in dust covers and the beds stripped. On the arrival of Augusta there was a call for sheets. None could be found. The princess was laid on a bed between two table cloths. A messenger was sent to find Mrs. Cannons, the midwife. Implements were borrowed from surgeries near St. James's Palace. At the same time messengers were sent to the London residences of Lord Privy Seal Godolphin, Lord Chancellor Hardwicke and Archbishop of Canterbury John Potter requesting their immediate presence at the palace. Hardwicke was away from town, but both Lord President of the Council Wilmington and Lord Privy Seal Godolphin reached St. James's in time to be official witnesses of the genuineness of the birth.

At one side of Augusta's bed stood the Griff. At the other side were Lords Godolphin and Wilmington. While the midwife worked, Augusta complained of increasing pain. At 10.45 p.m. the Griff asked whether the child had been born and the midwife replied, 'Don't you hear her cry?' Then from between the tablecloths the midwife, like a conjuror producing a rabbit, drew out the baby and thrust it into the arms of astonished Lord Privy Seal Godolphin. Fifteen minutes later the sixty-three-year-old Archbishop Potter came puffing and blowing into the palace to congratulate the exhausted mother, to admire the minnow-like baby and in a grave voice to pronounce a blessing. There was, apparently in the royal traditions of the day, a call for more bishops and, according to Egmont, four more had reached the palace while the day was still young.

Soon after the secret departure of the Griff and Augusta from Hampton Court all the card-playing ended. The king and queen went to bed. They had no reason to doubt that their son and daughter-in-law had also retired, or were at least in their private drawing room with Desnoyers and other friends. The king and queen were asleep when at 1 a.m. they were awakened by knocking on their bedroom door. It was Mrs. Titchburne, one of Caroline's dressers. Mrs. Titchburne hurried excitedly into the room, causing the queen to ask: 'Is the house on fire?' Mrs. Titchburne replied that she carried a message from the prince that he wished them to know the princess was in labour.

'My God, my nightgown!' cried the queen.

'Your nightgown, madam,' said the dresser, 'and your coaches too. The princess is at St. James's.'

The king and queen then learned that the message had not come from the prince's rooms in Hampton Court but by courier from London.

Soon after 2 a.m. there was an exodus of indignant personages from Hampton Court, led by the queen. All were bound for St. James's Palace. The exodus had followed an explosion of fury from the king at the message from the Griff brought to the bedroom by Mrs. Titchburne. The king scolded Caroline for allowing herself to be outwitted so thoroughly by the Griff and Augusta. He warned Caroline that when their other children heard about this they would be ashamed of her. The unhappy Caroline dressed quickly while prematurely awakened servants banged on the bedroom doors of those commanded to drive through the night with her to London. It was to be an unfortunate expedition, ill-planned and the result of irrational panic stirred by the fury of the king.

In the coaches trundling through the narrow bumpy thoroughfares from Hampton Court to London were the queen, Princess Amelia, Princess Caroline, two ladies-in-waiting, Lord Hervey, the Lord Chamberlain, the Duke of Grafton, and Lord of the King's Bedchamber, the Earl of Essex. Unaware, of course, that Augusta's baby had already arrived, all were doubtless hoping to participate in the drama inside or in the ante-chamber of Augusta's bedroom. The queen and princesses and Hervey were still suspicious that this might all be a fraud, that if there were a baby at all it might not really be Augusta's. The Duke of Grafton and the Earl of Essex had, indeed, been detailed to observe everything closely and to speed back to the king as soon as was feasible with a detailed report.

The queen and her party reached St. James's Palace soon after 4 a.m. The vast interior seemed dank and chilly at this early hour. Lord Hervey told the queen he would have a fire lighted and hot chocolate prepared for her in his own suite. She expressed her thanks, adding that he need not fear that she would be tasting anything on this, the Griff's, side of the palace, as if he were a Borgia poisoner. The queen then went upstairs to the ante-chamber of Augusta's bedroom. There the Griff met her. He wore a night-cap and his 'nightgown', the robe thrown over the more simple attire for the bed. He respectfully embraced his mother with kisses on hand and cheeks in conventional Hanoverian royal fashion. Then he told her that Augusta had given birth to a baby girl nearly six hours ago. This was bitter news to the queen who had vowed: 'At her labour I positively will be, let her lie-in be where she will.' Yet the exchange of words with the prince had at least broken the ice of silence which had existed between him and the queen since the quarrel over his allowance in the previous February. Within a few more moments Caroline was at the bedside of her daughter-in-law, smiling and congratulating her. Next Lady Archibald Hamilton entered the room, the baby in her arms, dressed only in a red cloak and nappies. 'May the good God bless you, you poor little thing,' said the queen in French after giving her tiny grand-daughter a kiss. 'You have arrived in a nasty world.' Referring to the ordeal of Augusta's night drive from Hampton Court, Caroline remarked that 'apparently you suffered terribly'. 'Not at all,' was Augusta's reply. 'It was nothing.'

A torrent of words poured from the Griff, who had not conversed with his mother for so long. He described the journey with Augusta, her sufferings and the anxiety these caused. The queen, intent upon keeping the peace, uttered no reproof to her son or demanded any explanation. Instead she turned on Lady Archibald Hamilton, saying she was astonished that a mother of ten children, experienced and mature, should have allowed 'these people to act such a madness'. The conversation was ended by the arrival in the room of Lord Hervey, the Duke of Grafton and Lord Essex to stare at the mother and the baby. Finally Caroline gave Augusta an affectionate kiss of farewell with this equally affectionate farewell speech: 'My good princess, is there anything you want, anything you wish, or anything you would have me do? Here I am; you have but to speak and ask: and whatever is in my power that you would have me do, I promise you I will do it.'

The queen and the princesses, before finally driving back to Hampton Court, hurried into Lord Hervey's apartments. They enjoyed a cup of hot chocolate and a cosy gossip with him and the Duke of Grafton before the fire. Between sips the queen pronounced the baby definitely to be Augusta's own. 'Well, upon my honour,' she chattered, 'I do no more doubt this poor little bit of a thing is the princess's own child, than I doubt of either of these two being mine, though, I owe to you, I had my doubts upon the road that there would be some juggle. And if, instead of this poor, little, ugly she-mouse, there had been a brave, large, fat, jolly boy, I should not have been cured of my suspicions. Nay, I believe that they would have been so much increased, or rather, that I should have been so confirmed in my opinion, that I should have gone about his house like a madwoman, played the devil, and insisted on knowing what chairman's brat he had bought.' Next the queen had a few pertinent remarks for her cronies regarding her son and his latest exploit: 'But, altogether, was there any such a monstrous conduct? Such a fool, and such an impertinent fool? And such impudence, to receive us all with such ease, as if nothing had happened, and that we were the best friends in the world?'

At five o'clock that morning Sir Robert Walpole arrived at St. James's Palace. Lord Harrington also was added to those collecting information for reports to the king. The two saw the mother and baby. Then they were called by the Griff to his bedroom, where he lay exhausted from the drama of the past hours. The Griff disclosed to the two that twice during the past week he had taken his wife from Hampton Court to London but did not add that this was for her to obtain special medical advice and attention. Walpole and Harrington were later to tell the king of these trips as evidences of the Griff's callousness and of his defiance of his father's wishes. The two also saw the queen in Hervey's apartments. Soon after this Caroline, Hervey and the princesses swept back to Hampton Court. 'I am glad we came,' she said to Hervey, summing up their visit to her son and daughter-in-law. 'For one who does not care a farthing for them, the giving oneself all the trouble is *une bonne grimace pour la publique*. And the more impudences they do, and the more civilities we show, the more we shall be thought in the right and they in the wrong, when we bring it to an open quarrel.'

Later in the morning large numbers of people were outside St. James's Palace. News of the birth, spreading incredibly fast by word of mouth, excited London. Seeing and hearing the jubilation of these ordinary, unimportant people, the Griff must have felt that he, his wife and baby were really among friends. At Hampton Court he and Augusta had been ignored by the king and queen. The baby would have been born in an atmosphere of disdain and ridicule. The queen would, as she had vowed, been at Augusta's bedside, saving up every detail of the *accouchement* for a humorous description to Hervey. Augusta—as she herself said later—had wanted the baby to be born at St. James's rather than at Hampton Court. In the warm atmosphere of the love of London the Griff and Augusta would have been thrilled by the cries of public jubilation at the gates of the palace. But now events at Hampton Court and elsewhere began to move quickly. These would end in the ignominious eviction of the lovable but disobedient Prince and Princess of Wales.

Before the queen had got back to Hampton Court two polite

and friendly letters from the Griff had been delivered there by
a messenger. These had been written and dispatched immediately after the birth, hours before the arrival of the queen and
her party at St. James's. The letters, containing no mention
of the rebellious flight of his son and daughter-in-law to
London, only added to the anger of the king. Next came another message from the Griff that he would 'wait upon' his
parents at Hampton Court in three days' time. In reply to this
the king sent Lord Essex to the Griff, telling him not to come,
and condemning him for allegedly risking Augusta's life. He
also told the Griff how the king 'resented to the highest degree'
the indignities to which he had been subjected by his son. The
Griff hurried back to his father a written reply. The letter
apologised for having upset the king. 'But for some days the
princess had suffered from colic. Mrs. Cannons, Dr. Hollings
and Mr. Broxholme were consulted several times. They
assured me that she was not near her time and the two doctors
still held this opinion at midday on Sunday. But they had
advised that if she had pains other than colic she should
be given a stimulant and taken as soon as possible to town.
I did all this and am very upset that circumstances should
have arisen in which my love for the princess might seem to
have put aside my first thought, which except for that I should
have had, to always show my devotion to your majesty. And
further, if I dare say so, the princess wanted me urgently at
that moment to take her to London, where help would be
nearer, that I could not resist her appeal. For if, because of my
refusal, anything had happened to her, I should never have
forgiven myself.' The letter asked the king that 'you will
permit me to pay my respects to you at your levee, which I
should not have failed to do on Monday if the queen had not
commanded me to do so only today'.

The king's only reply to this letter was a message telling him
not to come to the levee. Next the prince was appealing to
Lord Chancellor Hardwicke to try to heal this breach with
the king. The prince was now under strong pressure from his
advisers to try to appease his father's anger. Pulteney, Chester-

field and Lord Carteret all thought that his precipitate flight with Augusta had given his parents cause for resentment and displeasure. And they realised that leaders of the king's party could damage the prince's popularity with the public by spreading stories of his 'cruelty' to Augusta by bringing her to London while in labour.

The king would not countenance the presence of the Griff at Hampton Court. Nevertheless the queen, together with daughters Princesses Amelia and Caroline, could not resist personally investigating what was happening to the Griff, Augusta and baby at St. James's Palace. Nine days after the birth all drove there on a rainy muddy morning, their arrival watched by a big crowd gathered about the gates. The queen again inspected the baby. The baby was in the arms of Lady Archibald Hamilton, who drew attention to 'her prettiest little hands', tactlessly comparing them with the beauty of the Griff's hands. The Griff formally received his mother and sisters at the entrance to his wife's bedroom, but throughout their visit never addressed a word to them. Yet on their departure he accompanied them from the palace into the street, kneeling in the mud in respectful farewell when the queen entered her coach. The crowd were touched by what they mistook to be an act of devotion of a loving son to his mother.

Back at friendlier Hampton Court, the queen indignantly related to the king how, except for her arrival and departure from St. James's, the Griff had insultingly ignored her. His majesty's comment was that Caroline was 'well enough served for thrusting her nose where it had been shit upon already'.

To the Griff there seemed to be a lull in the war. No hints had reached him so far of dark plans that would result in his eviction from St. James's and in his being banned from entering any other residence of the king. In mid-August George was even sending commands to his son naming the date when the baby should be baptised and graciously appointing himself as the godfather. The godmothers, said the king, would be the queen and the Dowager Duchess of Saxe-Coburg. The baptism was performed by the Archbishop of Canterbury Dr. Potter in Augusta's bedroom, ornately decorated for the occasion. None of the godparents was present. The Duke of Burlington stood in for the king, Lady Burlington for the queen and Lady Torrington for Augusta's mother, far away in Saxe-Coburg. The baby was christened Augusta. Defying Hanoverian tradition, the pro-British Prince of Wales said that his daughter must not be called 'Princess' but addressed in English style as 'Lady Augusta'.

The Griff wrote to both his father and mother, thanking them for becoming godparents, even though they did not attend the christening in person. He was unaware that they would not have been godparents at all but for the persuasion of Sir Robert Walpole. The Griff asked the forgiveness of the king and also inquired sympathetically regarding the queen's worsening gout. Meanwhile, as plans were being developed for revenge on the Griff, monarch, queen and toadies at Hampton Court seemed to talk of nothing but his wickedness. Hervey composed a poor and almost meaningless verse about him entitled *The Griff to the Queen*. In this verse the Griff was apparently wishing that the gout would leave Caroline's feet and fly to her head. But the queen needed no encouragement in her growing condemnation of her son. Pausing from her breakfast, she said: 'I hope in God that I shall never see the monster's face again. . . . And yet once I would have given up all my children for him. I was fond of that monster. I looked upon him as one that was to make the happiness of my life, and now I wish he had never been born.' And the Princess Caroline, praised by many historians for her gentle disposition, broke in with, 'Pray Mamma, do not throw away your wishes for what cannot happen, but wish he may *crever* and that we may all go about with smiling faces, glad hearts and crape and hoods for him.' Alas for daughter Caroline. Only too soon she would be wearing crape and hood, not for her brother, but for her mother.

Hervey, the king, queen, Walpole and the Cabinet Council all helped to sharpen the knife which, it was hoped, would leave the Griff prostrate. Hervey produced a draft of a message to the Griff formally expelling him from St. James's Palace. This underwent some re-writing and polishing by Walpole. On September 9th, 1737, a meeting of the Cabinet Council put finishing touches to the message which was handed to the king for his signature. On the following evening it was carried from Hampton Court to the prince in St. James's Palace by the Duke of Grafton (Lord Chamberlain), the Duke of Richmond (Master of the Horse) and Lord Pembroke (Groom of the Stole). They did not immediately hand the message to the prince. The Duke of Grafton read it to him first. This eviction order from the king to his son began with the accusation that his professions made in recent letters were contradictory to all his actions. It continued:

You know very well you did not give the least intimation to me or to the queen that the princess was with child or breeding until less than a month of the birth of the young princess; you removed the princess twice in a week immediately preceding the day of her delivery from the place of my residence (Hampton Court) in expectation, as you have voluntarily declared, of her labour; and both times upon your return you industriously concealed from the knowledge of me and the queen every circumstance relating to this important affair. And you at last, without giving any notice to me or to the queen, precipitately hurried the princess from Hampton Court in a condition not to be named. And having thus, in execution of your own determined measures, exposed both the princess and her child to the greatest perils, you now plead surprise and your tenderness for the princess as the only motives that occasioned these repeated indignities, offered to me and to the queen your mother.

This extravagant and undutiful behaviour in so essential a point as the birth of an heir to my crown is such an evidence of your premeditated defiance of me, and such a contempt of my authority and of the natural right belonging to your parents, as cannot be excused by the pretended innocence of your intentions, nor palliated or disguised by specious words only.

The king's message went on to chide the prince as undutiful and told him 'that I have long had reason to be highly offended with you'. And now followed the expulsion order coupled with a side blow for the members of the opposition party who advised the Griff:

And until you withdraw your regard and confidence from those by whose instigation and advice you are directed and encouraged in your unwarrantable behaviour to me and to the queen, and until you return to your duty, you shall not reside in my palace, which I will not suffer to be made the resort of them who, under the appearance of an attachment to you, foment the division which you have made in my family, and thereby weaken the common interest of the whole.

In this situation I will receive no reply; but when your actions manifest a just sense of duty and submission, that may induce me to pardon what at present I most justly resent.

In the meantime it is my pleasure that you leave St. James's with all your family, when it can be done without prejudice or inconvenience to the princess.

I shall for the present leave to the princess the care of my grand-daughter, until a proper time calls upon me to consider of her education.

The long recitation of the Duke of Grafton having ended, he handed the message to the Griff. According to a later report of Grafton, the prince had changed colour several times during its reading. The dramatic interview ended by the prince asking the visitors to convey his humble duty to the king and to express regret for what had happened.

The king still burned with wrath and vindictiveness. He felt that simply to expel the Griff and Augusta from their St. James's Palace home was insufficient punishment. He scoured his mind for other moves that might add to their discomfort, embarrassment and disquiet. The king had given an assurance that they could leave at a time convenient to Augusta. But now she and the Griff were ordered to be out of the palace within two days. Another order forbade them to take away any furniture. Hervey boldly suggested to the king that they should be allowed to remove 'chests and those sort of things' into which their clothes could be packed. The couple's clothing, he argued, could hardly be carried from the palace 'like dirty linen in a basket'.

'And why not?' replied the king. 'A basket is good enough for them.'

Next, on command of the king, the Secretaries of State informed all foreign diplomats in London that they should not wait upon or have any social contacts with the Prince of Wales. At the same time the king's messengers were preparing to deliver a message from George at the front doors of scores of members of the nobility. It ran:

Notice is hereby given to all peers, peeresses, privy counsellors and their ladies and other persons in any station under the king and queen that whoever goes to pay their court to their royal highnesses the Prince and Princess of Wales will not be admitted into his majesty's presence.

Those friends of the Griff who could have best defended and advised him in this weekend of crisis were unavailable. Lord Chesterfield was ill with a high fever. Both Pulteney and Carteret were away in the country. Throughout Sunday the home of the Prince and Princess of Wales in the palace was in a turmoil as they prepared to leave. The Duke of Grafton all the time kept surveillance over the couple, having been ordered by the king to ensure that they took away nothing that was not their personal property. On the following day, amid emotional scenes, the evicted prince and princess left for Kew.

The king had planned an ignominious farewell from St. James's for his son and daughter-in-law. The prince's personal guards had already been withdrawn. And the king's own palace guards had been ordered not to present arms, salute or in any other way show respect to the couple when they left the premises. By this time, however, the news of George's treatment of Frederick had spread throughout London. A big crowd had gathered outside the palace. First they watched a few wagons rolling out with his and Augusta's personal possessions, bound for Kew. Next came members of his household. Lastly came Frederick and Augusta, with baby, nurse and others in their large coach. A mob surged about this coach with cries of 'God bless you!'

The prince's surprising reply was a shout of 'God save the

king!' followed by 'God bless the poor!' And now many in the crowd were weeping. The couple were no sooner off the palace precincts than one of its sentries was crying too. He had planned to disobey orders and to present arms as the prince and princess passed. But, as he later regretfully confessed, he had not carried out this resolve because all the time the eyes of his captain were upon him. Yet while those who were almost strangers to the Griff wept, his parents celebrated.

'Thank God tomorrow night the puppy will be out of my house,' the king had said. And the queen had several times repeated: 'I hope, in God, I shall never see him again.' And as time proved, God helped this hope to be fulfilled. She never saw the Griff again.

10

Caroline Dies

Sentence of banishment from the court had been pronounced by the king on the Griff as a terrible punishment. The foolish George II had learned nothing from his
own experience. His father George I had similarly banished
him when he was Prince of Wales. This had resulted in the
opposition rallying round him and in the establishment of a
rival court to that of his father. George II cast the Griff into
outer darkness without apparently believing that he could
quickly grope his way into the light again. He thought his
son lacked sufficient ability and personal appeal to rally a
formidable opposition. The fiasco of the Griff's attempt to
win parliamentary support for a bigger allowance seemed a
proof of this lack. Then the king absurdly believed that his
warning to the nobility to shun his son would have devastating
effect. He thought that the power and prestige of himself and
Caroline would frighten society from having any association
with the prince and princess. Very soon after the Griff's
banishment the king was told about important people seen
driving towards the lodge at Kew. The king, however, thought
that 'all too soon they would be tired of the puppy'. This,
added the king, was because that besides being a scoundrel, his
son was also a fool and would 'talk more fiddle-faddle nonsense
to his visitors' in a day than 'any old woman talks in a week'.

Yet the king's banishment of Frederick and Augusta drove
them into an atmosphere of happiness and freedom. They had
no longer to suffer existence in St. James's and the other royal
residences so near to the coarse, mischievous and hostile king
and queen and the tittle-tattle of Lord Hervey. The Griff's

love-hate relationship with his mother was finally ended by her acquiescence at his expulsion and the indignities that were heaped on this. The psychological unbilical cord between mother and son was finally severed. He had gone into banishment with this final benediction from his mother, uttered to Lord Hervey: 'My dear first-born is the greatest ass, and the greatest liar, and the greatest *canaille*, and the greatest beast, in the whole world, and I most heartily wish he was out of it.' The mother hated the son. The son now regarded her with a cold insensibility that might have been mistaken for hatred. Yet, unlike his parents, the Griff, with all his irritating weaknesses, was a poor hater. From the immutable ceremony and protocol of the royal palaces, the Griff and Augusta were pushed by the revengeful king into a more relaxed world where they could enjoy naturalness and freedom, and where they could fashion their own home environment. And friends did not desert them *en masse*. The couple and their baby were no sooner established at Kew than many people, unafraid of the king, arrived to pay their respects.

Chesterfield was still ill in bed. But when news reached Carteret and Pulteney in the country of the eviction of the prince they hurried back to London and out to Kew. They were joined there by Sir William Wyndham, a powerful member of the opposition party and close friend of Lord Bolingbroke, dreaded scheming enemy of Walpole. So many other politicians were also reported coming and going from Kew that both the king and Walpole became alarmed. Matters were not working out as George had anticipated. The king and Walpole imagined the Griff to be involved in vile plots against their policies with his political cronies. It was said he might support agitation for the repeal of the Test Act which prevented Roman catholics from sitting in parliament. He was also suspected of supporting the widespread desire among British people to remove Hanover from the rule of their king. The link between Great Britain and the electorate was becoming increasingly burdensome. Hanover took a lot of British money in addition to involving the United Kingdom in unpopular and dangerous foreign policies. George was enraged by rumours that the Griff might promise to renounce all sovereignty over Hanover when he became king, and even send William Duke of Cumberland there to rule a Hanover which would be independent. It was galling to George that the Griff might be thinking of such a fate for William whom he and Caroline adored. In the past the king and Walpole had, indeed, talked much about trying to make William heir to the British throne while shipping the Griff to Hanover for life as its elector.

Before the close of this fateful September the king was angered by the acceptance by the Lord Mayor and Council of London of an invitation from the Griff to dinner at Carlton House. The dinner was ostensibly a gesture from the prince in gratitude for their congratulations to him and Augusta on the birth of their daughter. Because of the rules of protocol the Griff did not eat with his guests, but leaders of the opposition were there in force, almost turning the celebration into a political rally. Every guest was handed what at first looked like a party pamphlet. But it was a copy of the king's eviction message which had been read to the Griff by Lord Chancellor Hardwicke. And Lord Carteret rose to tell the lord mayor and aldermen that the real reason for the king's persecution of the prince was the latter's unswerving loyalty to the opposition. After the meal the prince joined his guests. They received him with prolonged and boisterous applause. He made some amusingly snide allusions to Sir Robert Walpole. The king, queen and prime minister, feeling that only half the story had been told, soon published the entire correspondence and letters exchanged by the prince and themselves during their recent dispute. This delighted the nation's gossips. It became the dominating topic of society in the Pump Room at Bath.

For a while Sir Robert Walpole had to leave George and Caroline alone in their fears and perplexities. His wife had died and he retired to Houghton Hall in Norfolk for a period of mourning and melancholy reminiscence. Yet the bereaved Prime Minister could not on England's stage lament his dead wife and enact the broken-hearted widower for too long, for another woman was waiting impatiently in the wings. This was May Skerrit, his faithful mistress. Walpole doffed his mourning and married May in the following year.

Although visited by many members of the opposition party, the Griff was not at this time interesting himself much in politics, except perhaps to disseminate rumours in mischievous psychological warfare against his father. The Griff and Augusta were engrossed in their own domestic affairs. on where and how to live now that they were safely free of the bondage of the court. They wanted a residence in London. Why they were not content only with Carlton House, still in possession of the Griff, is a mystery, unless they thought it too small. Anyhow, they approached the Duke of Bedford with a view to leasing his imposing residence, Southampton House. So frightened was the duke of offending the king that he frustrated the couple with ingenious but polite reasons why they could not occupy his mansion. Next the Griff asked the Duke of Norfolk if he would let him Norfolk House, his mansion in St. James's Square. The duke consented, but only after his duchess had called on the queen to ask whether there were any parental objections to the arrangement. The mansion had a particularly magnificent drawing room where the Griff could hold receptions in competition with those of the king.

The house at Kew and its gardens, although so attractive, were uncomfortably close to the White Lodge of George and Caroline at Richmond. Besides the house was too small, and it lacked the grace and grandeur of the country mansion of which the prince and princess dreamed. In their search for such a place they chanced upon Cliveden (often spelt Cifden) in Buckinghamshire and were enchanted. Cliveden House was built in the seventeenth century by George Villiers, 2nd Duke of Buckingham. It passed into the possession of Lord George Hamilton, later the Earl of Orkney. The earl was responsible for many dramatic additions and alterations. One addition was a large gazebo. Another was the Blenheim Temple in commemoration of the battle at which Orkney commanded a brigade. There was a terrace stretching 440 feet with an imposing view of the countryside and Thames from the balustrades. Cliveden, like Norfolk House, had palatial-looking reception rooms. Early in 1737 Orkney had died, leaving Cliveden to his daughter Anne. She willingly rented the property to the prince and princess, even without obtaining prior permission of the king and queen. The Griff and Augusta loved Cliveden at first sight. Over the years it grew still more in their affections. Many of the happiest interludes of their marriage and family life were spent there. Incidentally, after the death of Frederick Cliveden had a curious history. It twice suffered ravaging fires and was twice rebuilt. In the course of the present century Cliveden moved into the possession of the Astor family. Before the Second World War it became famous as the rendezvous of those politicians and statesmen known collectively as 'the Cliveden Set'.

In the first weeks following the eviction of the prince and princess, large numbers of the nobility flocked to the king's receptions. These record attendances caused Hervey and other courtiers to believe that George was triumphing over his son. Many were without doubt being intimidated by the warning against associating with Frederick delivered at their houses by palace messengers. However, when the nervousness died down many of the nobility fell for the temptation of 'waiting upon' the Prince and Princess of Wales as soon as they were in Norfolk House. They knew the atmosphere there would be bright and sparkling compared with the dreariness of the official court. Both old and young were impressed when they met Frederick and Augusta, so much more self-confident and happier looking in their new surroundings. Augusta, although quiet and restrained in manner, was meeting with noteworthy social success.

As the summer passed the spirit of peace seemed to be blessing the household of the king as it was also blessing the Griff and Augusta. Active hostilities between the two sides had ceased. George and Caroline were increasingly glad that the hated Griff was now out of their sight. They were less worried about the possibility of his committing political mischief in the near future. The Griff and Augusta were on their part still relieved to be free of the palace protocol and receptions, the uncouth rudeness of the king and queen, and from the observation of Hervey and other court spies. There seemed now to be a sweet unwritten truce which might give king and queen, prince and princess, tranquillity for a long time. But, alas, for the king and his family, 1737 was the year of disturbance. The crisis over the alleged disobedience of Frederick and Augusta was only two months later succeeded by the crisis over the queen.

In the second week of November 1737 the Griff was spending some days at Kew. Early on Friday November 11th he heard that his mother was seriously ill. Although now an outcast to his parents he nevertheless hurried to London, staying at Carlton House without Augusta. Dutifully that evening the Griff sent Lord North, one of his equerries, to St. James's Palace to enquire about the queen and, despite the quarrel, to convey his concern and sympathy. Lord North was moreover instructed to ask if the Griff might visit his mother. This message was passed from person to person in the palace until it finally reached the king. 'He wants to come and insult his poor dying mother!' roared the indignant George. 'But she shall not see him. I could never let that villain come near her. And whilst she had her senses she would never desire it. No. No! He shall not come and act any of his silly plays here, false, lying, cowardly, nauseous puppy.' Thereupon a message was prepared by the king and others and was read by Lord Hervey to the startled Lord North. 'His Majesty', it said, 'does not think fit that the prince should see the queen, and therefore expects he should not come to St. James's.'

The queen was indeed dying. She had been ill two days while a legion of doctors gave her an assortment of medical cordials, patent medicines, purges, blisterings and bleedings. They were not aware until told to their astonishment by the king that she had suffered from an umbilical hernia since the birth of their youngest daughter Louisa in 1724. She had kept this secret from all but a few in the belief that such an affliction was repulsive. The hernia had now strangulated. At last, aware of the queen's complaint, the doctors called in surgeons, led by the royal family's favourite, the ancient Paul Busier, described by Hervey as aged eighty and by Horace Walpole as nearly ninety. While Busier was holding a candle and directing his colleague John Ranby to lance the swelling on the queen's body his wig caught fire. Accordingly the agony of the queen was intermingled for a few moments with merriment. This clumsy surgery was useless, but it had grossly repugnant results.

The queen lived on until the night of Sunday, November 20th. Much of the time the sixteen-year-old William Duke of Cumberland was at her bedside, together with his elder sisters Amelia and Caroline. But the name of her elder son was often on her lips. Soon after the king had sent his snub to Frederick through Lord North, Caroline was saying, 'I wonder that the Griff hasn't sent to ask to see me yet. It would be so like one of his filthy *parotres*.' Then the king told her of Lord North's visit, adding that she could see the Griff if she really wished it.

But Caroline replied: 'I am so far from desiring to see him that nothing but your absolute commands could ever make me consent to it.' Then, in talking on the probability of her death, Caroline said that 'at least I shall have one comfort in having my eyes eternally closed. I shall never see that monster again.' Since the deeds of ownership of the White Lodge at Richmond were in her name, the queen expressed anxiety that upon her death the Griff might inherit it. She was assured, however, that the White Lodge would go to the king, although after his death, alas, it might fall into the hands of the Griff.

The Griff was not rebuffed by the king's snub. He continued to send members of his entourage to St. James's Palace at close intervals, throughout day and night, for the latest information on his mother's condition. The king raved against these callers from Carlton House, who, he said, had no right to enter the palace. They still came; they still said how very much the prince wanted to be at the bedside of his dying mother. Meanwhile the unpredictable Griff was behaving at Carlton House in a manner which even his best friends thought was callous and even interpreted as manifestations of 'indecent rejoicing'. He would predict 'some good news soon' because it was 'impossible she can hold out long'. And in justification of his attitude he boasted, 'I'm a very good son; I wish her out of her pain.' The Duke of Marlborough, wincing at these recitals, repeated them to Lord Hervey. Lord Archibald Hamilton challenged such stories, insisting that the Griff was really grieved over his mother. Hervey in his memoirs added: 'But when Lady Archibald was asked if the prince was really concerned for the queen, she laughed and said: "He is very decent." '

While the dying Caroline had only the worst wishes for the Griff, she had expressions of deep love and noble advice to give to her husband and the other children. She told the king that he should marry again. And through his sobs he made the well-intentioned reply so often quoted by his biographers: 'No, I shall have mistresses.' At this the queen cried, 'Oh my God, that needn't stop you!' And it was strange that although when in normal health the queen had enjoyed the company of many scholarly clergymen, she had no wish to see them on her deathbed. Ordinarily she met Dr. Joseph Butler, her Clerk of the Closet, every morning, but now he was kept from her presence. It was only when this absence of any clerical attention became known to pious people outside the palace that the queen was persuaded to admit Archbishop Potter to her bedroom, following the advice of cynical Sir Robert Walpole to Princess Amelia that, 'Pray, madam, let this farce be played'. It was reported by some but denied by others that during his ministrations the archbishop persuaded the queen to forgive the Griff his alleged wrongs towards her and to send him her blessing. Horace Walpole was one who told this story. As son of the Prime Minister, he may have been correctly informed.

On the night of Sunday, November 20th, the king was

lying in the queen's bedroom on a makeshift bed on the floor. On a couch in a corner of the room was Princess Amelia. Suddenly Mrs. Purcel, a woman-in-waiting, cried, 'She is dying!' The king and Amelia went to the bedside. In another few moments Princess Caroline and Lord Hervey were in the room. The queen gasped: 'I've now got asthma. Open the window.' She added one word—'Pray!' Amelia opened a prayer book and started to read. Queen Caroline was dead, at the age of fifty-five. One of the staff of the Prince of Wales, lingering in the palace lobby, soon heard the news. He hurried back to his master at Carlton House.

The Griff had been refused a place at the bedside of his dying mother. Yet with indelicate audacity he next attempted to attend her funeral as chief mourner. He sent his equerry to Sir Robert Walpole and Lord Hardwicke with a message proposing this role for himself. He supported his application with the statement that King Charles I while Prince of Wales had been chief mourner at the state funeral of his mother, Anne of Denmark. In reply the prime minister and lord chancellor said that the king had already arranged for Princess Amelia to be leading mourner so that they did not think it advisable to pass on the message to him. They also disputed the assertion that King Charles was leading mourner when his mother was buried. The big funeral of Queen Caroline was celebrated in black splendour in Westminster Abbey. Her embalmed body was laid in a new vault in the abbey's Henry VII's Chapel.

To numerous historians of the eighteenth century Queen Caroline was a great woman. By her support of Sir Robert Walpole and by tactfully exercising statecraft of which the king was mentally incapable, the former princess of Anspach served her adopted country well. Nevertheless she secretly despised and disliked the British people, even scolding Walpole for his 'partiality to England'. Caroline retained the trust and affection of the king by flattery and by acquiescence to his affairs with other women. Up to the queen's death in her middle fifties the king, in his fashion, adored her despite his uncouth pronouncement that 'it's unreasonable a women after fifty should expect her husband to lie with her'.

The queen after her death was called 'Caroline the Good' as well as the Great. Yet her greatness and goodness seem to disappear from her attributes when her relations with her elder son are considered. She never tried to see the Griff during his boyhood in the isolation of Hanover. When he eventually moved to England she treated him with near contempt. She connived with the king in keeping the Griff from responsibility, from inviting him into the affairs of state. Her love of power destroyed all chances of his acting as regent during the king's absence in Hanover. Caroline could have influenced the king in the Griff's favour, just as she had succeeded in turning her husband's early hostility to Robert Walpole into approbation. Caroline supported her husband in the controversy over the prince's allowance. She was infatuated by Lord Hervey, the enemy the Griff so much disliked. The perpetual presence of the malevolent Hervey in her palace apartments prevented any trust and affection which the Griff might have developed for his mother. This foolish, cold and unfriendly attitude to the queen for the Griff, shown in all these ways, encouraged his dislike for his father and for her. Their refusal to give him any serious responsibilities of state drove him, from sheer boredom, into dissipation and acts of mischief. Held at arm's length by the influential queen, by the king and prime minister, no wonder that the Griff was so warmly embraced by the opposition. Caroline's foolish treatment of her son created problems which were not fully realised until she lay dead.

A Prince of Wales was needed to advise the king, calm the family hysteria and advise Sir Robert Walpole and the other ministers in their immediate decisions. The bereaved king spent most of his time in sentimental chatter and fits of weeping in the apartments of Princesses Amelia and Caroline. Even the Prime Minister had difficulty in reaching him. Neither the excited eccentric Amelia or the ailing Caroline had the mental balance to advise the king or even to act as intermediary between him and the ministers. It had rarely been widely admitted, but it was the queen who had often directed the decisions of the king. Now, bereft of her, he felt lost and without powers of resolution. In Holland was his eldest daughter Anne Princess of Orange, a woman of some wisdom and calm. But she would not even come if invited and anyhow the king was prejudiced against her. The king loved his younger son William, but at sixteen he could not be helpful. How easier the situation would have been if there had been a friendly Prince of Wales at the monarch's side!

The Dukes of Newcastle and Grafton were two members of the Council who thought that Princess Amelia, despite her uncertain temperament, might replace the dead queen as the king's guiding influence. But Sir Robert Walpole met this suggestion with the question: 'Does your Princess Amelia design to commit incest?' Walpole insisted the king's temperament was such that he would have to go to bed with any woman who might advise him as did the queen. Finally it was agreed that the king would at least forget his grief and behave with more normality and co-operation if his German mistress Madame Walmoden was brought as soon as possible from Hanover. Princesses Amelia and Caroline were scandalised when soon afterwards the earthy prime minister told them that until Madame Walmoden's arrival their father should, 'for the sake of his health', revive his intimacies with Lady Deloraine. 'People must wear old gloves till they can get new ones,' added Walpole with diplomatic finesse.

The feeling of the British masses had never warmed towards the king until he became a widower, for then the majority of the people with their natural kindliness felt sorry for him. There had been a spontaneous and touching display of this sympathy, and sorrow also, when the funeral procession moved through the crowds to the abbey. And this sudden wave of compassion and interest in the king appeared to have reduced their affection for the Griff. There were evil but inevitable rumours that he had refused to visit his dying mother, and these were never contradicted. By a few human gestures of appreciation for the sympathy being shown him the king might have at last won the affection of the nation. But wallowing in his grief this monarch of a country he disliked saw promise of consolation only in the mistress who would come to him from Hanover. There were, however, cynical men and women in London who felt no pity for George. These were exemplified by the following posted one morning at the Royal Exchange:

O Death, where is thy sting,
To take the queen and leave the king?

The court went into mourning, but there was no mourning in the household of the Prince and Princess of Wales. Before the elegant backgrounds of Norfolk House and Cliveden they gaily received a wide assortment of friends of society, politics, literature and art. At Norfolk House there were large receptions. Lines of grand coaches would move towards the mansion as they had moved towards St. James's Palace before the death of Caroline and the period of mourning. One who investigated the new 'court' at Norfolk House was the busybody Dowager Duchess of Marlborough, then aged seventy-seven. She had such a terrifying personality and made such pitiless judgements that among her many nicknames were 'Old Mount Aetna', the 'Beldam of Bedlam' and 'Her Graceless'. The duchess was no prude, but the German coarseness of the court of George II had often turned her stomach. She had always liked the Griff because socially he was wholesome and charming, despite his moral lapses and boyish pranks. Towards the end of 1737 the duchess wrote to a friend:

As to Norfolk House, I have heard there's a great deal of company, and that the Princess of Wales, tho' so very young, behaves so as to please everybody; and I think her conversation is much more proper and decent for a drawing-room than the wise Queen Caroline was with, who never was half-an-hour without saying something shocking to somebody or other, even when she intended to oblige, and generally very improper discourse for a public room.

At the approach of Christmas 1738 the king still mourned. There had been the dramatic decision immediately after Caroline's death 'to send for Madame Walmoden'. But there were second thoughts about hurrying her entrance while the queen's death remained so recent. It was decided that the king must exercise self-restraint and be content with Lady Deloraine during the period of mourning. Then, when England began to forget Caroline, Amelia would journey from Hanover to fall into the arms of the waiting king without dangerous public resentment. But the Princesses Amelia and Caroline, much as they had loved their mother, were rebellious. They were defying the mourning regulations to enjoy the theatre and opera.

Indeed, it was at the theatre one December night that the two elder princesses, with William Duke of Cumberland, came face to face with the Griff for the first time since his expulsion from their father's court. The confrontation took place in the royal box in full view of the audience. Unfortunately the Prince and Princess of Wales and the other three had separately decided to occupy the royal box. Accordingly when Amelia, Caroline and William made their entry they were astounded to find Augusta sitting there. A few moments later the Griff appeared. He bowed to his two sisters and brother. The sisters ignored the bow. Seeing their beloved Prince of Wales thus snubbed, the audience hissed the princesses in protest. This was too much for the sensitive Caroline, who thereupon fell into a swoon. To the fascinated audience the royal box had become a miniature stage. When Caroline recovered from her faint she and Amelia were hustled from the royal box by the embarrassed William. The comedy played in the box ended when William returned alone, giving the Griff and Augusta a respectful bow.

The new year of 1738 found Frederick and Augusta busy improving their new properties and active in the social life of both town and countryside. Augusta was again pregnant. She was told by her doctors that the baby could be expected in July. The Griff, now thirty-two, had more of the silly moods to which previously George Bubb Dodington had pandered. He liked to roam the town by night with young boon companions, not in immoral sexual pursuits but in holding up strangers in the street with foolish sallies and playing practical jokes. At that period many wealthy young men, who would now be described as playboys, mischievously roved the streets in the darkness. A group called the Hectors would smash windows and tear knockers off doors. They would, by prodding the bottoms of passers-by with swords, make them spin like tops. But the Griff's pranks were never cruel and generally he reserved them for his friends. One night, for example, he crept stealthily through the darkness to the house of his friend the dancing master Philip Desnoyers. Then he smashed its windows, knowing that the sound of shattering glass would awaken and terrify Desnoyers. Lord Egmont recorded in his diary details of what he called 'the prince's frolick'. Egmont damned the 'frolick' as 'a silly demeanour and of ill example for an heir to the crown, in his thirties and married'.

Augusta gave birth to her baby prematurely at Norfolk House on the night of May 24th. It was a difficult birth. The doctors feared that the baby might last only a few hours. For the sake of his little soul he was given a precautionary private baptism. Yet this baby, George Frederick William, was king of Great Britain for nearly sixty years before dying at the age of eighty-one. The birth was announced while the life of the baby still flickered precariously. The king, in his palace, treated the news of an heir for his son as a joke. 'A saddler's wife has been brought to bed,' he quipped, for the Prince of Wales was honorary president of the Company of Saddlers. Nevertheless the king allowed guns to be fired in honour of the baby. Londoners were quick to recognise the significance of the cannonading. They rushed in their thousands towards St. James's Square to cheer and demonstrate. While the king remained indifferent, the English crowds, with their unfailing sense of history, realised the significance of the birth to the nation and were strangely moved. George I, George II and even Prince Frederick had all been born in Hanover. Now, people said, there would one day be a king who was English born and English bred. And indeed this infant, later George III, loved England so deeply that he would never go abroad.

George II could at the time have been too emotionally

unbalanced and upset to rejoice at the birth of his male grand-child. At one moment elated, at another cast down, he was in a morbid and potentially dangerous condition. This condition led him into a grisly adventure. One Saturday night he went to bed, but between 1 and 2 a.m. awoke from what was apparently a terrible and frightening dream. For, calling an equerry, he ordered that the vault containing the body of Queen Caroline in Westminster Abbey be broken into immediately and the coffin opened. At this unsuitable hour abbey officials and labourers were awakened and set to work in Henry VII's Chapel. Later the king called not for his coach but for one of the shabby hackney sedan chairs which plied for hire all night in the streets of London. In this chair he was carried from St. James's and through the Horse Guards to the abbey. There in eerie candlelight he gazed at the embalmed body of Caroline in her coffin, apparently satisfying himself that she was not still alive. He was then carried back to the palace where he returned to bed. Despite the number of persons involved, the story of the king's morbid excursion was not made public for a long time. But the facts were outlined by Lord Wentworth, one of the royal pages, in a confidential letter to his father.

But in June 1738 George was able to forget his gruesome obsessions about his dead wife for the smiles and kisses of his living mistress. Madame Amelia Walmoden was at last allowed to leave Hanover for Helvoetsluys to be discreetly smuggled aboard a vessel bound for England. On arrival she was not escorted to the palace but to a dingy house in nearby St. James's Street to await his majesty's pleasure. The old Duchess of Marlborough described this temporary abode as 'a mighty mean dirty lodging'. Walpole and other ministers were, indeed, following the Roman Fabius's philosophy of the 'inevitability of gradualness' in establishing this German courtesan on English soil. It was thought that the moral temper of the British people would not flare up at her and the king if she rose to national and social heights in almost imperceptible stages. However, it became increasingly difficult successfully to pursue such a cunning policy while gossips such as Lady Marlborough were on the prowl. It was not long before nasty items were appearing in the newspapers. And one day on Kensington Gate appeared this notice:

Here lies a man of fifty-four,
Whose Royal Father's will he tore,
Who thrust his children out of door,
Then killed his wife and took a whore.

Not gradualness but immediacy became inevitable. Madame Walmoden was welcomed as a resident of St. James's Palace where she would be secure from public assault and insult. The king honoured his mistress by giving her the large and luxurious apartments which had been occupied by Melusine von Schulenburg, Duchess of Kendal, favourite mistress of his father George I. Later he gave his Amelia a mansion in Hyde Park. Next he honoured her with the title of Countess Yarmouth. Even in the eighteenth century Yarmouth was renowned for bloaters. In the English scene Amelia proved to be a surprising success. She was a quiet tactful woman. Content with being the king's mistress and domestic companion, she did not interfere in national affairs beyond earning some pin money by the sale of honours. For a little bribery she would acquire titles for appropriately wealthy applicants by whispering their names into the ear of her master the king.

The widower king was now happily occupied with Amelia. The widower prime minister was preparing to take as his bride his faithful mistress May Skerrit. Prospects for the two seemed bright, although Sir Robert Walpole was aware that Pulteney, Carteret and other members of the opposition were working hard for his overthrow. Thus he was paying out record bribes to politicians for continued support and to spies for any information concerning opposition plans.

The opposition were truly plotting against Walpole. Early in 1738 the Prince of Wales was visited by the brilliant Lord Bolingbroke, the most bitter and dangerous of the prime minister's enemies. Bolingbroke had been Secretary of State under Queen Anne. He had played a leading role in 'welcoming' King George I to England from Hanover. But later he was impeached for plotting to make pretender James Stuart the monarch. He fled to France. On obtaining a pardon, however, Bolingbroke was, through Walpole's influence, barred from sitting in the House of Lords. Bolingbroke continued to spend most of his time in France, but nevertheless played an influential part in guiding the policies of the opposition. He even wrote the speeches for some of its members. Bolingbroke was on a visit from France when in 1738 he had this meeting with Frederick, hailing him as the hope of the opposition. Bolingbroke predicted that the prince with his ability and charm would one day as king lead the nation to true happiness and freedom.

An important result of the Frederick-Bolingbroke meeting was a plan for a secret conference of opposition members to work out strategy for ensuring Walpole's early downfall. Since the prime minister's spies and informers seemed so active in London, it was decided that the talks should furtively be held in Bath, England's most fashionable and gayest resort, at the height of its autumn social season. 'A more convenient spot could not have been chosen', wrote Lord Chesterfield years later, recalling this autumn cabal. 'This elegant town much resembles the Bajae of the luxurious Romans. Like that, it is distinguished by its waters, its magnificence and its pleasures.' Moreover, it was often frequented for pleasure and society by members of the opposition. Lord Chesterfield had a house there in Pierrepont Street. Pulteney (later the Earl of Bath) was the local M.P. Pitt often frequented Bath.

An announcement was made that the Prince and Princess of Wales would visit Bath for health and relaxation. It was added that after the recent stress of childbirth the princess would benefit from the salubrious air and invigorating waters of the spa. Another story was that the couple would turn their visit into a great social celebration over the birth of their son and heir. Again in the words of Chesterfield, 'An event so interesting to the nation afforded a favourable opportunity of assembling the prince's friends. and concealing business under the appearances of festivity of joy.' The coming visit of Frederick and Augusta threw Bath's society and corporation into a whirl of excitement. The famous Beau Nash, King of Bath, was granted a large sum of money for their entertainment. Banquets, balls and gala breakfasts were organised. At the same time the political conspirators arranged the secret meetings they would have with the Griff.

The prince, princess and their attendants moved to Bath from Cliveden in an imposing procession of coaches and outriders. They were greeted at the city gates by Beau Nash, mayor, corporation, choirs and music. Both the Griff and Augusta during the following days were tireless in smilingly fulfilling their social obligations. Everywhere the Griff—modest and charming—was received with adulation. People compared him unfavourably with his quarrelsome and bumptious spinster sister Amelia who had been in Bath some years previously to take the waters. Her trip had inspired the sinister Lord Hervey to comment that 'the hot spring that would cure her might be found nearer than Bath'.

Lord Chesterfield arranged for his own personal servants to 'assist' at the sumptuous entertainments provided by Nash and the corporation for Frederick and Augusta. They were really there as opposition spies to eavesdrop on the conversation of supporters of the king's party in Bath for the season. These bewigged lackeys of Chesterfield in their velvet suits, silk stockings and buckled shoes were stationed like museum statues around those notorious centres of gossip, rumour and scandal, the Pump Room and Assembly Rooms. Through the ingenuity of Nash and Chesterfield the Griff would be wafted away from the public festivities to preside over the anti-Walpole conspirators. The drama and the cloak-and-dagger atmosphere of the cabal and its gay, luxurious background naturally appealed to the prince with his love for all things theatrical. The fact is, however, that these elaborately planned but rather absurd proceedings in Bath accomplished little. When parliament reassembled the gross but massive figure of Walpole was not toppled. Indeed he continued as prime minister for nearly four years. But he was gradually to be worn down and overcome, like a bull in a Spanish ring. Despite the very limited success of its secret purpose, this visit to Bath of the Griff became a personal triumph. Under Nash's leadership the town showed its gratitude and affection for him by raising an obelisk to commemorate the visit. Bearing an inscription written by Pope, this seventy-foot obelisk still stands. This was long an object of veneration among debtors. For on his historic visit to Bath the Griff had persuaded the authorities to release all the local debtors from prison.

I I

Sugar Plum Bombardment

The social pleasures and the intrigues at Bath had been agreeable diversions. In the following year, however, the Prince of Wales was watching events with more resolve and certainty regarding his own position in the nation. He was a happier, more confident person. The obstacles to his personal freedom and to his influence as Prince of Wales were one by one being removed. In 1737 the king had tried to disgrace him by the eviction from St. James's Palace, by the attempts to make him a social outcast. But these spiteful moves had given the Griff a court of his own attended by a host of loyal political and social friends. Queen Caroline, the mother who so hated and scorned him, had died. With her death the power of her beloved Lord Hervey to harm him through influence and slander had greatly declined. Hervey was still a personality in the House of Lords, but in the eyes of the king and Walpole he was now only of small importance.

Yet there was still an enemy and obstacle in the path of the Griff other than his father. This was, of course, the prime minister Sir Robert Walpole. Friendly to his face, Walpole would invariably behind his back speak evil of him. Walpole could have used his powerful influence over the king to soothe and heal the quarrel with the Griff, to settle the old problem of the allowance. But, in the belief of the Griff, Walpole would always support the king in any move against him, however unfair. Thus from the new year of 1739 the Griff was watching, aiding and abetting the efforts of the opposition to drive Walpole from power. These did not succeed until 1742.

Early in 1739 there were skirmishes between the opposition and Walpole, but these were too small to have decisive results. Then a crisis arose which, it was felt, might well shatter Walpole for good. This sprang from the allegedly growing arrogance of Spain. She challenged Britain's sovereignty over Gibraltar and Minorca. She was jealous of fast-increasing British commerce and colonial expansion. On the other hand, there was a popular outcry against Spain in England for interference with British shipping. Feeling reached fever heat when English sea captain Robert Jenkins appeared dramatically before the House of Commons bearing one of his ears in cotton. The yellowing ear had, according to Jenkins, been cut off by Spaniards who boarded his ship off Havana and accused him of smuggling. Throughout the country there arose a cry for war against Spain. This had the full support of the opposition. Walpole, however, wanted the rusty sword of Great Britain to remain in its sheath. He was proud of his long maintenance of the peace. This had contributed enormously to the nation's economic prosperity.

Frederick was often in parliament to listen to these debates on peace or war. He openly praised the now belligerent opposition. Despite his German birth, Frederick had long been proud of Britain's greatness. He was always insistent that no challenge to her prestige should ever go unanswered. Accordingly the stand he took in this crisis was sincere and was not solely motivated by his desire that Walpole should be driven from office. Eventually the peace-loving Walpole became swayed by the cries for war, particularly in the then powerfully influential House of Lords. 'It is your war,' he told the Duke of Newcastle, 'and I wish you joy of it.' The decision to hit back at Spain brought cheering thousands into the streets of London. Amid the jubilation suddenly appeared the Griff, waving his hat and shouting 'Hurrah!' He believed that having surrendered to the opposition party's demands, Walpole would feel it his duty to resign. But Walpole clung to office. His post as prime minister had become more important to him than his own honour.

The War of Jenkins' Ear, as it was called, was characteristically British in its start. There was total unpreparedness. In the long years of peace Walpole had allowed the Navy and Army to degenerate into bumbling uselessness. The task of fitting out modest fleets for warfare in the East Indies and Pacific took eight months. Shortage of men resulted in the recruitment of ancient veterans, some of whom were crippled. One ship sailed with a contingent of marines who had only just enlisted and had never fired a rifle. Lack of hygienic precautions were soon decimating the crews on their voyages. Death from scurvy and other diseases in three of the ships commanded by Admiral George Anson reduced a total of 961 men and boys to 335. This was almost wholly a naval war. Anson was in spectacular action sailing around the world attacking Spanish outposts and shipping. Admiral Edward Vernon seized Porto Bello on the Isthmus of Panama with only six ships. His attacks on Cartagena and Santiago de Cuba failed.

The merciless opposition blamed Walpole for lack of preparedness for the war and for everything that went wrong in the fighting. The reputation of the opposition as the party of true patriots was rising. The national influence of the Prince of Wales appeared to be rising with it. In 1741 there was a general election. In keeping with the lack of political morality of the day both the king's and opposition parties paid out enormous sums in bribes. Walpole was returned to power but with a greatly reduced majority. His prestige had fallen low. He had become the subject of derision rather than of respect. M.P.s were making fun of him, while Lord Carteret was pleading that he be 'dismissed from the king's presence and councils for ever'.

Walpole, who had in the past spurned the Griff as weak and irresolute, was now looking pathetically towards him as his possible saviour. A result of the new attitude of the beleaguered prime minister towards the Prince of Wales was the mission to Norfolk House of the Bishop of Oxford, Thomas Secker, who had been one of the episcopal cronies of his mother. Secker, as the emissary of Walpole, came to the prince with a tempting and astonishing proposition. This was that if Frederick wrote an apologetic and deferential letter to the king he would be forgiven his alleged offences of the past. He would be granted the £100,000 a year for which he had unsuccessfully pleaded for so long. He would also without delay be presented with £200,000 towards the repayment of his many debts. And finally the bishop assured the Griff that the king would in future treat his advisers with favour and eventually make them 'a suitable provision'. This bribe from Walpole was munificent and apparently had the king's concurrence. Frederick, however, put principles before his personal interests and those of his friends.

Frederick told Bishop Secker that he would negotiate nothing while Sir Robert Walpole remained prime minister. He blamed Walpole for the nation's troubles, for the alienation which existed between the people and their king. Grimly the bishop returned to his waiting coach. Walpole's ingenious plan for the purchase of the Griff's support for his continuance in office had failed. He resigned before an opposition majority in February 1742. Walpole had served George I and then George II over twenty years. For fourteen years he had been belittling and obstructing the Prince of Wales. Yet the prince did not, like so many others, kick the giant who was down. He wrote him a friendly and respectful letter.

The new prime minister was sixty-nine-year-old Lord Wilmington, the former Sir Spencer Compton, who had been supplanted by Walpole early in the reign of George II. Several members of the opposition were given positions of power. The new Secretary of State was the Griff's friend Lord Carteret whose ability and charm made him virtual leader of the cabinet within a few weeks. Pulteney had surprisingly rejected an approach from the king to become prime minister. This vitriolic orator, whose condemnations had done so much to undermine Walpole's power, preferred to move into the House of Lords as the Earl of Bath.

Towards the king, as well as towards Walpole, the Griff showed magnanimity and the spirit of forgiveness. He wrote his downcast father a letter of submission. He begged to 'wait upon' him at St. James's Palace with some of his friends of the opposition. The king could no longer afford to treat as an outcast a son who was on the crest of such great popularity. A message informed the Griff that his majesty would be graciously pleased to give him an audience together with some of his friends. News of the coming reconciliation was made public. The lord mayor ordered that London be decorated for a general jubilation.

Nearly four and a half years previously the Griff and Augusta had been driven from St. James's Palace in disgrace, without even the guards at the gate giving him a farewell salute. They had been denied chests in which to carry away their clothing and linen. Now in February 1742, after such a long banishment, the prince in his coach moved into the palace courtyard to the salutes of the guards, officers and the presentation of arms of the sentries. Inside the palace he was escorted into his father's presence. The king was surrounded by ministers and other attendants. Among them the Griff saw the smiling face of his friend Pulteney and by what Horace Walpole described as 'the commanding beauty' of his friend Carteret. The Griff stopped and kissed the hand of his father in the ritual of loyalty and humble submission. This was an embarrassing moment for both father and son. The father broke the silence of four and a half years with a question. 'How does the princess do?' he asked. 'I hope she is well.' It was a very formal ceremony of reconciliation, with no promises from the father of an increased allowance or a gift for the payment of debts. The prince did learn, however, that his personal guard of troops would be restored.

There followed one of those London public rejoicings which the Griff enjoyed so much, particularly when he was their centre. He picked up Augusta at Norfolk House for the drive through the decorated streets past cheering crowds. They were in the course of this hysterical day formally congratulated by the lord mayor and corporation which also sent a loyal and grateful message to the king. During the afternoon the

Griff and Augusta boarded their ornate barge to be rowed to Greenwich with an orchestra playing in an accompanying craft. Crowds lined the river banks to watch and to cheer.

The king soon received Augusta as if there had never been any estrangement. He talked with her about the downfall of Sir Robert Walpole. He begged her to prevail upon her husband to dissuade opposition members from demanding that Sir Robert should be impeached. And soon the Griff and Augusta learned that they could live in Leicester House which had been George's official residence when he was Prince of Wales. This was a large mansion on the north side of Leicester Square. The king's display of 'goodwill' was outwardly impressive, but it did not mean that his almost pathological dislike for his elder son had been overcome. Since the young man seemed so popular with such men as Carteret and Pulteney who were now so important, it was only sensible to offer him a little appeasement. Otherwise the king had no intention of consulting the Griff on political or state affairs, of giving him any important responsibilities. Very soon after the formation of the new ministry the Griff found himself kept in ignorance of its deliberations and intentions. Those opposition leaders now in the king's service felt they could not pay so much attention to the Prince of Wales and his views. Like a breaking wave, the Griff's influence had fallen very quickly from its impressive crest.

The Griff, however, was not without his political friends. He could still preside at their meetings and contrive to have raised in parliament issues likely to embarrass the new government. These meetings were attended by those politicians known as the 'boy patriots', who had been ignored by old Lord Wilmington, the new prime minister. There was Lyttelton, still one of the Griff's most intimate friends and a member of his household. There were Pitt and the Grenville brothers. Then there was still Lord Chesterfield, a consummate master of political plotting and mischief-making and an active enemy of the king. In the shadows there was George Bubb Dodington on his way back into the prince's favour. There had been the bitter break between the two when Dodington had been forbidden further entry into Carlton House in 1734. But since then they had often been in touch, even though Dodington had refused to support him in the parliamentary debate over his allowance. There were bonds of memory between the Griff and Dodington. They had shared literary and artistic interests. They had together gone whoring and had indulged in other foolish but nevertheless enjoyable adventures. The Griff had been dazzled by Dodington's wealth. Dodington, on his part, had genuine affection for the Griff.

In the year that followed there arose a rival to Frederick in the affections of the British people. This rival was his blue-eyed younger brother William Duke of Cumberland. William had joined the Navy in 1740 at the age of nineteen. With the amorous precocity of his family he had some two years earlier taken the first of a succession of mistresses. She was Mrs. Nancy Wilson, an actress who had formerly been an orange-seller. More manly than the Griff in appearance, but too pudgy to be handsome, Cumberland could exhibit a charming manner when so disposed. His naval career lasted but a year. In 1741 he was serving in the Coldstream Guards with the rank of colonel.

Lord Carteret, who had been so close to Frederick, was indirectly responsible for the rise to national renown and popularity of young Cumberland. The War of Jenkins' Ear had through the belligerent policies of Secretary of State Carteret become part of the War of Austrian Succession. Frederick the Great of Prussia had invaded the Austrian territory of Silesia. Britain aligned herself with Austria and Holland against Prussia, France and Spain. Through Carteret's persuasion Prussia came to terms in the Treaty of Berlin. Now Britain's big effort was directed against France.

In the spring of 1743 the king went to Hanover, impatient for an opportunity to be with his troops in the field and to win glory in battle. With him went the Duke of Cumberland, also thirsting for military adventure. Carteret appeared in Hanover soon afterwards. He saw much of Cumberland,

showering both him and the king with flattery. At the same
time came a message from Frederick asking that he be allowed
the privilege of any army command in this war. The request
was politely refused, and with reason. Frederick had never
received even the most elementary of military training. Then
came the Battle of Dettingen, with George in command of
British, Dutch and Hanoverian troops. Cumberland was in
charge of this army's left wing. Both father and son fought
with outstanding gallantry. Cumberland was wounded in a
leg by a misdirected bullet of an allied soldier. The king,
leaping off his bolting horse, rallied his troops with a cry of
'Now, boys, now for the honour of England! Fire, behave
bravely and the French will soon run.' The French, fighting
courageously, were defeated.

The king and his younger son returned to England in
triumph. They made a grand entry into St. James's Palace. The
Prince of Wales stood at the door of the great drawing room
at the top of the flight of marble stairs to greet and congratulate
the conquering heroes. He smiled at the approach of the little
king. The king walked haughtily past him. Now that he and
Cumberland were such heroes and had become so popular
with the masses, he doubtless felt he could safely snub his
hateful Griff. The two warriors were receiving widespread
acclamation, a novel experience for them both. The twenty-
two-year-old Cumberland, soon to be promoted to the rank
of lieutenant-general, received the biggest roars of approval,
specially when his limp reminded the spectators of the wound
received in gallant combat. He was given the nickname of
'Billy the Bold'. Many rhyming and prose tributes to Billy the
Bold were soon being hawked on the streets of London.
A year later Cumberland, following strong pressure from
the king, was appointed commander of the allied forces in the
Netherlands.

The outlook for the Griff which had seemed so hopeful
on Walpole's fall became increasingly depressing. During the
summer Lord Wilmington had died. Carteret had expected
the premiership, but the king passed him over for Henry

Pelham, brother of the Duke of Newcastle. Frederick and his political cronies plotted for the fall of Pelham. However, Pelham consolidated his position and Carteret was forced out of the ministry. Later Pelham was heading a new ministry which became known as the 'Broad Bottom Administration' because of its mixed composition of whigs and tories. Into this government, of which Frederick strongly disapproved, were drawn not only Lord Chesterfield but also Lyttelton to whom he had been so close. Frederick ordered Lyttelton to leave his household. Their social meetings with their many literary and artistic friends ceased. Lyttelton, a religious man with a strong sense of honour, had considered it his duty to accept the call to become a Lord of the Treasury in the new administration. But the Griff regarded his conduct as the ungrateful desertion of a faithful friend. Lyttelton blamed others for making mischief and turning the prince against him. In his suffering he wrote to the Griff: 'It has been my misfortune to have my conduct much misrepresented to your royal highness, but, however I may suffer under your unmerited anger, I shall always continue to preserve the most grateful sense of your past goodness to me, and the most sincere, disinterested zeal for your service.' With the sensitive Lyttelton gone, the Griff was even more enthusiastically seeking a renewal of his close alliance with Dodington.

In this period of surprising changes Lord Hervey, once such an influential figure, vanished from the scene at the age of forty-six. Always a delicate man, he died and left a mourning widow and family but an indifferent court and nation. Some attributed his early death not wholly to physical ailments but to repressed fury and frustration at the cessation of his national importance. His great power in court and politics perished with the death of his patroness Queen Caroline in 1737. He joined the cabinet as Lord Privy Seal in 1740, serving without distinction until the fall of the Walpole administration. Hervey had briefly been one of the Griff's best friends and then for so many years his worst enemy. Through his influence over Queen Caroline, Hervey undoubtedly did more harm to the Griff than any other slanderer and mischief-maker, effectively poisoning any goodwill that his parents and sisters bore towards him. Hervey died as an unhappy and hate-obsessed failure. Yet the brilliance of his memoirs, unpublished until 1848, were to win him lasting fame as historian and writer.

In March 1745 Robert Walpole died. Given a peerage on the fall of his ministry he had, as Earl of Orford, sat glumly in the House of Lords, only rarely rising to make a few remarks. Then one afternoon when the Prince of Wales was present Orford aroused the peers with a startling speech in which all his old powers of eloquence and persuasion had returned. He warned that Prince Charles Edward, known as the Young Pretender, was in Dunkirk preparing to invade England with powerful French support. Since the British Army was on the continent, there were only 7,000 adequately trained men available to defend England against this invasion. Walpole warned that at any moment enemy forces might be 'ravaging the country with fire and sword' and be preparing to enslave the population. This speech made a tremendous impression. The House sent a message to the king pledging loyalty in the coming attempt to place the catholic Prince Charles on the British throne in his stead. The Griff, aroused to the gravity of the crisis by his old enemy Walpole, discussed it with the king. However, a storm ravaged the fleet of France and caused her to think again. She decided to postpone the invasion.

The impetuous and confident twenty-five-year-old Prince Charles decided he could reclaim the British throne for himself and the House of Stuart without such massive French support. The tall, blue-eyed, fair-haired prince, whose grandfather had been James II, was sure that once he was on British soil, Scots and English enthusiasts would rally round him. Thus three months after the death of Walpole he landed with a few supporters in the West Highlands and made his headquarters at Glenfinnan. There the Macdonalds, the Camerons and members of other clans joined him.

The king was in Hanover when the Young Pretender landed.

And it was two weeks before he was back in London, at first contemptuously dismissing any chances of success for the invader. The Duke of Cumberland was in the Netherlands. The French, under Marshal Saxe, had defeated his allied army of British, Hanoverians, Dutch and Austrians at Fontenoy. As the French won more victories, the out-generalled Cumberland and his British soldiers were recalled to resist the invasion of their own homeland. The Griff had in the absence of his father and brother studied closely all the reports of the invasion. He had been impatient to get into the battle for the defence of the throne to which he was heir. On the king's return Griff begged him the privilege of military service in the campaign. The king replied with an emphatic refusal. This meant that the Griff, although Prince of Wales, would at the command of the king remain inactive while his brother was given all the honour and responsibility in the war with Prince Charles and the rebels. It seemed that once again the king's hatred for his elder son, together with his extreme jealousy, had directed his decision. The Griff reacted strangely to this new rebuff from his father. He donned a psychological armour of exaggerated cynicism. He tried to give the impression that he cared nothing about the threat to the Hanoverian dynasty in England. He tried to treat the crisis and its warfare as a joke. His former demeanour of serious concern was changed into a demeanour of hilarity and gaiety.

Frederick and Augusta spent more time at Cliveden and Kew than in London during the struggle against the advancing Prince Charles. With a large number of attendants they organised parties, amateur plays and concerts. The war threatening King George's throne was treated with studied indifference, if not as a joke. The Griff made fun of his brother Cumberland who had failed so miserably at Fontenoy. Although this young man had been called upon to lead the struggle for the preservation of the Hanoverian dynasty his elder brother did not wish him well. When Frederick and Augusta did spend periods at Leicester House in London they behaved with light-hearted gaiety and often went to the theatre.

Charles Edward, hailed by the Jacobites as the real Prince of Wales, made triumphal progress early in his campaign. From Glenfinnan, where he had raised his standard, he marched to Perth and then on to Edinburgh, which promptly surrendered. The same night he was presiding at a victory ball in the ancient palace of Holyrood. Soon afterwards the English troops, commanded by Sir John Cope, were fleeing from the charges of the Highlanders at Prestonpans. Six weeks later the young Pretender and his army marched from Edinburgh and besieged Carlisle.

In London there were fears that those who secretly favoured the Jacobite cause were waiting for an opportune moment to rise in support of the Young Pretender. Pro-Jacobite posters, pasted by night on walls and buildings of the city, angered the majority who favoured the Hanoverian dynasty. There were large demonstrations of loyalty to George II. A hymn called *God Save the King*, with music arranged by Thomas Arne, was fervently sung on the stage and in the auditorium of Drury Lane Theatre. This hymn, which later became the National Anthem, was believed by most people to be new. Actually it had been sung fifty years previously by supporters of the fugitive James II and James III. It was founded on an old folk tune.

At this time of acute anxiety in the nation Cliveden had never been so jolly. The Cliveden set had lost most of its remaining inhibitions through the departure of Lady Archibald Hamilton who had served well as Lady of the Robes to the princess and before that as mistress to the prince. Apparently Lady Archibald had, at the age of forty-five, become too bossy and conservative. She left in indignation but also with a guarantee from the Griff of a pension of £12,000 a year. Her place was taken in the circle of the prince and princess by Lady Middlesex, described by Horace Walpole as 'very short, very plain and very yellow'. But Lady Middlesex was also a classical scholar and she shared with the Prince and Princess of Wales an appreciation for good music. Moreover, Lady Middlesex, despite her forbidding appearance, was bright and witty and would sparkle at some of the all-night supper parties of the Griff and Augusta.

Augusta had recently given birth to her fourth son Henry Frederick, who would one day become Duke of Cumberland. This was her sixth child. There were Augusta and George, and after these had come Edward Augustus, later Duke of York and Albany, Elizabeth Caroline, and William Henry, later Duke of Gloucester. The Griff had planned to give a big supper on the night of the christening of Henry Frederick. As this christening was coinciding with the Young Pretender's siege of Carlisle, the Griff decided that this should be the motif of the party. Thus he ordered his household's pastry cooks and confectioners to make a large edible model of the fortress of Carlisle to be served as the supper dessert. At the same time he ordered provision of a large quantity of sugar plums. A big company sat down to supper that night. It included Lady Middlesex (now Lady of the Robes), Lord Stair, Sir William Stanhope the Duke of Queensberry and Augusta with five of her maids of honour. One of these maids was the lovely but wayward Elizabeth Chudleigh. The first courses at the supper ended. The dessert in the substantial iced-sugar model of the citadel of Carlisle was carried proudly into the dining room by liveried servants. This was placed on the table. Immediately the maids of honour started bombarding it with sugar plums. Soon the Griff, Lord Stair and others were joining in this hilarious siege of the sugar citadel. Another surprise of the occasion was the exhibition of new-born baby Henry Frederick in a cradle under a large canopy in the middle of the drawing room. Not realising this was the genuine child, the ageing Sir William Stanhope astounded the company with the remark: 'In wax, I suppose?'

Frederick was at that time annoyed with William Pitt, formerly a loyal friend, for following Lyttelton into the Pelham ministry. Pitt became Paymaster of the Forces, but on the day of the christening party there were rumours he was to be Minister for War. At his mirthful supper the prince declared that Maid of Honour Chudleigh was far better suited to be Minister for War than was Pitt. He told Miss Chudleigh that she must immediately apply for that post. He dictated a letter on her behalf for delivery to Lord Harrington of the Cabinet Council. When the maid of honour had signed the letter the prince asked all those at the dining table to add their signatures in support of her becoming Minister for War. The Duke of Queensberry, a friend of Pitt, refused, as did the more humble Mrs. Layton, one of Augusta's dressers. The letter was handed to a footman for delivery. Incidentally, this Elizabeth Chudleigh had the year previously become secretly the wife of a son of the late Lord Hervey. Years later her bigamous marriage to the Duke of Kingston won her national notoriety.

Like the sugar fortress on the Griff's supper table, Carlisle was overwhelmed. Prince Charles's forces then moved on and took Manchester. Everywhere, except in the home of the Prince and Princess of Wales, there was acute anxiety as the Young Pretender moved on to Derby, which was only 130 miles from London. On December 4th, 1745, he reached Derby. When late next day the fateful news reached the government in London a messenger was dispatched to inform the Prince of Wales. The messenger, entering the drawing room at Leicester House, came upon a blindfolded figure pawing at those who pranced hilariously around him. The Prince of Wales was playing Blind Man's Buff with his pages.

There were no drawing-room games being played at St. James's Palace. The king, in a panic, was preparing to flee London. He believed that the Young Pretender and Jacobite hordes would be arriving within a few days. Similar panic swept the population of London. On what became known as 'Black Friday', early in December, 1745, people besieged the banks trying to exchange their paper money for real coin. The Griff continued to enact the role of the indifferent playboy, although years later it became known that he had practised some deception. A note in the diary of the then deceased Earl of Marchmont told how Frederick, despite the rebuff from his father, made another attempt to join the Army.

To the delighted surprise of the king and many others, the tide in the war suddenly turned. Prince Charles retreated from Derby on persuasion by the Scottish chiefs who warned him of insufficient English support. At the same time many of the Jacobite rank-and-file deserted and returned home. Nevertheless, with more recruits the Jacobites won a victory at Falkirk. On failing to capture Stirling Castle they started a retreat to the Highlands. And now came the Duke of Cumberland's golden hour. His army crushed the enemy at Culloden Moor near Nairn and the Young Pretender fled the battlefield.

This younger brother of the Griff celebrated the first victory he had ever won in a bath of blood. Thereafter he was known as 'the Butcher'. On the encouragement of Cumberland his soldiers slaughtered hundreds of Scots prisoners and wounded. Then for the fun of it they waded through the pools of blood, laughingly splashing one another like children paddling in the surf. Many other Highlanders who survived bullets and bayonets were clubbed to death. A hut full of wounded men was wantonly set alight. James Wolfe, later the posthumous hero of the Battle of Quebec, was disgusted by the callous behaviour of his royal commander.

Coming upon a wounded Highlander on the Culloden battlefield, Cumberland ordered Wolfe to 'shoot that insolent scoundrel'.

Wolfe refused, with the reply: 'My army commission is at the disposal of your royal highness, but I cannot consent to become an executioner.'

Cumberland, however, was a dashing hero in the eyes of heartless and vicious soldiers and officers. He encouraged them in cruel and shameful antics. For example, he had a number of terrified young Scots girls brought into camp and stripped naked. They were then thrown on to the backs of horses to ride races while the onlooking troops roared with laughter at the plight of the girls. It was said that on learning the details of Culloden, the Griff expressed regret that his brother had been the victor. This regret was attributed to jealous motives, but more likely it had arisen from the stories of Cumberland's atrocities and the terrible human suffering that followed the victory.

The episodes ending the daring invasion by Prince Charles were followed with fascination and unabashed sympathy by Frederick. The Young Pretender did not make his escape from Scotland until nearly six months after the slaughter of Culloden. He owed much to the remarkable gentlewoman Flora Macdonald. The twenty-three-year-old Flora was one of his companions when he escaped from Skye wearing women's dress as 'an Irish spinning maid, Betty Burke'. When Flora was arrested, brought to London and lodged in the Tower the Griff insisted upon visiting her. He protested when Augusta told him that in her opinion Flora was a traitress undeserving of sympathy.

'I hope,' he added, 'that if I had been in Charles Edward's plight you would have behaved as did Flora Macdonald.'

It was largely due to the Griff's efforts that Flora was released from the Tower, finally regaining her full liberty through the Act of Indemnity of 1747.

Nearly eighty prominent rebels were tried and executed. The views of the Prince of Wales clashed with those of the king and the Duke of Cumberland in his belief that only forgiveness and magnanimity in victory could win true respect for the crown and the Anglo-Scottish union from the defeated Jacobites. The prince's passionate intercession saved at least seven rebel lords from the axe or hangman's rope. His biggest fight was made for the life of the Earl of Cromarty, condemned to death with Lords Kilmarnock and Balmerino in a cruel and theatrical trial in Westminster Hall. Cromarty had pleaded that he had been 'seduced from his loyalty to King George II in an unguarded moment by the acts of desperate and designing men'. Frederick also adopted desperate and designing methods to win Cromarty a pardon. He approached the king's ministers personally and individually. He threatened them with 'the utmost of his vengeance' if they permitted Cromarty to die. Eventually they gave way and procured the condemned man a king's pardon.

Frederick could have saved still more lives had it not been for the insistence of the Duke of Cumberland on a policy of the utmost vengeance. Culloden had not slaked his thirst for blood. He wanted the axe to fall—with the mob watching—on as many rebel necks as possible. There was a discussion between mayor and aldermen on a proposal to honour the duke with membership of some city company. 'Let it be the Butchers',' suggested one alderman. The public butchery of the rebel lords in London was an ignoble spectacle, although they behaved with exemplary courage.

'God bless King George,' intoned the chaplain in a funeral prayer preceding the execution of Lord Balmerino.

'God bless King James,' responded Balmerino loudly.

While the seventy-eight-year-old Lord Lovat was being driven to the Tower from his trial a woman shouted, 'You'll get that nasty head of yours chopped off, you ugly Scottish dog.'

He replied: 'I believe I shall, you ugly old English bitch.'

The spirit of compassion and disgust at the continued persecution of the helpless Jacobites led the Griff into more actions which resulted in fantastic rumours that he was himself a supporter of their cause. The Earl of Westmorland, who had dared to be a Jacobite, was invited by the Griff to join his household staff. Welcomed as a maid of honour to Augusta was Catherine Walkinshaw. Her sister Clementina was the Young Pretender's mistress. The Griff continued to argue that in the cause of national unity it was the duty of the victors of 1745 and 1746 to forget the past and to treat former enemies as friends. Supporters and admirers of his brother Cumberland villified him for this.

More and more people were singing *God Save the King* as the horrors of the years 1745 and 1746 receded into the past. In 1748 the War of the Austrian Succession was at last ending. The British Navy triumphed. In a succession of victories it had swept all enemy fleets from the high seas. In warfare on land the achievements of Great Britain had been dismal. Her subsidies to her fighting allies had been more useful than her armies. Because of the strain upon the economy of these subsidies a spirit of rejoicing swept the nation when in October 1748 the war ended with the signing of the Peace of Aix-la-Chapelle. The king made this an occasion for glorifying his reign of twenty-one years. He was showing more goodwill towards the British people, despite his past tirades against them in the privacy of his household. The warm-hearted British people were on their part quick to appreciate indications of such kingly goodwill. The anthem *God Save the King* was now sung with fervour, and in the king's celebrations over Aix-la-Chapelle and his reign, the Griff generously and whole-heartedly joined.

Preparations for the spectacular festivities took so long that they did not begin until 1749, the year after the signing of the treaty. All London was illuminated. A display of fire-works was described as the biggest ever. People, in the cockney manner, sang and danced in the streets. The Griff appeared among them, joining in the fun like any ordinary citizen. And in this year of celebration the pleasure gardens of Rane-lagh, first opened in 1742, reached the height of their splendour. There was a great masked ball 'in the Venetian manner'. Gliding about the Ranelagh lake was a giant gondola, illumi-nated, beflagged and beribboned, carrying an orchestra.

'It was the prettiest spectacle I ever saw', wrote Horace Walpole. 'Nothing in a fairy-tale ever surpassed it.'

The Griff and Augusta joined in the dancing and the all-night revels unrecognised in their masks. As in this joyous year celebrations became wilder, conservative people began to complain that even the Treaty of Aix-la-Chapelle was no justification for immodesty. It was felt that the limit had been reached when Elizabeth Chudleigh, maid of honour to Augusta, appeared almost naked at another masquerade attended by the king.

Soon all London was humming the *Firework Music* written by Handel for the celebrations. The composer was fully in favour again with both the king and the Griff who had treated him so disgracefully. The road back to acceptance and

affluence had been hard. Recovering from his stroke, Handel
had returned to England. In 1743 he seized the opportunity
offered by the king's bravery in battle to compose the *Dettingen
Te Deum*. In 1745 he composed *Judas Maccabeus* as a tribute to
the king's triumph over the Young Pretender. All these
efforts flattered and pleased the king. But, above all, George
found it impossible to ill-treat Handel after he had attended a
performance of *The Messiah* during which he rose from his
seat to clap with uncontrolled enthusiasm and appreciation
at the composer's genius. The king could, indeed, have fairly
claimed to have been the salvation of *The Messiah*, an oratorio
which had been condemned by many of the clergy as
'irreligious'.

12

Country Gentleman

During the late 1740s Frederick became obsessed by the feeling that the time was drawing near when he would be king. The late 1740s were to him years of planning, of the framing of detailed policies which would be put into effect upon his succession to the throne. The king, born in 1683, was well on the way to seventy, yet, except for his haemorrhoids, he seemed strong and vigorous, despite rumours and gossip that he was becoming senile. A symptom of this 'senility' was said to be revealing itself in his pursuit of young girls. Anyhow, the Prince of Wales felt sure he would soon occupy the throne and acted accordingly.

From 1747 onwards he was in almost constant discussion with political friends, new and old. In what became known as the *Carlton House Paper* he informed members of the opposition what his policies would be as king. He would try to abolish party, investigate bribery and corruption in government, strengthen the militia and ban army and naval officers of lower rank from parliament. He even insisted that he would need a civil list far smaller than that enjoyed by his father. He displayed a passionate devotion to Great Britain her people and institutions. He was a pioneer of the 'Buy British' movement. Both the Griff and Augusta insisted upon wearing clothing made only from British materials and of British design. While often speaking French in his family circle and with close friends, he loved the English language and its literature. He objected to the use in court of German, his native tongue. He wanted to become the 'patriot king', as described by Bolingbroke in this work of that name.

The Griff had his own periodical *The Remembrancer* to strengthen the influence of his party and to publicise his own political ideals. *The Remembrancer* was edited by his friend James Ralph under the name of George Cadwalader. It was through Ralph that the prince persuaded Dodington to resign his post as Treasurer of the Navy to return to him as a political adviser. Another who became increasingly influential in the prince's political circle was Dodington's friend Sir Francis Dashwood, a man of ability, but a rake, stories of whose Medmenham orgies have become progressively exaggerated by time.

During this period of the Griff's intensive preparation for the kingship a powerful new influence entered the lives of himself and Augusta. This was James Stuart, 3rd Earl of Bute. The Griff had gone to the Egham races from Cliveden when heavy rain drove him into a tent. Deciding to pass the time in a game of whist, he asked an attendant to find him a congenial partner. Lord Bute was presented to him. The ensuing game of cards developed into a close friendship. Six years younger than the prince, Bute was a handsome man with a proud and somewhat impertinent air. In those days of knee-breeches, when male calves were on constant display, Bute won the reputation of possessing 'the most elegant legs in London'. Augusta, who shrank from some of her husband's friends, was immediately captivated by Bute. He was to exercise a powerful influence over her in the next reign when their close relationship led to widespread suspicion that he had become her lover. Bute was married to a daughter of Lady Mary Wortley Montagu, who had been so enchanted by the Griff when she met him in his boyhood in Hanover. The friendship between Bute and the prince and princess grew quickly in warmth. Then his appointment was announced as Lord of the Bedchamber to Frederick. Lady Mary Wortley Montagu was unimpressed by her son-in-law's honour. To a friend she wrote: 'I hope it may prove yet more fortunate in its consequence, tho' court favour is as little to be depended on as fair weather at sea.'

During the late 1740s a big change came over Frederick. He had at last reached a maturity and a way of life that brought him tranquillity and happiness. He seemed to have become completely anglicised, with his affection for the countryside and for its ordinary working folk with whom he loved to mingle. He developed the Englishman's passion for games, particularly cricket. He became a devoted family man, delighting in sharing in the fun and recreation of his children. From time to time he still played foolish pranks with Dodington, Desnoyers and other cronies, but any marital infidelity seemingly had ended. This was remarkable for the son of womanising George II and grandson of sensual George I. Lady Archibald Hamilton was certainly the Griff's mistress when she became an attendant to Augusta, but this relationship lapsed long before her dismissal. Lady Middlesex has often been described as the mistress of the Griff, but there is no sound evidence of any immoral relationship between them when she was a member of his household, beyond snide semi-humorous suggestions of Horace Walpole and others. He may have had an affair with her years previously. However, in the Griff's household his friendship with this physically unattractive little woman appears to have been solely intellectual.

Notwithstanding his acts of unfaithfulness, the Griff had always been in love with his wife, who was unfailingly loyal and devoted. Outside their household she was inclined to nervousness and reserve. People complained that despite a surface friendliness she was difficult to get to know, if indeed she possessed anything worth knowing. Earl Waldegrave saw Augusta as one who 'was represented as a woman of excellent sense by those who knew her very imperfectly; but in fact was one of those moderate geniuses, who with much natural dissimulation, a civil address, an assenting conversation and a few ideas of their own, can act with tolerable propriety so long as they are conducted by a wise and prudent counsellor'. Chesterfield summed up Augusta as 'an ambitious and busy woman, with parts, and with an appearance of cold insensibility'. Yet the Griff adored her for

. . . that gentleness of mind, that love
So kindly answering my desire;
That grace with which you look and speak and move,
That thus has set my soul on fire.

These were the prince's feelings about Augusta as expressed in an ode he wrote on her under the title of *The Charms of Sylvia.** It was imperfect poetry, but nevertheless a revealing picture of this woman as seen by her husband, bereft of that 'cold insensibility' imagined by Chesterfield.

Frederick and Augusta rejoiced in their growing family. Four years after Henry Frederick, whose arrival in 1745 was celebrated so mirthfully, came their seventh child Louisa Ann. Louisa was followed in 1750 by Frederick William. The Griff never saw their ninth child, Caroline Matilda, born after his death. She became a tragic, persecuted queen of Denmark.

In studying the personality and activities of Frederick in these later years the influence upon him of religion cannot be ignored. Like his mother, the Griff had long been interested in philosophy and theology as an interesting intellectual exercise without these having any practical effect upon his life. He and Augusta were regular in their attendance at services of the established church, although they invariably arrived late. But the Griff, like many others, found no true inspiration in the church and clergy of the day. The bishops and other high church dignitaries of his acquaintance were clever but conventional men living in luxury and enjoying the fleshpots of society. The names of some of these eighteenth-century dignitaries became tainted by scandal. Lord Egmont wrote of a Bishop of Bristol who 'would get the finest women he could and afterwards marry them off'. Finally his debauchery brought 'such infirmities upon him' that he had to go abroad, leaving behind a bastard.

While church-going among the upper classes was a convention or social grace, among the servant classes it was an obligation. They were herded to services by their masters and mistresses as necessary for their betterment. Horace Walpole,

* See Appendix, page 221.

saying that 'a good moral sermon may instruct and benefit' servants, went himself to church only to encourage their attendance. One axiom of the aristocracy was that the working classes were wicked. Ladies and gentlemen were generous contributors to the Society for Promoting Christian Knowledge (founded in 1688) which showered upon the poor such tracts a *A Caution Against Drunkenness, A Kind Caution to Profane Swearers* and *A Persuasion to Serious Observation of the Lord's Day.*

Frederick was always quick to recognise humbug. He saw the Church of England flattering the rich while patronising without really helping the poor. Thus when the voices of John Wesley and George Whitefield started to thunder through the country he was thrilled. In the Church of England boisterous enthusiasm and booming oratory from the pulpit had been regarded as ill-mannered. But the Methodists, smashing convention, were in their emotional and dramatic preaching making thousands of converts, transforming thousands of lives. The Griff went secretly to hear Whitefield preach. He was deeply stirred. He also attended services conducted by aristocratic Methodist Selina, Countess Huntingdon, where worshippers of high birth often concealed themselves behind voluminous chapel curtains. These Methodists moved him as had none of the scholarly Anglican bishops and clerks of the royal closets.

The prince enjoyed meeting Lady Huntingdon at court receptions which she had long graced as a personage of noble birth and marriage. He was worried on learning that notoriety and criticisms arising from her unconventional evangelistic activities were causing her to stay away. When one day the Griff commented on Lady Huntingdon's absence to Lady Charlotte Edwin she laughingly replied, 'I suppose she is praying with beggars.' The Griff made this reply: 'Lady Charlotte, when I am dying I think I shall be happy to seize the skirt of Lady Huntingdon's mantle, to lift me up with her to heaven.' But any religious intolerance repelled the Griff. He annoyed orthodox Anglican churchmen by receiving Quakers and allowing them to pour out to him complaints regarding the disabilities to which they were subjected.

The prince was almost foolishly generous. As one who was often in debt himself he contributed large sums towards assistance for imprisoned debtors. And as on his visit to Bath he would never let pass an opportunity for pleading for the release of debtors from prison. A special interest of his was the Georgia Society through which many debtors were assisted in emigrating to the American colony of that name. The town of Augusta, Georgia, was named after his wife. The Griff was what is known today as 'a soft touch'. He paid all the debts, amounting to £500, of the poet Richard Glover. He endowed many needy and also improvident people with pensions. Wherever the prince moved he was pursued by beggars, aware that he never refused a plea for alms.

Seduced in his boyhood and over the years indulging in many sordid pursuits and encounters, the Griff in this later period of his life was becoming repelled by the moral cesspools of England. In his *Carlton House Paper* of 1747 he attributed the difficulties of Great Britain not only to the strife and bitterness of party and faction but also to 'a great depravity of morals diffused throughout the country'. This was not hypocrisy. He was becoming changed. He was, with the change, seeing his country with new vision.

Returning to the Griff's joy in the countryside, it delighted him to escape the sophistication of London for his gardens at Cliveden and Kew, for country lanes and inns. He was the first English royalty to mingle with the 'common people', talking naturally with them and even sitting with them around the tables in their cottages. Like the English countrymen of today, he enjoyed visiting 'the local' and chatting with any other men who happened to be there. His favourite drinking places while at Cliveden were the Three Feathers (named after himself) and the Chequers, where he mingled with local farmers and their labourers. From Kew House he would take long walks into the countryside, sometimes accompanied only by a beloved dog. The dog was very ordinary, except that it had been a gift from the poet Pope and bore on its collar this announcement:

I am his highness's dog at Kew.
Pray tell me, sir, whose dog are you?

The Griff was not a devotee of hunting and other field sports, although, as a sop to convention, he joined in them from time to time. He was, however, a keen player and pioneer of cricket. The rules of the ancient game were codified in 1744, but Frederick had played with a Surrey group before that. In 1735 he and the Earl of Middlesex had brought two teams together for a bet of £1,000. In 1746, enthusiastic on cricket becoming an organised national game, Frederick was patron of a match between Kent and All England. In the egalitarian spirit of village cricket the Kent captain was Rumsey, the Earl of Derby's gardener, while among aristocratic members of his team was Lord John Sackville, later the Duke of Dorset. The county won by one wicket. Although in the 1740s the Griff organised village games at Cliveden and Kew, the honour for the founding of the first village cricket club belongs to Hambledon, Hampshire. This was established in 1750.

Despite the efforts of Frederick and other pioneers of cricket, it was often a rough and unruly game or an excuse for subsidiary vulgarities. For example, the *Penny London Morning Advertiser* in its issue of 11th June 1744, under the headline of 'Excellent Sport', announced:

This day will be played on Walworth Common a great cricket match between 11 gentlemen of the Borough of Southwark and 11 gentlemen of High Kent and Blackman.

The gentlemen who play this match have subscribed for a Holland smock of one guinea value, which will be run for by two jolly wenches, one known by the name of The Little Bit of Blue (the handsome Broom Girl) and the other, Black Bess. They are to run in drawers only, and there is excellent sport expected.

Captain Vinegar, with a great many of his bruisers and bull-dogs, will attend to make a ring, that no civil spectators may be incommoded by the rabble.

When the weather at Cliveden was too wet for cricket

Frederick, his children and friends would go into a huge bare room to play what they called 'baseball'. Far from being the baseball known to Americans today, it was nevertheless a species of rounders. They also played another game called push-pin.

Cliveden in the country and Leicester House in London were centres for private concerts, plays, masquerades and even ballets by both amateurs and professionals. The prince and Augusta would invite into their homes large numbers of friends to enjoy these entertainments. The couple had not been long at Cliveden before they made an open-air theatre, with a chalk cliff shaped and smoothed by workmen to improve the acoustics. It was here in 1740 that the stirring words and music of *Rule Britannia* were first heard. The prince had suggested to poets James Thomson and David Mallet that they collaborate in the writing of a masque based on the life of Alfred the Great. Thomas Arne, friend of Handel and later the arranger of *God Save the King*, was commissioned to write the music. Arne had written many popular works, particularly for the theatre. The masque was a great success, the Cliveden audience being stirred by *Rule Britannia* and other patriotic airs. But whether Thomas or Mallet wrote the words of *Rule Britannia* has long been a subject of controversy. Unfortunately each poet later claimed to have been its sole author.

Entire orchestras performed inside or on the long terrace of the Griff's Cliveden mansion. Sometimes he would himself take over the baton from the conductor. He wrote a little light music, but this had no special distinction. He also for many years practised hard on his 'cello. Although he could command the services of the nation's greatest musicians, he always had time for the struggling amateurs like himself. He obtained great pleasure in playing a 'cello in a village amateur orchestra trying obediently to respond to the wild baton waves of the lay conductor.

The cultural activities of the Griff have long occasioned sneers from superior people because of suggestions by Horace Walpole and others that he was a poseur who wanted to be accepted by society as a devotee of arts and letters. This criticism is obviously nonsense. The Griff throughout his life showed indifference both to public opinion and to that of people in authority. Criticism and scorn from the king, queen, sisters, Walpole, Hervey and many others failed to move or influence him. The Griff was, for better or for worse, always himself. He was no friend of pretence. Anyhow, whatever the judgement of others, the children of the Griff found it exciting and delightful to possess such a father. In adulthood they cherished memories of the pleasure brought to them by their father, even though they were very young in those years.

He joined them in cricket and baseball, in practical jokes and uproarious laughter. He also encouraged the amateur theatricals to which they were devoted. He even obtained the help of the famous actor James Quin to improve their elocution. They never forgot how in 1749 they gave a performancof Joseph Addison's *Cato*. Prince George, aged eleven, was Porteus. Prince Edward, ten, was Juba. Princess Augusta, twelve, and Princess Elizabeth, seven, were also in the play. Their father and Lord Bute wrote a special prologue, spoken by George, and an epilogue spoken by Edward and Augusta. Each rang with pride in England. In the course of the prologue George declaimed:

> *What, though a boy! it may with pride be said,*
> *A boy in* England *born—in* England *bred;*
> *Where freedom well becomes the earliest state,*
> *For there the love of liberty's innate.*

And in the epilogue Augusta regretted that as a princess she would have to wed some foreign royalty. She recited:

> *Could I have one of England's breeding,*
> *But 'tis a point they're all agreed in,*
> *That I must wed a foreigner,*
> *Across the seas—the Lord knows where—*
> *Yet, let me go where 'ere I will,*
> *England shall have my wishes still.*

Added Edward:

In England born, my inclination,
Like yours is wedded to the nation;
And future times, I hope, will see
The general, in reality.
Indeed, I wish to serve this land,
It is my father's strict command;
And none he ever gave will be
More cheerfully obeyed by me.

The Griff had known parental neglect, hate and scorn but never parental love. His own childhood deprivation of fatherly interest and affection had the psychological effect of his wanting to shower loving attentions on his sons and daughters. The eldest child Augusta, later the Duchess of Brunswick, seemed to be an almost constant companion of her parents, and sometimes she delighted in wearing identically the same gowns as her mother. George, who was to reign so long as king, was a serious-minded boy but inclined to indolence. Although an intelligent talker he had unusual difficulty in learning to read. His brother Edward was a more attractive personality. But he grew up to be idle and immoral and died as Duke of York and Albany at the age of twenty-eight. Little Elizabeth was a weak and deformed girl, but regarded as the mentally brightest of all the children. Her life of semi-invalidism ended in 1761.

Evidence of the Griff's absorbing interest in his children has survived in the form of memoranda and letters in his handwriting. Lord North had been appointed to supervise the studies and daily routine of the boys George and Edward. Even Sunday was included in the routine which Frederick wished his elder children to follow. Thus:

'On Sundays, prayers exactly at half an hour past nine above stairs. Then the two eldest princes and the two eldest princesses are to go to Prince George's apartment, to be instructed by Dr. Ayscough in the principles of religion till eleven o'clock.'

The extant letters of Frederick to his son George are undated. They often refer to incidents or affairs of which today we can know nothing. For example:

You can't imagine how happy you made me yesterday, any mark of a sincere, or a sensible, feeling heart gives me much more joy than any signs of wit or improvement in your learning which I daresay will come also in time. You have a father who loves you all tenderly and (who tho' peevish against your faults, because he wants you should shine) always by the father again, when he sees you mend.

Thank God you are all well, we are too. How do you advance in English history and in what reign are you, and why don't you write me what you have learnt. . . . As you and Edward are both in town, I think one might speak of everybody's health, and the other acquaint me with the progresses you make with your masters, but Edward has forgot me, and has given me no signs of life this fortnight, which hurts me. For the future I beg both may take it by turns to tell me in writing once a week what you have read; it will imprint it better on your mind and convince me that you both apply, which will make me happy, as nothing can do that more, than a prospect, to say my children turn out an honour to me and a blessing to my country.

Chiding Prince George for 'not sparing a quarter of an hour' from his activities to write to him, the father concludes a letter with:

You of all people should take more trouble, as God has given you so high a mark to govern one day so many nations, and if you do not please them, they won't please you in return. Read this carefully, and keep it as it comes from a father who (what is not usual) is your best friend.

He wrote this advice to George in the consciousness that the boy would one day be king:

Flatterers, courtiers or ministers are easy to be got, but a true friend is difficult to be found. The only rule I can give you to try them by is, if they tell you the truth and will venture for your sake to risk some moments of disagreeable contradictions to your passions, through which they may lose your favour if you are a weak prince, but will settle themselves firmer in it, if you turn out that which I hope God will make you.

In this period of their lives both the prince and princess found great happiness in a multitude of activities. But not all was well among their friends. There were jealousy and animosity between Dodington and others close to the prince, such as the 2nd Earl of Egmont and Lord Bute. The former had recently inherited the Egmont title from his father the 1st Earl from whose informative diaries we have quoted. This younger Egmont had grown greatly in favour with the Griff. Both Egmont and Dodington claimed to be his chief political adviser. The Griff was in fact consulting more with Egmont on opposition strategy than with Dodington. He had placed his handwritten text of the *Carlton House Paper* in Egmont's safe keeping. Matters were further complicated by efforts being made by the rejected Lyttelton to win his way back into princely favour. The poets and other writers introduced to the Griff by Lyttelton were still welcomed at his homes in London and in the country. Lyttelton, however, remained unwelcome. And at about that time the Griff stopped his £100-a-year pension to Lyttelton's protégé poet James Thomson. This has been denounced as an act of spite. But more likely Thomson did not need this pension any more. He was better off, 'the good Lyttelton' having in 1745 obtained for him the £300 a year sinecure of Surveyor-General of the Leeward Islands which, incidentally, he never visited once.

Dodington was, it seemed, relegated to the role of the prince's companion in his more trivial amusements, and as a convenient figure for practical jokes and mirth. Dodington's protruding stomach, his snub nose and ready wit, gave him a resemblance to the cheeky circus clown who, amid roars of laughter, receives rains of blows from an inflated bladder. Yet even in that harmless office he was still treated with coldness by jealous men in the prince's social and domestic circle. The diaries of Dodington reveal his pride when occasionally given more serious duties, and his pain at the resentment shown him in Leicester House, Kew and Cliveden. Proudly he recorded one day how as the reputed adviser to the Prince of Wales he had dined with the Lord Mayor of London, Sir Stephen Pennant. Another day he wrote: 'Lord Talbot informed me of the many lies told of me to the prince and the unalterable inveteracy of the family (meaning the Griff's friends and advisers) against me. God forgive them, I have not deserved it of them.'

But for Dodington it was not all booby traps and being rolled down steps in blankets. There were unconventional parties in improbable places, and practical jokes against other people than himself. For example, his diary tells of a mysterious night party at a London dressmaker's. He wrote: 'At eight o'clock undressed by order. Waited upon Their Royal Highnesses at Carlton House where came Lords Inchiquin and Bathurst and Lady Middlesex, in whose landau we six, Her Royal Highness and Lady Middlesex, His Royal Highness and we three gentlemen went to Mrs. Glass's in Tavistock Street, a maker of habits, where we stayed till near twelve, and then we hurried in the same manner to Carlton House, where we met Lady Howe and Lord Bute and supped.' In those days some dressmaking establishments had staffs of seamstresses, chosen for their saucy attractiveness as well as for their skill at the needle. They would have contributed much towards a gay party, even in such high male and female company. And on that night Bute might well have been the target of the Griff's fun, as well as Dodington. Bute had such a pompous and self-important air that the Griff liked to deflate him with such insults as, 'You would make a good ambassador in some paltry little court where there is nothing to do.'

As a companion with the Griff in light-hearted and often foolish amusement, Dodington often met the French dancing-master Philip Desnoyers. The Griff and Desnoyers were now friends of long standing. Desnoyers was three times a week giving lessons in deportment and dancing to Princes George and Edward and the elder princesses. He was regularly seeing Frederick and Augusta for conversation, games and other diversions. Dodington's diary tells how he was guest at a dinner party in Desnoyer's London house with the prince and princess. It also describes a hoax played upon Madame de Munchausen, wife of the Hanoverian minister in London, in connivance with the Griff and Augusta. They arranged for Philip Desnoyers to sit in the home of Lady Middlesex disguised as a fortune-teller. They then drove Madame de Munchausen there for a session with the 'fortune-teller', having told Desnoyers in advance to give her some 'surprising' predictions. The unsuspecting diplomat's wife listened and, in the measured words of Dodington, was 'surprised sufficiently'.

In July the Griff and his wife paid their second visit to Bath, this time accompanied by their eldest daughter Augusta. Their stay ended with a giant picnic on the banks of the river Avon at Saltford, a few miles from the city. All the neighbouring country folk were invited to drink beer with the prince and to listen to a non-stop band. The hundreds who gathered around him were thrilled and enchanted. They agreed says a record of the day, that 'there never had been such a prince'.

The couple and their daughter proceeded to the Isle of Wight and Portsmouth. Again the prince delighted men, women and children by moving among them in walk-about fashion, frustrating fussy officials and courtiers who, faithful to their traditions, feared that his dignity might suffer.

A better financial position contributed towards the content of the Prince and Princess of Wales during those last years. The king had at last been prevailed upon to increase his son's allowances. Although the Griff was in debt, the threat of complete financial disaster had been removed.

13

The Griff Flies Away

Frederick was showing far less interest in politics during the last months of 1750 and the first months of 1751. Earlier he had been full of plans for his actions and policies as soon as he came to the throne. Every detail of the *Carlton House Paper* would be discussed with its custodian Lord Egmont. He would also confer on his future as king with his legal expert and adviser Dr. George Lee, a friend of many years. The Griff had shared the belief of others that his father George II had not long to live. He had expected to ascend to the throne at any time, certain that he would achieve much in the creation of a greater and happier England. He visualised himself as 'the people's monarch' uniting every class and faction of his subjects. Then suddenly all his national hopes, plans and expectations ended. This was because of a premonition that he himself would soon die. He had with Dodington still been visiting professional seers and fortune-tellers. From this fact arose a story never confirmed, that one of these had predicted an early death.

The Griff told others of his premonition as he worked feverishly to complete extensive landscaping and building plans in his gardens at Kew. He gave it as his reason for wanting the work completed as soon as possible, as if it were to serve as a kind of memorial. For a long time, however, he had been conscripting even his most distinguished guests—both ladies and gentlemen—to toil alongside labourers in his grounds. Even the enormous and overdressed Dodington was set to work, much to his private indignation. Now, after the premonition, the Griff was hurrying to line a new aqueduct with busts of history's philosophers from Confucius onwards. They were being specially sculptured from pictures of these thinkers assembled for the prince by George Vertue, his artistic adviser. The area around the aqueduct had years previously been lovingly laid out under the direction of the designer William Kent. Now it was being re-landscaped in order to accommodate the philosophers. Despite the premonition, Frederick appeared then to be in good health as in his shirtsleeves he bustled among his mixed army of workers.

But despite Frederick's declining interest in politics, his opposition party was keeping busy. Its biggest target was his brother the Duke of Cumberland. Billy the Bold, it was charged, was becoming too bold and too powerful in his role as captain-general of the British land forces at home and abroad. The charge was supported by the Griff's party journal *The Remembrancer*, particularly during the debate over the Mutiny Bill. The Griff himself, however, remained on comparatively friendly terms with Cumberland, as if the fires of this controversy were not worth fanning. Then the anti-Cumberland campaign reached a new, mysterious phase in February 1751 as the Griff laboured in his gardens at Kew. A circular was dropped by night at the doors of hundreds of London houses asking questions about Cumberland, with the inference that with his growing power over the British fighting forces he might one day be tempted to seize the throne. The question in the circular which caused most offence was,

Whether a younger son of the crown should ever be invested with absolute power over the army, and at the same time by a factious connexion make himself master of the fleet, our lives and fortunes might not be dependent on his will and pleasure, and the right of succession have no other security than his want of ambition.

The popularity of Billy the Bold had declined among masses of the British people since his cruel excesses after Culloden had become more generally known. They preferred to call him Billy the Butcher. However, the king, court and members of the Pelham administration were outraged by this sinister circular. Of course there were suggestions that it had been inspired by the Prince of Wales. Accordingly suspicion fell upon his closest political collaborator Lord Egmont of having been its author. Nevertheless the mystery of the circular's authorship remained unsolved. Unable to arrest a culprit, the Houses of Lords and Commons voted for a meaningless but painless *auto-da-fé*. This was that a copy of the pamphlet be publicly burned to cinders by the official hangman.

The Griff was lying ill on February 22nd, 1751, the date of this absurd ceremonial burning. All January and into the first half of February he had been working ceaselessly in his grounds at Kew where, in icily cold weather, some order seemed to be emerging from the chaos in the area of the aqueduct. He had seemed so well and unaffected by the sleet and the cutting winds. Then one evening he started to wheeze and to cough. He had developed pneumonia or pleurisy. Inevitably, in obeyance to the medical superstitions then prevailing, the patient was blooded. He remained in bed, seething with impatience at being kept away from his labours in the Kew grounds. But on Friday, 8th March, he was up and around again, although feeling unsteady. Four days later he insisted he was well enough to return to state and private duties, the first of which was to be in official attendance on the king in a function at the House of Lords. He wore his heavy and cumbersome robes as Prince of Wales. In comparison with the cold outside, the atmosphere in the House of Lords was hot and stuffy. As he sweated, together with the overdressed nobility in this fetid ceremonial, his thoughts were without doubt at Kew where the busts of the philosophers were going to dominate the aqueduct and gardens. For upon leaving the House of Lords he was driven to Carlton House where he threw off his heavy robes for a light coat and waistcoat. A few minutes later he was on his way to Kew. There in the cold open air he worked and talked with his labourers and gardeners. He returned to Carlton House for the evening, feeling terribly tired and unnaturally hot. He went into an unheated room that opened on to the garden and dropped on to a couch. Lord Egmont happened to enter this room and, seeing the prince, warned him that it was unwise to rest there. Nevertheless the Griff ignored Egmont's warning. He fell asleep and did not awaken for three hours.

He awoke with paroxysms of coughing. His coach carried him to Leicester House to rejoin his wife and children. Augusta, seeing his condition, summoned doctors. They warned Augusta he was very ill. They bled him twice. They raised blisters on each of his legs believing that when these burst the body would be relieved of nauseous poisons. Augusta, knowing the tendency of her husband to get excited, ordered that no one should visit him except immediate members of the family. Reports of the prince's condition were sent to the king who surprisingly conveyed his sympathy and best wishes. Calling at Leicester House on 15th March Dodington was relieved to be told that the Griff was out of danger. Like twentieth-century naturapaths, eighteenth-century doctors believed in the curative properties of clean bowels. Thus Dodington thought it worth noting in his diary for the enlightenment of posterity how 'plentiful' a movement of the patient's bowels had been.

During those days in bed, with his political advisers and other visitors kept away from his room, the Griff was generally quiet but content. It seemed he was resigning to a feeling that his premonition was close to fulfilment; and that, after all, the remaking of his Kew gardens would never be completed in his lifetime. He would never see the rows of sculptured heads of the world's greatest philosophers lining this aqueduct. It was doubtless with this feeling that one day when his eldest son entered the bedroom he beckoned to him with the words: 'Come, George, let us be good friends while we are permitted to be so.' George came close to his father. The Griff had never been known to talk to his family about the desperate loneliness of his childhood in Hanover, with his later realisation that his own father and mother had no love for him. But now he was confiding these sadnesses to his gentle and understanding thirteen-year-old son who many years later, as king, never forgot them.

Only a few years previously Frederick had said that when he was dying he would be happy to seize the garments of the Methodist Lady Huntingdon to be raised with her to heaven. But on the night of Wednesday, 20th March 1751, the Royal Griffin flew away unaided and alone. Anyhow, there was an appropriate musical prelude to this flight into the unknown. Earlier on that night the prince had happily asked to see some friends. He chatted with them while eating bread and butter and drinking coffee. When the friends had gone Philip Desnoyers brought his fiddle into the bedroom and played quietly to the patient. In an ante-room courtiers and other attendants settled down to a game of cards. The prince's doctors, Wilmot and Hawkins, paid him their final visit for the night. Suddenly the Griff started coughing while Pavonarius, his *valet de chambre*, supported his body in a sitting position. Dr. Wilmot, observing the still coughing invalid in the dim candlelight, said: 'Sir, I hope this will be over in a quarter of an hour and that your royal highness will have a good night.' But in the ante-room Dr. Hawkins was heard to mutter: 'Here's something I don't like.' Meanwhile Augusta entered the room. She stood at the foot of the bed while the Griff coughed on. Then he put a hand on his stomach, saying, '*Je sens la mort*' ('I feel death'). As the Griff shivered, Pavonarius gave a cry of 'The prince is going!' The princess snatched up a candle and rushed to the side of her husband. He had already gone.

During the same night there was a card party in the apartments of the king at St. James's Palace. The king was leaning over a table watching the play of his daughter Princess Amelia, the Duke of Grafton and the Duchess of Dorset. They were interrupted by the appearance of Lord North from Leicester House. North broke the news of the death of the Prince of Wales. With a look of astonishment the king exclaimed: 'Why they told me he was getting better!' The king hurried from the room to find his mistress Lady Yarmouth, the former Madame Walmoden, to tell her in shocked tones: '*Il est mort*.'

Meanwhile at Leicester House Augusta had shut herself up

alone in the death chamber while outside reigned confusion and bewilderment. The news of the Griff's death had spread with incredible speed. Friends, bishops, diplomats and others were arriving at Leicester House, even at that late hour, to pay their condolences. All were told that Augusta could not be seen. No one dared to disturb her as she remained by the corpse of her husband in the closed bedroom. Four hours had passed before she opened the door to pass through the throng in the ante-room and corridors outside. Augusta's ladies-in-waiting persuaded her to go to bed. They were worried over the effect which the strain of the past hours might have upon her pregnancy, a baby being expected in the following July. However, after only two hours' rest she was up again talking in her closet with Dr. Lee, legal adviser to the late prince, William Breton, long a member of his staff, and others. The shock of death often leads the bereaved to hasty, illogical deeds which later are regretted. Thus Augusta in her grief made a rash decision. With Lee, a doctor-at-law, who should have known better, she burned the private and political papers of the Griff that very morning. Up in flames went letters, notes, memoranda and documents which her husband had kept under lock and key for many years. Egmont, Dodington and others who had been trusted by the prince were given no chance to study the mass of papers and to save all that might be worthy of preservation and of use to future historians.

The boy George, now the Prince of Wales, was told gently of his father's death by his tutor Dr. Ayscough. The boy turned white, placed his hand over his chest.

When the anxious tutor said, 'I am afraid, sir, you are not well,' the prince replied, 'I feel something here, just as I did when I saw the two workmen fall from the scaffold at Kew.'

A few days later the king himself was at Leicester House prevented by his own tears from consoling George, his daughter-in-law and other members of the family. He came after Augusta had sent him a letter to thank him for his written condolences. 'I throw myself with my children at your feet', declared this unusual letter. 'We commend ourselves, sire, to your fatherly love and royal protection.' Despite the tears that fell from the king's eyes in Leicester House, he was planning to ensure that his dead son be dishonoured by an inferior funeral. And by the end of 1751 he was saying: 'This has been a fatal year in our family. I have lost my eldest son, but I was glad of it.'

As if there was any mystery about the cause of Frederick's death, the king ordered a post-mortem. The learned pathologists found in the side of the body signs of an abcess. In the words of Dodington, 'the breaking of this abcess suffocated the prince'. It was recalled that three years previously he had been struck hard by what was variously described as a cricket ball and tennis ball. He had also suffered a fall. Later, however, medical opinion was that the Griff was killed by a straight case of pneumonia. Since in this posthumous examination the prince's bowels had been removed from his body, these were reverently placed in a box covered with red velvet to await the funeral.

The masses of London were grieved at the passing of the member of the royal family who had been closest to them. Leaders in the world of art and letters were also quick to pay tribute to his memory. Printed eulogies to the Griff and his life were numerous. Some were spoiled by eighteenth-century floweriness and exaggeration. Those produced in Oxford and Cambridge—some in Greek and Latin—seemed little more than formal and conventional exercises in classical composition. Nevertheless the jealous king who had graciously shed a few tears over his dead son did not relish the idea of the whole nation mourning him. Accordingly he used his influence to prevent the funeral from becoming too memorable. He could rely upon assistance in this matter upon the more spiteful government leaders who had suffered from the Griff's active sponsorship of the opposition party. A council was nominated to plan the funeral, arranged for the 13th April. Although Dodington and other friends of the late prince were members of this, they met with many obstructions and delays. The peers were obviously being warned to shun this funeral The bishops, who ordinarily swarmed like black locusts on such occasions, were also advised to stay away.

The body of the Griff, together with the appendages in the velvet-covered box, were on the night preceding their Westminster Abbey burial taken to his own chambers in the House of Lords. All the gentlemen of his bedchamber were instructed to keep vigil around it from ten in the morning until an hour or so before the funeral in the late afternoon. No arrangements had been made to give these exalted gentlemen decent refreshments, so that, in the words of Dodington, they were forced to send out 'for a great cold dinner from a common tavern in the neighbourhood'.

The funeral procession from the House of Lords started in pouring rain. There was a meagre display of troops. Except for the pall-bearers there were no English peers walking behind the coffin, but one bold Irish peer—Lord Limerick. The sad Princess Augusta rode in one coach, but the crowd looked in vain for any other member of the royal family. The king, Duke of Cumberland, the Princesses Amelia and Caroline and other sisters were all absent. For all were being embodied in these obsequies by one representative, the Duke of Somerset. And fortunately all the children of Augusta and the Griff were being kept at home away from this dismal and disgraceful spectacle. Of the entire Privy Council only two members were present. One of these was Dodington. All the bishops stayed away except for Joseph Wilcocks, who was both Bishop of Rochester and Dean of Westminster. He was to take the funeral service for £3 instead of his customary fee of £2. The usual deal covers to protect such processions in Parliament Yard in rainy weather had not been erected. The sad parade, dripping wet, entered the south-east door of the Abbey and turned into Henry VII's Chapel. There the body of the Griff would lie in the same vault as that of his mother Caroline and near the grave of Fitz Frederick, his illegitimate son by Anne Vane. Strangely, a small choir was in attendance, although there was no organ music and no hymns were sung.

Handel, who had composed an anthem for the Griff's wedding, had offered no dirge for his funeral.

The desolate Augusta and the other mourners now endured the funeral service of the established church as read by Wilcocks, who had been dean of the Abbey for twenty years. Finally came the scene at the open grave when, in the words of the Book of Common Prayer, 'the corpse is made ready to be laid in the earth'. Again the tired voice of the old dean was raised:

'Man that is born of a woman hath but a short time to live and is full of misery; he cometh up and is cut down, like a flower. . . .'

Appendix

[1] *The Charms of Sylvia*

This ode, written by Frederick, was dedicated to his wife Augusta:

'Tis not the liquid brightness of those eyes,
   That swim with pleasure and delight,
Nor those heavenly arches which arise
   O'er each of them to shade their light:
'Tis not that hair which plays with every wind,
   And loves to wanton round thy face;
Now straying round the forehead, now behind
   Retiring with insidious grace.
'Tis not that lovely range of teeth so white,
   As new-shorn sheep equal and fair;
Nor e'en that gentle smile, the heart's delight,
   With which no smile could e'er compare.
'Tis not that chin so round, that neck so fine,
   Those breasts that swell to meet my love,
That easy sloping waist, that form divine,
   Nor ought below, nor ought above:
'Tis not the living colours over each
   By nature's finest pencil wrought,
To shame the full-blown rose, and blooming peach,
   And mock the happy painter's thought:
No—'tis that gentleness of mind, that love
   So kindly answering my desire;
That grace with which you look, and speak, and move,
   That thus has set my soul on fire.

[2] *Venez, Mes Chères Déesses*

This song, composed by Frederick, expresses his preference for love compared to war. It was written after the Battle of Fontenoy:

Venez, mes chères Déesses,
Venez calmer mon chagrin;
Aidez mes belles Princesses,
A le noyer dans le vin.
Poussons cette douce ivresse
Jusqu'au milieu de la nuit,
Et n'écoutons que la tendresse
D'un charmant vis-à-vis.
Quand le chagrin me dévore,
Vite à table je me mets,
Loin des objets que j'abhorre,
Avec joie j'y trouve la paix.
Peu d'amis, restés d'un naufrage,
Je rassemble autour de moi,
Et je me ris de l'étalage
Qu'a chez lui toujours un Roi.
Que m'importe que l'Europe
Ait un ou plusieurs tyrans?
Prions seulement Calliope
Qu'elle inspire nos vers, nos chants.
Laissons Mars et toute la gloire,
Livrons-nous tous à l'amour;
Que Bacchus nous donne à boire;
A ces deux faisons la cour.
Passons ainsi notre vie,
Sans rêver à ce qui suit;
Avec ma chère Silvie
Le temps trop vite me fuit.
Mais si par un malheur extrême,
Je perdois cet objet charmant;
Qui, cette compagnie même
Ne me tiendroit un moment.
Me livrant à ma tristesse,
Toujours plein de mon chagrin,
Je n'aurois plus d'allégresse
Pour mettre Bathurst en train.

Ainsi pour vous tenir en joie,
Invoquez toujours les Dieux,
Qu'elle vive et qu'elle soit
Avec nous toujours heureux.

[3] *Here Lies Poor Fred*

Many verses were written about Frederick following his death. The following epitaph, obviously written by a Jacobite, has survived to be often quoted. It has damaged the prince's reputation by representing him as a negative character of which 'no more can be said' other than that he lived and died.

Here lies poor Fred
Who was alive and is dead:
Had it been his father,
I had much rather;
Had it been his brother,
Still better than another;
Had it been his sister,
No one would have missed her;
Had it been the whole generation,
Still better for the nation;
But since 'tis only Fred
Who was alive and is dead
There's no more to be said.

Bibliography

Arkell, R. L. *Caroline of Ansbach*, 1939.

Barbeau, A. *Life and Letters at Bath in the XVIII Century*, 1904.

Cowie, L. W. *Hanoverian England 1714–1837*, 1967.

Coxe, W. *Memoirs of Sir Robert Walpole*, 1798.

Cumberland, Richard. *Memoirs* (2 vols.), 1807.

Dutton, R. *English Court Life*, 1903.

Edwards, Averyl. *Frederick Louis Prince of Wales*, 1947.

Egmont, Earl of. *Diaries 1730–1747* (3 vols.). Historical Manuscripts Commission, 1920 and 1923.

Grant, Charles. *England Under the Hanoverians*, 1949.

Hervey, Lord John. *Some Materials Towards Memoirs of the Reign of George II* (3 vols.), Ed. Romney Sedgwick, 1931.

Ilchester, Earl of, Ed. *Lord John Hervey and His Friends*, 1950.

Marples, Morris. *Poor Fred and the Butcher*, 1970.

Marshall, Dorothy. *English People in the Eighteenth Century*, 1956.

Melcombe, Lord (G. Bubb Dodington). *Political Journal*. Ed. T. Carswell and L. A. Dralle, 1965.

Montagu, Lady Mary Wortley. *Complete Letters*. Ed. Robert Halsband (3 vols.), 1966.

Petrie, Charles. *The Jacobite Movement*, 1959.

Redman, Alvin. *The House of Hanover*, 1960

Thackeray, W. M. *The Four Georges*, 1861.

Toland, W. *Account of the Courts of Prussia and Hanover*, 1714.

Vehse, E. *Geschichte der Höfe des Hauses Braunschweig in Deutschland und England*, 1853.

Walpole, Horace. *Memoirs of the Reign of King George II*. Ed. Lord Holland, 1847. *Letters*. Ed. Peter Cunningham, 9 vols, 1891.

Walters, John. *Splendour and Scandal: the Reign of Beau Nash*, 1968.

White, T. H. *The Age of Scandal*, 1950.

Williams, E. N. *Life in Georgian England*, 1962.

Young, George. *Poor Fred, the People's Prince*, 1937

Dictionary of National Biography.

Gentleman's Magazine (from 1731).

Allgemeine deutsche Biographie, 1878.

Index

Compiled by Gordon Robinson